JAMES MORTON OMNIBUS

East End Gangland
Gangland International

JAMES MORTON OMNIBUS

East End Gangland
Gangland International

JAMES MORTON

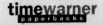
timewarner
paperbacks

A *Time Warner* Paperback

This omnibus edition first published in Great Britain by
Time Warner Paperbacks in 2003
James Morton Omnibus Copyright © James Morton 2003

Previously published separately:
East End Gangland first published in Great Britain in 2000 by
Little, Brown and Company
Reprinted 2000
Published by Warner Books in 2001
Copyright © James Morton 2000

Gangland International first published in Great Britain in 1998 by
Little, Brown and Company
Published by Warner Books in 1999
Reprinted 2000, 2001
Copyright © James Morton 1998

A CIP catalogue record for this book
is available from the British Library.

ISBN 0 7515 3516 8

Printed and bound in Great Britain by
Clays Ltd, St Ives plc

Time Warner Paperbacks
An imprint of
Time Warner Books UK
Brettenham House
Lancaster Place
London WC2E 7EN

www.TimeWarnerBooks.co.uk

East End Gangland

For Dock with my love and thanks

Contents

Introduction

My father, who was a spice merchant, had a warehouse and office in Mitre Street just around the corner from where Jack the Ripper killed Mary Kelly. Although I went frequently to his warehouse – where as a child it was my delight to feed the cats since we did not have one at home – he never pointed out the connection with local history when we went to the Square to collect his car. He was a singularly incurious man and I doubt whether he even knew that, had he wanted, he could have touched the bricks of the house where she died. Certainly if he did know, he did not pass this intelligence on to me. Now it is too late. The whole area has been pulled down to ease the flow of the traffic speeding – well, that is certainly not the correct word – towards the heart of the East End.

My father's connection with the East End terminated when in late 1962 some stray members of the Richardson gang accidentally blew up his premises. He was certainly not their target but had the misfortune to be located across the road from a warehouse which was part of a long-firm

fraud they were running at the time. A long-firm fraud
is a scam whereby goods are bought on credit and sold
at a knock-down price. The vendor is never paid and in
the 1960s, if it was properly organised, it was rare that
the principals or indeed anyone else was convicted. On
this occasion the idea was to remove the goods from the
warehouse and have a fire, thereby doubling the profit
by claiming from the insurance company for the so-called
lost goods.

Apparently the plan had been to torch the empty warehouse at a weekend when no one was around, so the risk
would be minimal. Unfortunately, after petrol had been
poured all over the premises, the arsonists saw a courting
couple in the street and, so to speak, held their hand. By the
time the pair had gone the fumes had risen and so, when a
Guy Fawkes rocket was aimed at a semi-basement window,
instead of igniting a fire which would burn nicely the place
literally blew up and demolished much of the street. The cats
were unharmed. My father moved what was left of his stock
to the generally much healthier area of the Borough.[1]

Just why over the years has the East End offered so
much fascination for outsiders when other areas, such as
the Elephant and Castle which have also had more than
their fair share of crime and major criminals, have failed to
generate any real interest? Perhaps it is a matter of semantics
and it is the very word East which carries the air of the
Orient with it. It was another world, one filled with the
unknown and therefore the spice of danger, which gave it
an attraction. Just as Harlem in the 1920s was the place for
smart white New Yorkers to end their evenings, so was the
Railway Tavern in the East India Dock Road (and known
as Charlie Brown's) the place for London's café society to

---

[1] See Robert Parker, *Rough Justice*, pp. 90–91; Charles Richardson, *My Manor*, pp. 124–5.

visit for a *frisson*. The proprietor, in evening dress, would show them his collection of curios in what was in effect a museum and they would proudly sign the visitors' book. To have visited the East End, where policemen only went in pairs, and to have survived the experience was something to speak about. To an extent the East End was seen as another land and its inhabitants a race apart. Their poor physical condition was seen as one reason for British defeats in the Boer War, and in 1912 the convenient Anon was quoted as saying:

> The first stage of decay had already been reached when the stolid, God-fearing puritan of two and a half centuries ago has given place to the shallow hysterical cockney of today.[2]

Jack London, who lived for a short time in the East End and described life there, wrote that to exist in the day-to-day wheeling and dealing and fighting for food and work required a social personality that was voluble and aggressive. Those outside the area had a fear of the socially deprived mob dating back to 8 February 1886, when the London United Workmen's Committee march to Trafalgar Square demanding employment took place. The meeting had been addressed by Ben Tillett and John Burns, but afterwards a small group went on a rampage overturning carriages, looting and, worst of all, breaking the windows of the Reform and Carlton Clubs. The demonstration was badly mishandled by the police. In charge was the 74-year-old District Superintendent Robert Walker in civilian clothes. He was quite unable to cope and suffered the additional indignity of having his pocket picked. The demonstrators made their way to Oxford Street where they were turned back by Inspector Cuthbert and fifteen

---

[2] J.M. Whitehouse (ed.), *Problems of Boy Life*.

men from Marylebone police station who were due to go on night duty.

There were fears that this was the beginning of an uprising, but the majority of the marchers trotted off home singing 'Rule Britannia' and despite a careful lookout by the police over the next few weeks no further demonstrations took place. Nevertheless the incident was sufficient to establish the spectre of 'The East End Mob' as an early, if as yet unlabelled, folk devil. The Commissioner of Police Henderson resigned the next day.

Years later Tillett spoke again. This time it was at a meeting of dock labourers at Tower Hill on 7 August 1911 which was once more watched by the authorities with some apprehension, particularly when he urged that the Port of London should be brought to a standstill:[3]

> We are only fighting for the right to live; we are only fighting our employers because hitherto they have refused to recognise the claims we made. We were mere riff-raff, dockers, not men; now we are showing the employers that we are men with all the noble qualities that can be found in man. Brothers, we want to finish that period when the so-called docker or transport worker or coal porter or carman shall be looked upon as nothing. If we all drop tools the Lord Tomnoddys would rot from want of food.

This was one of the abiding fears of the general public, that the dockers would stop them from eating. It was also feared that the working classes would actually rise up out of the grinding poverty in which so many lived. It can be argued that many of the philanthropic improvement schemes had the ulterior motive of maintaining the *status quo* behind them. As the number of strikes at the end of the nineteenth century and in the first years of the twentieth

[3] PRO MEPO 3 206.

century show, improvement in working conditions came slowly. There were, for example, tailors' strikes in 1889, 1906, 1909 and 1912; cabinet-makers' in 1896, 1900, 1911 and 1913; bootmakers' in 1891, 1901 and 1912, and Jewish bakers' in 1906 and 1913. It is against this background that crime in the East End must be set.

But back in the 1880s Henderson's successor, Sir Charles Warren, whose qualification for the post had been the governorship of the Red Sea Littoral, had fared not much better in his dealings with the East End. He was under constant criticism for failing to find Jack the Ripper. One of his less thought through acts had been to engage a pair of bloodhounds from the entrepreneurial Mr Brough for £100. Their owner had a better sense of smell, at least for money, than his dogs, for they became temporarily lost.

The East End's reputation undoubtedly benefited from the rise in literacy and the growth of the popular lending libraries. Charles Dickens' unfinished *The Mystery of Edwin Drood* opens in an East End opium den. Later, in a Sherlock Holmes story, a respectable man is seen disappearing into another den when he is supposed to be working on the Stock Exchange. Many of the popular Sax Rohmer novels had an East End setting.

The East End has always had its share of the famous and infamous. The Old Gravel Lane murders are mentioned by Thomas de Quincey, himself an early casualty of the opium trade. Claude Duval, perhaps the most gentlemanly of the highwaymen, lived in Colchester Road, Leman Street. A little later in time, a one-legged Welshman named Hughes ran a thieves' kitchen in Catherine Wheel Alley and some maintain that it is he, rather than the usually favoured Ikey Solomons, who was the prototype for Dickens' Fagin.[4] The

---

[4] Millicent Rose, *The East End of London*.

lovely Madeleine Smith, who years later would perhaps be fortunate to obtain a 'not proven' verdict in Edinburgh where she had been accused of poisoning her now-unwanted lover, went to school in Clapton. She was to have a small industry created around her trial arguing the merits of her guilt or innocence.

On the theatrical front, the celebrated actor David Garrick made his first stage appearance as Harlequin in Alie Street. Later a playhouse was named after him in Leman Street where it was said 'ladies can seat themselves without rats running over them'.

A curious feature of the East End towards the end of the nineteenth century was the so-called penny gaff. It was a form of theatre often played in a shop with a back parlour, with the dividing wall knocked down. There were usually two performances nightly and the earlier house cost twopence. One very popular figure in this form of entertainment in which, like the Parisian Funambules, the players were not allowed to speak but could sign and discharge mock firearms, was Mrs Douglas Fitzbruce who appeared in such dramas as *Gentleman Jack or The Game of High Toby*.

James Greenwood describes her gallantly when she appeared as Dick Turpin:

Dressed in buckskin shorts and highly polished boots she could not have been more than forty-five. Her husband who had been seen earlier putting up the poster advertising the performance was Turpin's colleague Tom King whom he accidentally shot. When Mrs Fitzbruce let fly at point-blank range there was such a whistling and stamping of feet that the dust from the plaster wash of the walls blew up a storm of dust. Afterwards patrons, if they had sixpence, could purchase pictures of Mrs. F. as Cupid and Lady Godiva.[5]

In creating and maintaining its image the East End was also fortunate to have a series of very public incidents. In the 1890s Jack the Ripper, one of the great serial killers, fascinated the public. Here was a man killing not a mile from the great British institutions such as the Bank of England and yet operating in conditions which those who worked in the bank and their families could only read and have nightmares about. And read and theorise about him they have done ever since. Richard Whittington-Egan, in his mammoth compilation of books and articles on the killings, estimated that at the end of 1998 there had been no fewer than 500 publications about the case.

In writing a book on crime in the East End there is an immediate problem in defining just what was and is the East End. Some parts are easy – Aldgate, Limehouse, the Docks, Stratford, West Ham, Hackney and Hoxton all fit neatly, but what of Hackney's neighbour Stoke Newington which has an N postal code? What about Romford and Ilford? Surely those are in Essex, yet they have been inextricably linked with the East End, its *moeurs* and its villains, and all have influenced criminal life in the East End. I have adopted what critics may call a wide brush.

I had intended to confine this account to the twentieth century, but I have slightly enlarged the parameters to begin

---

[5] James Greenwood, *The Wilds of London*. Ned Wright describes a visit to a penny gaff where there was first a rough music hall and then the melodrama *Count Fribourg or The Murder in the Black Forest*. About a hundred young people sat on benches and there was also some sort of gallery. He thought that most had stolen the penny entrance money although he had been obliged to pay double. 'It is difficult to conceive the strange power of fascination places of this kind acquire over these poor misguided boys and girls who attend them.' A lady who danced the hornpipe to the point of exhaustion in the first half received six shillings a week and had to provide her own costume. *Cassell's Magazine*.

with the pogroms in Eastern Europe and the influx of the Ashkenazi Jews from the 1860s onwards – replacing the immigrant Irish who, with the successive Potato Famines of the 1840s and 1850s, had come to London and settled in the East End at the bottom of the social pile.

I have also included some of the particularly interesting domestic crimes such as the Lipski murder of his downstairs neighbour and the killing of Fanny Zeitoun, both of which give an insight into life in the late nineteenth and early twentieth centuries. I have, however, generally avoided the many non-gang-related East End domestic murders of the period and instead have concentrated on crime carried out for profit or by gangs. Until recently, and the rise of the drugs gangs, however, most of the East End gangland murders have not been commercially orientated but have resulted from disputes over wives and girlfriends and slights real and perceived. These have been included.

It would not be right, however, to omit the first murder on a railway. This world-wide distinction belongs to Franz Muller, a German tailor working in London who killed a jeweller, Thomas Briggs, in a railway carriage between Bow and Hackney Wick on 9 July 1864. Robbery was the motive and Muller snatched his victim's gold watch before throwing Briggs onto the railway line where, in fact, he died. In his haste, Muller overlooked £5 Briggs had on him and also took away the wrong hat. The watch-chain was eventually traced to a Cheapside jeweller with the appropriate name of Death, who described the customer as being foreign-looking and possibly German. Of course the case made the newspapers and a witness came forward to say he recognised the hat found in the railway carriage. He had bought two of them, one for himself and one for Muller. The police now discovered that Muller had sailed for New York and, anticipating the Crippen case by some fifty years, detectives took a faster ship. Muller was found with the missing watch in his possession.

He maintained his innocence and approached both Queen Victoria and German royalty to intervene on his behalf. At the end his nerve failed and, in one of the last public executions, he confessed before a large crowd. He was hanged by William Chalcraft on 14 November 1864. For a time, the type of hat he had left behind in the railway carriage was known as a Muller.

This informal history will end, as journalist John Diamond puts it, when

> . . . the Synagogues became mosques – broken-backed Jewish men who shuffled along Brick Lane have been transformed into broken-backed shuffling Bengali men.[6]

My thanks are also due to Harold Alderman, Albert Appleby, Steve Ashenden, Fred Bailey, Mickey Bailey, Frankie Bateson, Jeremy Beadle, J.P. Bean, Barbara Boote, Hilary Clarke, Dave Critchley, Alan Dixon, Peter Donnelly, Frank Fraser, Brian Hilliard, Rita Matharu, Jean Maund, Helen McCormack, Kelly Parkes, Silvia Perrini-Rice, Lillian Pizzichini, John Rigbey, Andrew Rose, Linda Silverman, Dot Swarc, Tony Thompson, John Warburton, Richard Whittington-Egan who kindly read the chapters on the nineteenth century, the Curator of the Jewish Museum, Sternberg Centre, the staff of the Tower Hamlets Library, Bancroft Road, the Public Record Office, the British Library and the Newspaper Library at Colindale as well as many others who asked they be not named.

Once again, this book could not even have been started without the total help and commitment of Dock Bateson.

6 John Diamond, 'The Last Cockney' in *The Times*, 14 March 1998.

1

The Nineteenth Century

The earliest of the great nineteenth-century East End murders were the so-called Ratcliffe Highway murders which Thomas de Quincey calls the Old Gravel Lane murders and took place in September 1811. On 7 September, a man named Marr sent his maidservant out to buy some oysters and when she returned she found the door locked. She went for help and when neighbours broke in they found that Marr, his wife, their baby and a 13-year-old apprentice had all been killed, their heads beaten and their throats cut. Now London was said to be in a state of terror with doors barred and gun dealers running out of stock as people prepared to defend themselves. On 19 September the bodies of the Williamsons – he was the landlord of the King's Arms in New Gravel Lane – and their elderly servant were found. They too had their throats cut. A lodger hearing noises went to investigate and, when he saw a figure standing over a body, escaped through a window and raised the alarm.

A labourer, John Williams, who was lodging at the Pear Street Inn near Cinnamon Street, was arrested. Within a matter of hours he hanged himself in his cell at Cold Baths Fields prison in Holborn. At any rate, that is the official story. What is certain is that his body was placed in a cart and escorted by parish officers and the High Constable of Middlesex (in full regalia) and driven through massed crowds past the homes of the victims. Since the practice was to bury suicides at cross-roads, the body was then interred at St George's Turnpike and a stake driven through the corpse. Over a hundred years later workmen disinterred the corpse and the bones were shared out as souvenirs with a local publican having the skull.

Whether Williams was the murderer is very much more open to question, as is his apparent suicide. The police historian T.A. Critchley and the crime writer P.D. James have put together an interesting argument that Williams was innocent and was killed in his cell as a convenient way of closing the investigation.[1]

It was shortly afterwards that the East End had its own version of Burke and Hare. In 1831 John Bishop and his brother-in-law, Thomas Head, also known as Williams, drugged a 14-year-old Italian boy, Carlo Ferrari, who made a living exhibiting performing mice, in Nova Scotia Gardens, part of the Old Nichol, which would later become Columbia Market. They killed him by first drugging him with rum laced with laudanum and then drowning him by lowering him head first into a well behind Bishop's House. They sold his teeth, but then asked the surgeons at King's College for nine guineas for his body. The staff – suspicious of receiving a new corpse and one which did not appear to have died naturally – called the police. The pair had previously had two successes, the victims being an elderly woman, Fanny Pigburn, and another young boy. A crowd of some 30,000 is said to have turned out for their turning-off at Newgate

---

[1] T.A. Critchley and P.D. James, *The Maul and the Pear Tree*.

on 5 December. Their bodies were handed over to King's and St Bartholomew's respectively. Bishop claimed he had been a resurrection man for some ten years, the last five of which had been in partnership with Head and a third man, John May, who gave evidence against them.

The same year, Eliza Ross killed the 84-year-old match-seller Caroline Walsh in Goodman's Yard, now Royal Mint Street, for her clothes which she promptly sold. Ross seems to have been a dreadful woman who dealt in cat skins and whose greatest claim to fame, before the murder, was to have strangled and bare-handedly skinned the cat belonging to the landlady of the Sampson and Lion in Shadwell with whom she had quarrelled. Her common-law husband, Edward Cook, was acquitted after the jury heard that he had stared out of the window and had taken no part in the killing of the match-seller. Ross was hanged on 9 January the following year.

The next case – which throws a little light on the emerging Metropolitan Police Force and their relationship with the community – came on 26 March 1863 when a respectable-looking man entered a shop owned by Matilda Moore and her husband at 96 Green Street, Bethnal Green, saying he wished to purchase some oats. Whilst she was looking for them he picked her pocket of a purse containing about £8. She discovered the loss immediately and, as he tried to leave the shop, hung on to his coat-tails. He then grabbed her by the throat and she had a heart attack. He escaped, leaving his coat and scarf behind.

Matilda Moore survived the immediate danger and went back to work, saying she could not identify the man, and it seems rather as if she told the police she wished the matter to be dropped. Inquiries into the scarf and coat came to nothing. Then on 7 January 1864 she died aged 55 years. The jury unanimously returned a verdict of wilful murder by a person unknown and the coroner suggested the only way to solve the matter was to offer a reward which would induce one of his 'Pals to Peach'. A reward of £100 was suggested, but there was a dispute as to who should pay for the handbills and eventually the work was undertaken by the Commissioner for Police, offering £50.[2] The reward was never claimed.

The same year Henry Wainwright, a brushmaker, died and left what was then a fortune of £11,000 to be divided between his five children. His son, also named Henry, had married two years earlier and carried on the business in the Whitechapel Road next to the Pavilion Theatre. A popular man locally, he owned a Georgian house in Tredegar Square as well as the shop. He gave readings of Dickens and lectured on 'the Wit of Sidney Smith' at the Leeds Mechanics Institute.

Unfortunately, after his marriage Wainwright had, in 1871, met Harriet Lane, the 20-year-old daughter of a gas manager. She was educated, attractive and apprenticed to a milliner. All went well for a time, with Mrs Wainwright completely unsuspecting of her husband's second home. He had set Harriet up in a house in St Peter Street, Mile End, and on 22 August 1872 they had a daughter. A second daughter was born the following year and they moved to Cecil Court in the Strand before returning to St Peter Street. A notice was published in the *Waltham Abbey Weekly* that she had married a Percy King of Chelsea.

And then things began to fall apart. Wainwright was getting into a financial tangle by running two (and possibly more) homes. His brother William dissolved the partnership, with the result that Harriet's £5 a week was cut. In turn she became quarrelsome and turned to drink. Now Henry Wainwright introduced her to his brother Thomas whom, for the purposes, he called Edward Frieake. She supposed she was to be transferred; they thought they were going to kill her.

2 PRO MEPO 3 69.

In early September 1874 Harriet became very drunk, created a stir outside the lodgings which she now shared with an Ellen Wilmore and was given notice to quit. However, things improved and on 11 September her transfer to Frieake was apparently completed. She had tired of Henry and she was by no means averse to a new owner. That day she left to join Frieake and was never seen alive again.

Three weeks later Miss Wilmore received a letter from Harriet saying that things were even better. She and Frieake were off to the Continent and provided she renounced her old friends, marriage would follow. Both Miss Wilmore and Wainwright received confirmatory telegrams; but she was not satisfied and after consulting with Harriet's sister a private detective was instructed. All he discovered was that Edward Frieake was an auctioneer in the City and was certainly not the man with whom Harriet had apparently left the country. Her father called on Wainwright begging to know whether his daughter was alive or dead, and was told her former lover did not know.

Over the winter a paint room in the warehouse next to Wainwright's shop, also owned by him, began to develop a smell so strong that the tenants moved out from their rooms above it. As for Wainwright, things went from bad to worse and in June 1875 he was declared bankrupt. The warehouse was to be transferred to a new owner and it was imperative that Wainwright moved the body. Thomas, released from his role as Teddy Frieake and now the proud owner of an ironmongery at the corner of Southwark Street and Borough High Street, agreed to allow Wainwright to re-bury his mistress in the cellar of his shop. Unfortunately, it was not quite that simple.

On 11 September 1875, a year to the day after she had disappeared, the body of Harriet Lane came to light. Her body was dug up, but the quicklime in which she had been buried had preserved rather than destroyed the corpse which Wainwright now wrapped in several cloth parcels prior to moving it. In the annals of crime, Henry Wainwright's behaviour must go down as one of the more stupid examples, for he then called in a youth named Stokes and told him to watch the packages whilst he went and called a cab. It should, of course, have been Stokes who was sent for the cab. When the inquisitive youth looked in the parcel, a severed hand fell out. There followed a sequence worthy of the Keystone Cops. Wainwright drove off and on seeing a ballet-dancer friend, Alice Day, invited her to join him and Harriet in the cab. Now he lit a cigar in an attempt to hide the ever-increasing smell of putrefaction. The astute Stokes, who had chased after him on foot, found two policemen to whom to tell his story. They laughed at him, but the youth was determined and eventually found another pair who this time listened to what he had to say. Wainwright now stopped at an ironmonger's and, when the police caught up with him and asked to be allowed to examine the parcels, offered them £50 each to go away. They refused what was then an enormous sum of money. In fact, since he was bankrupt it must be doubtful if, had they accepted, they would have received the bribe. Off went Wainwright, Miss Day and the pieces of Harriet to Stone's End Police Station.

Wainwright was charged with Harriet Lane's murder on 21 September 1875. The forensic evidence showed she had been shot twice in the head and her throat had been cut. He was hanged at Newgate prison by William Marwood on 21 December that year, an event to which some 60 people had been invited. According to reports he behaved with some dignity on the scaffold, rounding on the spectators saying, 'Come to see a man die, have you, you curs?'

His brother Thomas, charged as an accessory to murder, received seven years. For once virtue was rewarded and Stokes received, not the £50 the constables were offered, but £30 out of public funds.

The last decades of the century produced a series of seemingly inexplicable events which became known collectively as the West Ham Vanishings. On 13 May 1881, 14-year-old Mary Seward, described as young looking for her age and a trifle backward, disappeared. She had been playing at home in West Road, West Ham, most of the afternoon, but at 6 p.m. her mother told her to go and look for her nephew who had wandered away from the house. The boy was found and given a ticking-off, but Mary disappeared. Later there was a suggestion that she had been seen with a gypsy at a fairground. The Home Office put up a £25 reward and this was supplemented by the proceeds of a local concert.

At 10 a.m. on Saturday 28 January 1882, 12-year-old Eliza Carter left her elder sister's house, also in West Road and only ten doors away from the Sewards, to go to her parents who lived nearby in Church Street. On the way she took some clothes to the laundry to put through the mangle. She was not seen again until at 5 o'clock she spoke to a schoolfriend in The Portway opposite West Ham Park, telling her she was afraid to go home because of 'that man'. At 11 p.m. that night she was seen in the company of an ugly middle-aged woman dressed in a long Ulster and a black frock.

The next day Eliza's dress, which had buttons all the way down the front, was found in a local football field minus the buttons. There were traces of arrowroot biscuits in her pockets and the police believed they might have been used to entice her into the park. The buttons had been cut off and were thought to be worth about sixpence.

There was now disquiet in the neighbourhood that the Home Office seemed to value the lives of young girls so poorly; but although questions were asked of the local Member of

Parliament, nothing came of it.[3]

Another in the series of vanishings was said to have occurred the day before Mary Seward went missing, but this time it was a 67-year-old lady who disappeared from her home in Keogh Road. In the evening she went to a local shop to purchase soap and candles but when the postman and milkman called the next morning they were unable to obtain a reply. In turn the police failed to get a response and broke in. The soap and candles were in place and the grandfather clock in the hall had been wound up. The washing-up had been done and the bed made, but of the lady there was no trace.

Then for a time the vanishings stopped, or at least they were suspended until, in January 1890, three young girls disappeared within a very short time span. The only one whose body was found was 15-year-old Millie Jeffs who had been working as a nursemaid after leaving school the previous year. Curiously she lived twelve doors from the Seward home. One Friday evening she met her father Charles, a railwayman, after he finished work, and he gave her threepence to buy some fish at Bowmans in Church Street. She had not returned by 7.30 and a search was instigated; it lasted until 2.30 a.m. but produced no result. On Valentine's Day, police officers searching for stolen lead broke the window of 126 West Road and found the body of Millie Jeffs in a cupboard. She had been sexually assaulted and strangled. At her burial in the East London cemetery a collection raised £250 as a reward, but her killer was never found.

[3] Curiously, on 13 September 1912 another Eliza Carter was murdered in West Ham. This was a lovers' quarrel and the 17-year-old was found with her throat cut in the arms of 20-year-old William Charles Beal who had also cut his own throat. She had been nearly decapitated but Beal's rather speculative defence was that it was she who had cut both his and her own throats. The jury made a strong recommendation for mercy on the grounds of his youth. It did him no good. Despite being described as not of very sound mind, he was executed at Chelmsford prison on 10 December 1912.

Probably the young girls who were never found were kidnapped and used for the purposes of white slavery or child prostitution; there was an unhealthy market in young prostitutes at the time, and indeed there is some evidence that prostitutes sold their children for the trade. The case of the elderly lady is by no means as well documented in the local papers as the other vanishings, and may be an example of an urban myth.

The case of Carl Wagner has often been included in the vanishings. He disappeared on 1 April 1882 and so fits neatly into the time scale, but his is a much more prosaic tale of childhood disobedience. The story is that his body, without any marks of injury, was found at the foot of a cliff in Ramsgate with no explanation as to how it got there.

In fact he had left his father's butcher's shop on 30 March with a bag containing the very substantial sum of £150 in gold and had gone to Ramsgate with John Walters, one of his father's employees with whom he had been told not to associate. The body was not uninjured; there was evidence that he had been beaten with a screwdriver. Walters was recognised in the town as having bought Carl a pair of trousers and paid in gold. When told that a body had been found under the cliffs, Walters had replied that he hoped it was not that of his friend who had been with him the previous day but who had gone off with a woman. Somewhat fortunately he was acquitted of murder, but was immediately re-arrested and convicted of theft for which he received five years.

Six years later came Jack the Ripper.

The Whitechapel Murders have, perhaps, been the greatest and most lasting contribution to the lore and legend of the East End. Most aficionados who call themselves Ripperologists believe that the five murders which took place over the relatively short period from 31 August 1888, when Mary Ann Nichols was killed in Bucks Row, to 9 November, when Mary Jane Kelly was killed and then mutilated in Millers

Court, Dorset Street, were the work of one man dubbed Jack the Ripper. The other three which are definitely attributed to him are Annie Chapman on 8 September at Hanbury Street and Elizabeth 'Long Liz' Stride and Catherine Eddowes at Berner Street and Mitre Square respectively, both killed on 30 September.

Two earlier murders took place which some attribute to Jack the Ripper. They were of Emma Elizabeth Smith on the night of 2–3 April and, four months later, on 7 August, Martha (or Emma) Tabram, who was also known as Martha Turner, in George Yard Building.

The first can certainly be ruled out, because Emma Smith survived after she was attacked and said she could identify one of the four men involved. She had been seen talking to a man with a white scarf shortly after midnight in Fairance Street, Limehouse, and then reappeared at George Street lodging house and told the deputy that she had been assaulted and robbed in Osborn Street. She was taken to the London Hospital where she was found to have had an instrument, not a knife, inserted in her vagina. She must have been in great pain as she staggered back to the lodgings, but had made no complaint to any police constable she must have passed in the street and was indeed reluctant to be taken to hospital. She died two days later of peritonitis. Unfortunately, it was not until 6 April that the police were informed. It is possible that her attackers were members of the Green Gate Gang or the Old Nichol Gang who operated in the area at the time as ponces and extortionists and as street robbers generally.

So far as Tabram was concerned, her body was first seen about 3 a.m. on 7 August on the first-floor landing of George Yard Building. She had been stabbed 39 times. Earlier in the evening, along with a colleague Pearly Poll, she had picked up two soldiers and had been drinking with them in the Angel and Crown public house. The soldier with Tabram was identified and produced an alibi. It was thought that

Tabram's killer was ambidextrous, and that two weapons of which one was a bayonet had been used. All soldiers then stationed at the Tower of London were put on an identification parade, but Poll failed to pick anyone out. She was ordered to attend the inquest on Tabram and went into hiding. Found in Covent Garden, she was made to attend another identification parade, this time at Chelsea Barracks where out of pique she identified the first two men she saw. In turn they were able to provide alibis.[4]

There was another little flurry over the death of Catherine Millett – the so-called Poplar or Rainham Mystery. Catherine, sometimes called Rose Mylett, was found fully clothed lying in Clarke's Yard off High Street, Poplar, on 20 December 1888 by a Police Sergeant Golding. The Divisional Surgeon Matthew Brownfield saw nothing suspicious and the body was removed for a post mortem, at which time he suggested she had been strangled. However, his assistant Dr Thomas Bond, who earlier had examined the body of Mary Jane Kelly, did not agree and the inquest turned into a medical battle. Four doctors thought she had been strangled with a cord of the type used in those days to cut a bar of soap. Bond and the Coroner Wynne Baxter, who featured in so many of the East End inquests of the time, disagreed. The jury returned a verdict of wilful murder but no suspect, if indeed there ever should have been one, was ever arrested and for a short time there was speculation that Jack the Ripper had changed his methods.[5]

When it comes to it there are perhaps seven serious or semi-serious suspects with little if any evidence against any of them. In descending order there is Montague John Druitt,

---

[4] Walter Dew, *I Caught Crippen*, pp. 95–103. Dew always believed that Emma Smith and Martha Tabram were genuine Ripper victims. He based this on the fact that both killings were on a Bank Holiday Monday.
[5] PRO MEPO 3 143. See also *The Star*, 24 December 1888; *The Advertiser*, 10 January 1899.

a failed barrister who committed suicide by weighting his pockets and drowning in the Thames. His cousin, Dr Lionel Druitt, at one time practised as a doctor in the East End, which gives him the opportunity to hide with his cousin and also to learn the rudiments of anatomy. At least he was favoured by the Assistant Chief Constable of Scotland Yard Sir Melville Macnaghten, but apart from opportunity, which is common to thousands, there appears to be no positive evidence against him.

Then there is public house landlord George Chapman, also known as Severin Antoniovich Klowoswki, who was favoured by Chief Detective Inspector Frederick Abberline, one of the few senior officers involved in the actual hunt not to write his memoirs. He remarked to Inspector George Godley when some years later Chapman was arrested for the poisoning of various wives, 'You've got Jack the Ripper at last.' Just why Chapman should change his *modus operandi* from vivisectionist to poisoner is not clear. Nor it is clear why he should abandon his first career. As for ability, he had been some sort of field surgeon in the Russian army and could have acquired rudimentary skills there.

Dr Thomas Neill Cream was later convicted of poisoning a series of prostitutes. The evidence against him seems to be based solely on the fact that when he was being hanged his last words were 'I'm Jack . . .' This may have been a muffled cry of 'I'm ejaculating', but his supporters take it as evidence of his guilt. A further complication to the flimsy case against him, in that he is recorded as being in prison in America at the time of one of the killings, is overcome by saying that bribery was rife and prison records inaccurate and he may have been released. There is also another fanciful theory, to which Sir Edward Marshall Hall subscribed, that he had a double, also a criminal, and they exchanged names and identities to provide each other with an alibi. Cream, when he was hanged, was repaying a debt by calling out 'I'm Jack the Ripper' – if that is what he intended to say – so clearing his *doppelgänger* of suspicion.[6]

The Duke of Clarence, whose fiancée Princess May of Teck changed her name to Mary and married his brother George V, is favoured by many. Unfortunately, there is an almost insuperable flaw in the argument against him in that he was dead when one of the murders occurred. This is overcome by the ingenious and entertaining conspiracy theory that he had gone mad from syphilis and was being held in a private mental hospital. If this is correct, it means he was from time to time released or escaped, killed and found his own way home again.

If you do not fancy his Royal Highness – or a Masonic connection which is also on offer and which includes the Queen's physician Sir William Gull – then there is an argument against a man who may have been his lover and was certainly his tutor at Cambridge: James Kenneth Stephen, the son of the High Court judge. The reasoning is that when the Duke became engaged he sacrificed 'symbolic' women. The best evidence is that after Stephen received a blow to the head in an accident in 1886 he became increasingly deranged and was committed to an asylum in November 1892, dying three months later. Quite where he obtained the medical skill thought necessary to dissect the poor women is not made clear.

There is, however, a doctor in the frame. Roslyn D'Onston Stephenson was certainly peculiar – a journalist, medico,

---

[6] The case against Cream may not be completely defeated by the fact that he was meant to be in prison. Certainly not if the case of John C. Colt, brother of the inventor of the revolver, is concerned. Whilst in The Tombs prison awaiting execution for the murder of Samuel Adams he appears to have contrived his escape, with considerable help it must be said, by staging a fire and apparently committing suicide but in reality exchanging his position with a corpse. The coroner was aware of the deception and the jury was specially selected to investigate his death. Colt fled with Caroline Henshaw, the woman he had married hours before his escape, either to California or Texas. See Charles Sutton, *The New York Tombs*.

mage and, as Richard Whittington-Egan puts it, 'Man about Whitechapel.' As part of the case against him, it is suggested that the murders were black magic rituals.

The case, such as it is, against each of the principal suspects has been rehearsed time and time again and it is entertaining although idle to look at some of the other names which have been suggested over the years. Sir Melville was by no means wholly committed to the theory that Druitt was the Ripper.[7] He also suggests a Polish Jew Kosminski, in which he is supported by Chief Inspector Donald Sutherland Swanson, and a Russian doctor Michael Ostrog as possible suspects. Martin Fido is on the same lines on the Polish Jew theory. He has traced an Aaron Kozminski as being admitted to Colney Hatch, the North London asylum, on 6 February but, when it comes to it, favours another inmate Nathan Kaminsky who died there in 1889 under the anglicised name of David Cohen.

Other potential claimants to the title have included Frederick Richard Chapman, a Brixton doctor who died of a tuberculous psoas abscess on 12 December 1888. Given his illness, he could easily be eliminated; he would have been hardly able to walk, let alone dart about the alleys of the East End. The evidence against him is based on the account of a former police constable Robert Clifford Spicer who said he had arrested a doctor with bloodstained cuffs and a prostitute, but the pair had been released on the authority of his superior. Spicer had been discharged from the police on 25 April 1889 for being drunk and interfering with two private persons. B.E. Reilly concluded from some research that Chapman was really Dr Merchant, his name being a pseudonym – a chapman was a merchant. This was smartly blown out of the water.[8]

---

[7] Confidential memorandum M.L. Macnaghten, 23 February 1894.
[8] See *Daily Express*, 16 March 1931; B.E. Reilly in *City*, February 1972; Nicholas P. Warren, 'Dr Merchant was not Jack the Ripper' in *The Criminologist*, Spring 1992.

Francis Thompson, the poet, was another off-the-wall suggestion. The evidence against him is that he had some medical training, was a drug addict and therefore unpredictable, had a friendship with a prostitute and 'possessed a chaotic sexuality'. He also had lived in the East End and this familiarity suggests he would have been able to elude the police by darting into the back turns and doubles.[9]

As the years have passed, more and more outlandish theories have been produced. One of the more acceptable is that of Jock the Ripper expounded by Molly Whittington-Egan: William Henry Bury, who killed his wife and was hanged on 24 April 1889. He is said to have been known in Whitechapel and to have left a detailed confession which was never published but which made startling revelations about the Ripper murders. Other less likely candidates have included Mary Kelly's boyfriend Joseph Barnett; George Francis Miles, who was Oscar Wilde's boyfriend; and Charlie the Ripper, a fishmonger who had sexual difficulties.[10] In recent years on the strength of a diary, the authenticity of which is jealously supported and challenged, James Maybrick, possibly poisoned by his wife Florence in Liverpool, has come into the reckoning.

In a compilation of theories of Ripperologists, amateur and professional, in 1995 the identities were, as might be expected, widely spread.

As Donald Rumbelow wrote:

[9] Joseph C. Rupp, 'Was Francis Thompson Jack the Ripper?' in *The Criminologist*, Winter 1982.
[10] Molly Whittington-Egan, *Scottish Murder Stories*, Chapter 16; *True Crime*, April 1982; mentioned but not adopted by Donald Rumbelow *supra* p. 141 and *Reveille*, 12 March 1976 respectively. In Camille Wolff's compilation *Who was Jack the Ripper?*, Wilf Gregg lists no fewer than twenty-five suspects against whom some sort of plausible or implausible case has been made, and the actual list of suspects is probably three times that length. Richard Whittington-Egan has produced an encyclopaedic reference book, *The Quest for Jack the Ripper*, of literature on the Ripper murders up to and including the spring of 2000.

I have always the feeling that on the Day of Judgment, when all things shall be known, when I and the other generations of 'Ripperologists' ask for Jack the Ripper to step forward and call out his true name, we shall turn and look with blank astonishment as he does so and say, 'Who?'[11]

PC Ernest Thompson was thought to be the only person to have seen Jack the Ripper. He had only been in the service for six weeks when on 13 February 1891 he went out on night duty alone for the first time. He was walking through Chambers Street when a man came running out of Swallow Gardens towards the Royal Mint. Thompson saw a man under a lamp with a bag in his hand and he ran after him, but fell over something which turned out to be the body of Frances Coles. He was so upset he wandered in a dazed state and was taken to the local station.

Over the years Thompson became convinced he would never die of natural causes, and indeed he was stabbed to death at Alder Street and the junction with the Commercial Road on 1 December 1900, at the age of 32. The man he apprehended was behaving badly towards some women at a night coffee stall and when questioned moved away to open a clasp knife and returned to stick his knife into Thompson's neck. Thompson held on to the man, calling for assistance, and died with his hands still on the assailant's collar. Barnet Abrahams, a 41-year-old cigar maker, was defended by Charles F. Gill. Abrahams claimed he had been given a severe beating by the police and so remembered nothing of the incident, and the judge directed that the jury should find manslaughter. He received 20 years' penal servitude and died in prison.[12] Thompson left four children

[11] Donald Rumbelow, *The Complete Jack the Ripper*, p. 141.
[12] See Tom Divall, *Scoundrels and Scallywags*, pp. 104–5, and Frederick Wensley, *Detective Days*, pp. 4–5.

all aged under four, and his widow benefited from a collection which raised £338. There is a small memorial to him and two other officers in Tower Hamlets cemetery.[13]

What is certainly apparent is that the Ripper murders produced another wave of anti-Semitic feeling in the East End.[14] It was believed that only a foreigner could have carried out such abominable crimes, a theory argued from time to time by an Assistant Commissioner, Sir Robert Anderson. The theory was based, in part, on a report from *The Times* correspondent safely in Vienna. In 1884 a Jew named Ritter had been tried for the murder and mutilation of a woman in a village near Cracow. The reasoning was that there was a belief amongst fanatical Jews that the Talmud required such an act of atonement by a man who had had sexual relations with a Christian woman. The Chief Rabbi was keen and quick to scotch such a theory. So far as the Talmud was concerned, there was no such direction. But for a time, fuelled by the fact that one of the bodies had been found by a Jewish cemetery in Brady Street, there was the belief that the murder had been committed by one of the *shochets*, ritual Jewish slaughterers, and suspicion fell on a man John Pizer (known as Leather Apron) who fitted the popular conception of Jack the Ripper.

A man of Jewish appearance he was known to have abused prostitutes and after the Mary Nicholls' (sic) murder he disappeared for a time. Rumour spread and many believed he was the Ripper. Eventually he was found by the police and taken into custody at Leman Street Police Station

[13] Other names on the monument are Richard James Barber who, on 2 March 1885, fell through a skylight when chasing James Smith, who received one year hard labour for theft, and William Paster who at the age of 43 drowned whilst on holiday at Margate; he had tried to save a swimmer in difficulties on 24 July 1890.

[14] *Jewish Chronicle*, 14 September 1888; *East London Observer (ELO)*, 15 September 1888.

which, within half an hour, was surrounded by a crowd 'clamouring to get at him'. He provided an alibi but was kept in a place of safety until his name was cleared at the resumed inquest on Mary Nicholls.[15]

The lot of the policeman in the East End at the time was not necessarily a happy one. Describing the Ratcliffe Highway as Tiger Bay, journalist James Greenwood interviewed a local police officer around 1870:

> At times it is unsafe for our men to perambulate it except in a gang of three. They'd have the hair off a man's head if they could get a penny a pound for it.[16]

Describing his time in the East End ten years later, Fred Wensley would have none of the officers walking in threes. He did allow, however, that an officer could expect a hard time.

> Lambeth, however, was a model of probity and decorum compared with Whitechapel. Most of the inhabitants of my new division considered that they had a natural right to get fighting drunk and knock a policeman about whenever the spirit moved them. Bruises and worse were our routine lot. Gangs of hooligans infested the streets and levied blackmail on timorous shopkeepers. There was an enormous amount of personal robbery with violence. The maze of narrow ill-lighted alleyways offered easy ways of escape after a man had been knocked down and his watch and money stolen.[17]

One of the local sports, and one which continued for many years, was stuffing policemen down sewers. Norman

15 Walter Dew, *I Caught Crippen*, pp. 109–11.
16 James Greenwood, *The Wilds of London*, p. 1.
17 Frederick Wensley, *Detective Days*, p. 8.

Nettaway, who later himself served throughout the East End, recalls that his grandfather as a special constable received a certificate for pulling a constable out of a manhole.[18]

Wensley went to Whitechapel shortly before the turn of the century and never really left it. However the area might have been regarded by the ordinary citizen at that time, there is no doubt that it was the finest training-ground imaginable for a young detective.

> Men and women ripe for any crime from murder to pilfering were to be found in its crowded slums and innumerable common-lodging houses. The off-scourings of the criminal population of Europe – Russians, Poles, Germans, Austrians and Frenchmen – found a refuge there. Many of them, British as well as foreign, carried knives or guns which they did not hesitate to use. Organised gangs of desperate men and lads, armed with lethal weapons, infested the streets, terrorizing whole areas, blackmailing tradesmen, holding up wayfarers, and carrying out more or less open robbery in any direction that offered.[19]

Murders probably went uninvestigated and unrecorded and, unless there was clear evidence of foul play, those whose bodies were found near houses of ill-repute received open verdicts.

To counter these hooligans there was a collection of what Wensley described, with perhaps some understatement in parts, as outstanding figures.

> Some of them, by present day standards, may have been a little rough and uncultivated, but they had the most wonderful knowledge of criminals ... They lived for their work.

18 Conversation with the author, 4 November 1999.
19 F. Wensley, *Detective Days*, pp. 13–14.

Wensley was proud to have graduated from the ranks of men like 'Chinaman' Thompson and 'Johnny Upright' Sergeant John Thicke:

> I myself early attained the distinction of a nickname amongst criminals of the district. Those who spoke English called me Weasel – which I felt to be something of a compliment – and the foreigners corrupted it into 'Venzel'.

An assessment of his position nearly a century later puts his nickname in a slightly different context:

> Wensley knew his ground well and seems to have had an exceptional memory for detail, but he was unpopular with the Whitechapel immigrants who suspected him of corruption. Probably he knew rather less about the ways of immigrants than he tried to make out.[20]

One of the more curious aspects of detective work at the time, and one against which Wensley rebelled, was the practice of keeping detectives confined to their own areas, which gave criminals a relatively free hand since they could move districts in the almost certain knowledge that they would not be recognised.

> A divisional superintendent did not like officers leaving his district to operate in another; and a local detective inspector resented detectives from other districts 'poaching' on his division. He would hint pretty broadly that if he wanted their aid he would apply for it.[21]

One of Wensley's earliest arrests as a young detective followed an attack on a Jewish shopkeeper and his housekeeper on

---

20 Andrew Rose, *Stinie*, p. 13.
21 F. Wensley, *Detective Days*, p. 39.

4 April 1896. With Harry Richardson, he was called to Turner Street between Commercial Street and the Whitechapel Road. They climbed into the premises through a back window and began opening the doors of the tenement. One was pushed back at them and when Wensley broke through they found the body of 75-year-old John Goodman Levy. Upstairs in the front bedroom, which had been ransacked, was that of his housekeeper Sarah Gale. There was a hole in the ceiling and when they heard sounds above them Richardson volunteered to climb up. Wensley followed him.

On the roof they found the murderer about to jump into the street 40 feet below, anticipating that the crowd of onlookers would break his fall. Wensley went back through the hole, down the stairs and was in the street almost immediately after the man jumped, knocking himself unconscious and injuring several of the spectators.

The robber was William Saunders (also known as Seaman), supposedly a sailor from Millwall but in fact a ticket-of-leave man who over the years had served 28 years of penal servitude. On the last occasion he had walked into a chemist's shop in Whitechapel and asked for the loan of a hammer. When handed it, he hit the shopkeeper over the head and ransacked the premises.

It seems that for a time at any rate Seaman played the wronged lover. The woman at whose rooms in Millwall he was staying was brought in to make an identification, and she asked him why he had killed the pair:

> 'Revenge,' he replied. 'He did me the greatest injustice one man can do another.'
> 'Why, was that woman your wife?'
> 'No.'

And unfortunately the officer in charge then put a stop to this rather interesting conversation.

Later, his version of the crime was that he had known both Levy and Sarah Gale for some time and that Levy owed him some £70. The implication was that Levy had been acting as Seaman's receiver. On the morning of the murder he was let in by Levy and went upstairs to the girl's bedroom. She began shouting and kicking before he killed her and then went downstairs and killed Levy. It was then that he heard someone at the door.

The story was false at least in parts. There was no evidence that Sarah Gale had been killed in her room. So far as Wensley was concerned, there was an anonymous letter to back Seaman's implication that Levy was a receiver but no hard evidence. Seaman's statement ended:

> I then got on the roof from the inside and saw my only chance was to dive down off the roof head first. If it had not been for someone breaking my fall I should not have been lying in here. But there it is. Everyone has to die sometime. I know I am going to get hung and would not care if it was now, for I am tired of life.

However, in a curious way Saunders/Seaman still had a part to play in life. At the time of the Levy killing there had been a murder in Muswell Hill involving Henry Fowler and Albert Milsom, who had battered a wealthy retired engineer, Henry Smith, to death. They had also tortured him to make him disclose the contents of his safe. Milsom had put the blame on Fowler, a giant of a man who in turn had repeatedly threatened his co-defendant. As the verdicts of guilty were announced Fowler threw himself on Milsom and, in a fight lasting some twelve minutes before he was subdued, the whole dock at the Old Bailey was smashed. When both were brought under heavy guard for sentence, Milsom made whining pleas for leniency which were mimicked by Fowler.

On 9 June, in the last triple execution held at Newgate,

Seaman was put between Milsom and Fowler to prevent any further trouble. He is alleged to have said, 'Well, this is the first time in my life I've ever had to act as a peace-maker.'

By the end of the century the Rev. Samuel Barnett of St Jude's, Whitechapel, feared he had made no progress in bringing Christianity to the area. In a lament to *The Times* he wrote:

> After six years of work, after everything has been done which money can provide or thought can suggest, I have to confess that in the past year the church has been as little used as ever.[22]

Of course, one of his problems was that now many of his potential congregation were Jewish. And those who were not still did not seem to appreciate things.

[22] *The Times*, 7 April 1897.

2

Immigrants

The great Jewish migration to the East End of London began in the 1860s and gathered pace after the assassination of Tsar Alexander II in 1881. There had long been a Jewish presence in the East End and City of London, but these were the Sephardic Jews. The seemingly uncontrollable influx was of Ashkenazi Jews and, in a matter of years, the once-important Sephardic congregation had been reduced to numerical insignificance.[1]

In the 1850s some 18–20,000 Jews had lived in London, around 12,000 of them in the City itself. By 1902–3 there were some 140–150,000 in the East End alone, with the area around Whitechapel High Street and Commercial Road East the most heavily populated.[2]

The Jews were the dispossessed. Following a series of

---

[1] D. Swarc, 'Background and conditions contributing to Jewish prostitution in the East End of London 1890–1914' (unpublished manuscript).

[2] In 1901 there were at least 42,000 Russian-born Jews in Whitechapel. They were generally accepted in the community and in 1894 there were only 99 Russians and Poles amongst the 1,972 aliens in British prisons. The number rose substantially and then, after the Aliens Act 1905, declined. Thomas Arnold, Supt. H Div. Evidence to the Select Committee on Emigration and Immigration (Foreigners) showed they were committing only petty crime which included counterfeiting and burglaries. They did not steal for food. The main complaint was that they did not wash. Parliamentary Papers X (1889).

anti-Semitic edicts by the Tsars who ruled not only Russia but Poland, for some years they had been restricted to an area known as the Pale of Settlement on the Polish–Russian border. They were debarred from taking employment in government projects such as roads and railways and state manufacturing – in effect, anything to do with modern industrial growth. This left them with traditional employment – tailoring, bootmaking, working in cigarette factories – and in all these endeavours they worked in competition with each other.

There were also other hardships and restrictions. Fit young Jewish men were subject to conscription at any age between 12 and 25, where they could be required to serve for a period of 35 years. The mortality rate was high.

After the assassination of Tsar Alexander II by Jessie Helfmann, a seamstress, on 1 March 1881, an anti-Semitic campaign was launched in an attempt to deflect popular discontent. Apart from the pogrom in Kherson there were others in Kiev, Odessa and Warsaw, with some two hundred communities being the victims of arson, pillage and rape. One stated aim of the revolutionists was to have the troops defend the Jews against the Christians. The troops would either refuse or there would be a general uprising; it did not matter which. Now the Jews fled to England to find either a home or a resting-place for the longer journey to America.

During the winter of 1886–7 some 70 per cent of dock labourers, building craftsmen, tailors and bootmakers in the East End were unemployed, many for over two months. Unemployment in the three preceding years was the worst continuous sequence of any period prior to the First World War.[3]

By 1887 it was estimated that one third of Tower Hamlets'

---

[3] See W.W. Roston, *British Economy of the Nineteenth Century*, p. 49.

population lived on or below the poverty line, and 55 per cent of East End children died before they attained five years as compared with 18 per cent of children from other parts of London.

Typical of pious sentiments uttered for the jubilee of Queen Victoria was that written by the Reverend Simeon Singer, who would play a major part in the murder trial of Israel Lipski the next year:

> We are Englishmen and the thoughts and feelings of Englishmen are our thoughts and feelings.[4]

Despite this, there was considerable anti-Semitic sentiment being bruited in some of the magazines of the time:

> Foreign Jews of no nationality whatever are becoming a pest and a menace to the poor native born East-Ender – [they have] greater responsibility for the distress which prevails there probably than all other cases put together.[5]

It was said of St George's in the East that a murder had been committed in every house in this depressing area just off the Commercial Road, and on 28 June 1885 one of the more famous crimes occurred there when the body of the six-month-pregnant Miriam Angel was found at 16 Batty Street where she lived with her husband, Isaac. She was 21 and came from near Warsaw. She had made him his breakfast overnight and he left her in bed when he went to work at 6.15 a.m.

Philip and Leah Lipski lived at 16 Batty Street and let the

[4] *Jewish Chronicle*, 25 June 1886.
[5] 'Judenhetze Brewing in East London' in the *Pall Mall Gazette*, 18 February 1886. See also Simeon Singer's reply in the edition of 23 February.

top room to Israel Lipski who was an unmarried stick maker – what we would call frames for an umbrella. Leah Lipski, his landlady who was no relation, told the inquest held on 29 June and 1 July 1885 before Wynne E. Baxter that Israel had been a lodger for the last two years. He was a good worker when there was any, was of good character and had a fiancée, Kate Lyons, who steadfastly believed in his innocence. Batty Street was one of the poorest in the neighbourhood; average wages would be between 18 shillings and a guinea and the rent six shillings weekly.

Shortly after 11 o'clock that morning, Mrs Angel's mother came round and went up to her daughter's room where she knocked and could get no reply. She and Mrs Lipski went into the room, saw Miriam on the bed and, thinking she had fainted, went for the doctor, John William Kay, in the Commercial Road.

He arrived at 11.30 and found a very different situation. Beside the German feather-bed was a glass tumbler containing stout. On the bed was the dead Miriam Angel. She had corrosive fluid running from her mouth and onto her neck and breast and her tongue was burned. Kay could find no bottle on the sheets, so he pulled them aside to see if it had fallen down and saw the face of Lipski, protruding from under the bed. He gave him two slaps and he started; his mouth was injured with corrosive fluid in the same way as Miriam Angel's. The bottle found at the foot of the bed under some clothes was labelled Camphorated Oil, Bell and Co., 100 Commercial Road, corner of Batty Street. As for Miriam Angel, on her right eye and temple were marks of a serious blow probably made by a fist. There were no marks of violence about the genitals, but there was what appeared to be semen in the vagina. The girl's thighs were wide apart, and legs, thighs and genitals exposed; what is now seen as a classic position for the victim of a rape murder. When Kay gave evidence at the inquest on the second day he said it might be semen but there was no spermatozoa. When asked, Isaac Angel said that he had not had intercourse – described euphemistically as connection – with his wife on the morning of her death or the previous evening.

When Lipski recovered, his statement to the police was that he had returned to Batty Street from work during the morning when two men had taken hold of him by the throat, poured poison into his mouth and asked for his gold chain. Lipski said it was in pawn. He said they had told him, 'If you don't give it to us you will be as dead as the woman.' He suggested one of the men was a Simon Rosenbloom.

There was indeed a Simon Rosenbloom, but he gave a very different version of events. He said that he and Lipski had previously been apprenticed together and Lipski had offered him work when he met him the previous Saturday. Lipski gave him some work on the Tuesday and then said he was going out to buy a sponge and vice.

The nitric acid, said Charles Moore of Bell and Co., had been bought by someone who was not English the previous Saturday. He knew the man was a stick maker from his clothes.

There does not appear to have been anything in the way of cross-examination of the witnesses, nor was there any evidence that Lipski had behaved oddly or shown any sign of sexual interest in Miriam Angel. The jury returned a unanimous verdict of wilful murder by Lipski, who was committed for trial at the Central Criminal Court.

He was tried in the July before Mr Justice James Fitzjames Stephen, who summed up heavily against him. In fact his whole trial was fraught with difficulties. A small public subscription raised enough money to pay for his counsel. His solicitor, a John Hammond who had a Jewish clerk, seems to have done the work unpaid. At first Gerald Geoghegan, one of the first-rank barristers at the Old Bailey, was briefed on Lipski's behalf; but unfortunately Geoghegan had a tendency to drink, particularly before a capital case which he feared he might lose. Although he was present throughout the trial he took no part and Lipski was defended by a commercial silk, A. J. McIntyre QC.[6]

At the time a prisoner was not allowed to give evidence on his own behalf. He could call witnesses and make an unsworn statement from the dock, but the danger in either of these courses was that the defence then forfeited to the Crown the final speech to the jury. Lipski remained silent.

The basis of the prosecution was that Lipski had seen the heavily pregnant woman through a window onto the stairs as he went to his attic room and, overcome by lust, had attacked her. The difficulty with this is that the purchasing of the corrosive argues a degree of premeditation. The other occupants of what was a small tenement building do not

---

[6] PRO Crim 1 26 5. For a full account of the case, which argues Lipski's innocence or at least that there was not sufficient evidence on which to hang him, see Martin L. Friedland, *The Trials of Israel Lipski*.

James Fitzjames Stephen (1829–95) who had no great practice at the Bar and craved the prestige of a position on the bench, has a number of claims, dubious and otherwise, to fame. Curiously, he wrote for the *Pall Mall Gazette* for five years from 1865 and, rather more wholly meritoriously, a number of legal textbooks including *Stephen's Commentaries of the Laws of England*, which was used as a basic text in law schools well into the 1960s. On the down side was his cruelly adverse summing up in the Mrs Maybrick poisoning which did for the poor woman. Within two years of that case he was in a mental asylum, following his son James Kenneth Stephen who is one of the more abstruse suspects – based on his once being the tutor of another vague suspect, the Duke of Clarence – of being Jack the Ripper. Stephen jnr had been hit on the head in 1886 and never really recovered, beginning to show dangerous signs in November 1891; he died three months later. Stephen J. was, however, never in doubt of Lipski's guilt.

A subscription was set up to thank Hammond for his tireless efforts for Lipski, but it closed with only three contributions. He died in 1917 leaving an estate of a little over £100.

appear to have noticed any previous conduct by Lipski to suggest he was a potential rapist.

For a while there was considerable agitation that Lipski's conviction had been wrong but on the day before his execution at Newgate, after days spent in prayer with the Reverend Simeon Singer, he made a full confession which satisfied some people for the time. His story was that he had gone into Miriam Angel's room to steal and, despairing of his impoverished situation, had taken poison himself. The confession has the smell of a compromise. It obviated the slur of an attempted rape, but it is difficult to understand since on the morning of the killing he had set himself up in a new business and had a loyal and supportive fiancée and her family.

It was rumoured that he had made an earlier confession which had been torn up whilst there was still hope of a reprieve. Was the confession genuine, or was it made when there was no hope of a reprieve on the instigation of Singer who feared public disorder in a climate of growing anti-Semitism?

Certainly the confession was wrong. In it Lipski said he had gone to the room to steal and had been surprised. He then poured the corrosive down Mrs Angel's throat and took some himself. This had taken place almost immediately before her body was found. The medical evidence, however, contradicted this. Mrs Angel had been dead some two to three hours before her body was discovered.

He was hanged by James Berry at Newgate on 22 August. Berry, who had a history of accidents when hanging prisoners, once again miscalculated the length of drop required to break Lipski's neck and instead nearly decapitated him. When the black flag signifying a successful execution was run up at the prison, the crowd outside gave three cheers. Berry – sickened no doubt by his mistake, and moved by the Hebrew prayers chanted from the condemned cell – said he would not execute another Jew.[7] After his death 'Lipski' became a Yiddish and anti-Semitic insult.

Curiously, some thirty years later the body of another pregnant woman was found in St George's in the East with a man lying by her bed. The circumstances were, however, very different from the Lipski case and, on 30 December 1920 at Pentonville prison, Marks Goodmacher became only the second Orthodox Jew to be executed for murder when he was hanged. Russian born, he had served in the Tsar's army from 1898 to 1899. He came to England in 1908 and worked as a ladies' tailor's presser; he was then 35. He lived at 57 Lambeth Street, Whitechapel, with his wife Sarah and they had a son and a daughter, Fanny. Goodmacher, a thoroughly evil-tempered man, drove his wife out of the home. When his daughter married Sion Zeitoun in 1919, at first they lived with her father at Lambeth Street but they soon moved.

Fanny had complained to a friend, Esther Albert:

Oh I can't open my heart to you but this I can tell you, that my father loved my mother and because she left him his love has grown for me. He does not like me to go out or speak to anybody as he is very jealous of me. I must leave home through him.

Goodmacher began telling Zeitoun that his wife was having relations with other men. When that did not seem to have an adverse effect on the marriage, he then took to calling his son-in-law a ponce and spitting at him in the street. Relations

[7] James Berry retired in 1892 following another partial decapitation, this time of John Conway in Liverpool. He then became a music hall lecturer and a lay preacher. He died in Bradford in October 1913. It is thought by many that Lipski was the first Jew to be hanged in modern times, but this is not correct. William Marwood hanged Isaac Marks on 2 January 1874. He had been convicted of the Lambeth shooting of Frederick Bernard, at one time his intended father-in-law but whom Marks came to believe had cheated him in business.

were cut off but, to his fury, the couple still visited neighbours of Goodmacher; he said that if they went again he would cut the baby out of his pregnant daughter's belly. It was apparently a threat he made regularly.

Despite his threats and behaviour Goodmacher expected his daughter to seek a reconciliation on the Day of Atonement that year. When she did not go round to Lambeth Street during the day, he was heard that evening cursing in his yard in Yiddish saying, 'Why don't she come and see me? Why hasn't she come today? I will kill her tomorrow. I will cut her in the stomach.'

At 8.30 p.m. on 23 September 1920, the police went to 17 Grove Street, St George's in the East, to the top-floor room where Fanny Zeitoun was lying fully dressed with her throat cut with a razor. Goodmacher was also lying by the bed with his throat cut. He was taken to hospital and survived.

He had cut all her clothes, torn a fur necklet to pieces, broken a set of spoons and generally done what damage he could to the room, almost certainly in her absence since there was little sign of a struggle. The police surmised that she had been in the lavatory in the basement when he arrived and returning to her room had found him there. From the bloodstains they concluded that her throat was cut from behind, right-to-left – Goodmacher was left-handed – near the fireplace, and it seems he then put her on the bed and tried either to staunch the blood or wipe it clean. He then cut his own throat. Blood dripped through the ceiling and when they went to investigate at about 5 p.m., incredibly the neighbours thought Fanny must have had a miscarriage and had gone out afterwards. Her husband came home at about 8 p.m. to find her body. Goodmacher was charged with her murder and also the then offence of attempted suicide.

The defence relied on a plea of insanity at the brief trial at the Central Criminal Court on 18 November 1920, but it did not succeed. Dr Griffiths of Brixton prison was called in the hope that he would say the man was insane, but instead he gave evidence that although Marks Goodmacher was an hysterical and passionate man he could find no trace of insanity. In those days, and for some years subsequently, prison doctors rarely found their charges to be unfit for punishment, capital or otherwise.[8]

At the turn of the century, a favourite form of robbery was with the garotte. It was not the Spanish form of execution which involved a mask with a metal pin slowly tightened, but a neck hold which, properly applied, brought about unconsciousness. 'Properly applied' was the key phrase. Too much force and the victim died.

> You would come up to a man from behind, put your arms round his throat, with your fists on his throttle. If it went on for more than a few seconds he would choke, so you had to be skilled.[9]

A convicted garotter could expect a heavy sentence; 5 years and, worse, a 'bashing', 18 strokes with the cat o' nine tails.

The Reubens brothers were not sufficiently experienced and they paid the penalty. On 15 March 1909 the steamer *Dorset* berthed at the Victoria Docks and that night two officers, William Sproull (the second engineer) and McEachern (the second mate), went off on what was to be a drunken spree. They were not complete innocents. They expected to be tapped for money, and since they regarded it as insulting to give beggars bronze coins they carried with them a supply of silver threepenny pieces.

Around 2.30 the next morning the body of Sproull was found in Rupert Street just behind Leman Street. A police-man called by the night-watchman who found the body

8 PRO MEPO 3 285A.
9 Raphael Samuel, *East End Underworld*, p. 112.

saw McEachern leaning against a wall in the Whitechapel Road. His almost incoherent story was that the pair had eaten somewhere in Aldgate and had then toured the public houses. They met two girls, Emily Stevens and Ellen Charge, and agreed to go home with them to 3 Rupert Street. Whilst they were with them the door burst open and in came the Reubens brothers, Morris and Marks.

Questioned by Inspector Wensley, who was called, the constable remembered that two rough-looking men had been peering through the shutters of a house in Rupert Street earlier in the night. From the place where Sproull's body was found, a trail of silver coins led back to 3 Rupert Street. Marks Reubens was arrested in the house and a young prostitute in Room 13 admitted that she had brought a man back to the room. As the police searched the remaining rooms Morris Reubens was found and admitted that Stevens and Charge had brought Sproull and McEachern back. When the men refused to hand over the rest of their money the brothers had attacked them.

When Morris Reubens was searched, a constable found that sewn into the leg of his trousers was a series of hooks on which swung Sproull's watch and chain. It appeared that after having sex with the girls, McEachern had decided to return to the ship rather than to stay the night, taking Sproull with him. The Reubens brothers had known the girls had gone back to Room 13 and probably one of them had signalled to the brothers who were listening outside the room. Instead of rolling the sailors whilst asleep, as would have been the normal practice if they wanted the remainder of their money – about £5 each – they were forced to attack them as they left. McEachern may have been hopelessly drunk, something which probably saved him, but Sproull put up serious resistance. Morris Reubens had a stick of hippopotamus hide and this was broken in the fight. Now Marks used a pocket-knife; Sproull was stabbed twice in the face and in the wrist as well as the body. They managed to get Sproull to the door and pushed him onto the street saying, for the benefit of a passer-by, 'Get out! You don't live here.'

At the trial at the Old Bailey Morris claimed he did not know his brother had a knife. Both said it was the sailors who had attacked them. They were unable to explain the watch and chain. The defence was not one which appealed to the jury, who convicted them both after a retirement of 12 minutes. Morris began to call out 'Mercy, Mercy' whilst Marks fought with the warders before they were led away screaming. They were hanged at Pentonville on 20 May by Henry and Thomas Pierrepoint. Marks is said to have apologised to Sproull's relatives and said, 'Goodbye Morris, I am sorry . . .'

Wensley wrote:

> From that date, robbery with violence grew unfashionable in East London and few unaccountable dead bodies were found in the streets.[10]

It may be that a small industry was born with the execution of the Reubens brothers. A little later Wensley was sent a whisky glass with a hanging man engraved on the base. The inscription was 'The Brothers Reubens – the last drop'. Similar items were a favourite gift at such events as Masonic ladies' nights until well into the 1960s.

By no means all immigrant crime was the fairly amateur mugging and rolling of sailors. In 1901 the middle-aged German woman Bertha Weiner, from Shadwell, came to grief along with her twelve-strong gang of housebreakers and thieves. Their targets were big suburban houses standing in their own grounds, and up to five of the gang would go

[10] See PRO CRIM 1 112/4; F. Wensley, *Detective Days*, p. 92.

on what were meticulously researched expeditions. The raids were carried out with seeming impunity.

Wensley claims that it was when he saw a number of men in the Shadwell area who appeared to have money and the leisure to spend it that he became suspicious. He began shadowing the area and discovered that many of the men lived in a house in Albert Street which was regularly visited by Bertha Weiner who paid the rent. She lived with a sailor, Rebork, in Ship Alley about a mile away. She had an auctioneer brother, Ludwig, who with his two sons lived in Tredegar Square, Bow.

According to Wensley, Bertha Weiner was the putter-up and financier. The men from Albert Street were the burglars and disposed of the articles to her. The better pieces were auctioned by her brother and nephews.

The raid scheduled for 28 October was aborted when Wensley's father was taken seriously ill and the next night a housebreaking took place in Willesden with the windows and doors forced, the silver and wines removed from the cellar and much of the owner's clothing taken. The police eventually raided on 31 October when eight men were arrested in Albert Street. One put on a pair of stolen socks and another had a hat taken in the burglary. Wensley went to Ship Alley and broke in on the home of Rebork and Bertha Weiner at the same time as other officers raided her relations in Tredegar Square. One of the curious pieces of evidence against them was a small badge which had been presented to Sir Montague Sharpe, then deputy Chairman of Middlesex Sessions, by his fellow judges. One of the gang, Wald, a professional wrestler, wore it with pride, claiming he had won it in a tournament in Germany.

Bertha Weiner received 7 years' penal servitude at the Old Bailey in December 1901 and, with the exception of a nephew, the others were sentenced to 5 years. The young Weiner received twelve months.

In his autobiography[11] published in 1931, Frederick Wensley wrote:

> Any reader of the daily papers these days might come to the conclusion that Chicago is the only place in which organised bands of desperate criminals ever existed. The public have a short memory. It is not so very long ago that we, in the East End and some other districts of London, were engaged in stamping out groups of criminals, many of whom carried arms, and who waged a sort of warfare among themselves and against the public.

He continued:

> In the early part of the century there was one gang of this class who had established a real reign of terror among certain people in the East End.

The victims were those same people who are always the victims:

> In the main, however, the victims were persons who for some reason or another were a little shy of bringing their troubles to the notice of the police. Keepers of shady restaurants, runners of gambling dens, landlords of houses of resort, street bookmakers and other people on the fringe of the underworld were among those peculiarly open to trouble.

And of the others:

> Sometimes small tradesmen were offered 'protection' against

[11] F. Wensley, *Detective Days*.

other gangs at a price. If they did not take kindly to
this blackmail all sorts of unpleasant things were liable
to happen to them ... Persons who had resisted their
extortions had been brutally assaulted, their premises
wrecked – in one case an attempt to burn down a building
had been made – and any portable property stolen.

The principal East End immigrant gang which operated
around the turn of the century was the forty-strong pack,
the Whitechapel-based Bessarabians, sometimes known as the
Bessarabian Tigers or the Bessarabian Fighters.

The Russian Jews with their ingrained terror of the police
would, in practically every case, rather put up with the
gangs than risk the consequences of complaining to the
police ... we were continually having to let cases drop
through lack of evidence.
   They levied a protection toll on timid alien shopkeepers, proprietors of coffee-stalls and so on. The faintest
shadow of protest on their part at this blackmail and the
gang descended on them in force armed with guns, knives
and such weapons as broken bottles.[12]

In *Lost London*, the former Detective Sergeant B. Leeson gave
another example of their methods:

Lists of people to be blackmailed were drawn up by the
gangsters, and amongst these prospective brides provided the happiest and most productive results. A few
days before the wedding ceremony a gangster would
approach the bride's parents and threaten to expose all
sorts of imaginary indiscretions of which their daughter
had been guilty if their silence was not bought. The

[12] George W. Cornish, *Cornish of the Yard*, p. 4.

victims, fearful of the scandal that might ensue, invariably paid up.[13]

They ruled for almost a whole decade with their chief rivals the Odessians, so named because a man, Weinstein – also known as Kikal, the proprietor of the Odessa – took on the Bessarabians. He refused to pay protection money and, according to Leeson, fought them off with an iron bar when they came to demand their wages. The rival gang, which did not include Weinstein, took the name as a tribute to his courage.

For the next year or so there were the usual gang skirmishes. The Odessians threatened to cut off the ears of a leading Bessarabian named Perkoff. He was lured into an alley and one ear was removed before the local police arrived. In return, a coffee stall under the protection of the Odessians was attacked.

One of the final exploits of the Bessarabians came in 1902 when Barnet Badeczosky, Joseph Weinstein and Max Moses (who boxed at Wonderland under the name Kid McCoy) attacked Philip Garalovitch in Union Street. This was also an example of the power the gang wielded.

It is not now possible to decide whether this was simply robbery or had a political motive because Garalovitch was an ex-Russian police officer. At the magistrates' court the former officer said that Weinstein had gone up to him saying, 'Hello, you gave me two years' imprisonment in Russia.' He had replied, 'I only did my duty.'

Badeczosky then knocked him to the ground and took his watch from his chain. Max Moses took £6, his hat and his umbrella. When Garalovitch's companion, a man named Rosenberg, tried to stop him Moses hit him.

By the time the case appeared again in the court witnesses

---

[13] B. Leeson, *Lost London*, p. 147.

had been threatened and Garalovitch had sensibly gone to South Africa. Barnet Badeczosky and Joseph Weinstein were discharged, and Max Moses was fined £3 with the alternative of one month's imprisonment for his assault on Rosenberg: so apart from having to pay a lawyer, he made £3 from the deal.

The effective end of the Bessarabians came in October that year following an attack by them on a Yiddish music hall held in the York Minster, a public house in Philpot Street off the Commercial Road, where a number of Odessians were thought to be. There had been trouble the previous Saturday and witnesses spoke of Bessarabians going up and down the Commercial Road asking the whereabouts of their rivals.

One man, sometimes called Henry Brodovich but also known as Kaufmann, was stabbed to death. In the ensuing confusion the public was either less discreet or more likely less frightened than usual and names were named. As a result Max Moses, Samuel Oreman and Barnet Badeczosky were arrested. 'If that man had not died £15 would have squared it,' said Moses. He was said to have shouted, 'I'll give you India Rubber Mob,' pulling on a knuckle-duster.

It was clear that witnesses were at risk and the stipendiary magistrate Mead issued a warning that those convicted of threats would face imprisonment. This intelligence failed to percolate to Woolf Selvitzky, a restaurant keeper said to be the leader of the Bessarabians, and Marks Lipman, because the following week they were promptly convicted of an assault on Marks Mieland. Selvitzky had punched him saying, 'My pal is in trouble through you.' Two months' hard labour each.[14]

The week after that Woolf Kigesky and Joe Zelkowitz each received a month's hard labour. They had been endeavouring

[14] *ELO*, 1 November 1902.

to raise funds for their friends' defence and Morris Goldberg had refused to pay until threats were made.[15]

Meanwhile the committal proceedings on the murder charge continued and, somewhat against the perceived wisdom, E.S. Abinger, who would later have difficulties in the defence of Steinie Morrison, called witnesses to show that McCoy was indeed the victim of a planned attack. Evidence was called that people including the dead man, Henry Brodovich, who was said to have been armed with an iron bar, had been out looking for and threatening to harm McCoy that night. For the present it did neither him nor the others any good. They were all committed for trial. What must be remembered is that almost all the evidence except that of the police was translated by interpreters.

Alleged heads of the Bessarabians kept popping up. Presumably after the imprisonment of Selvitzky, Woolf Schaberman had taken over, for he was described as the head of the gang when he appeared charged with being concerned in the robbery of Max Goldman, a butcher, and stealing the watch of Harris Harman. This seems to have been a curious affair. Schaberman is said to have knocked Goldman down and then bitten him before stealing £8 in gold and his chain. Harman's watch was found in Schaberman's possession. It is difficult now to say what exactly happened or, indeed, who was batting for whom, because the police officer in the case said that Goldman had been very drunk and despite the finding of the watch Schaberman was discharged.

With their leaders in prison the Bessarabians faded from power, although they were still hired to break up Anarchist and Social Democrat meetings. When not working they could be found playing cards in a Roumanian restaurant at the corner of Setters Street and the Commercial Road. Meanwhile the police chipped away at the Odessians. Many went to

[15] ibid, 8 November 1902.

America where they joined forces with the local crooks. One known as 'Tilly the Burglar' is said to have become a Chicago policeman.[16]

There is no doubt that the Odessians and the Bessarabians committed crime for money and perhaps power in the community. The position of the so-called Anarchists and Socialist Jews is less clear. Certainly the latter spent some time and effort in provoking the Orthodox. Troubles broke out in September 1904, when for a week the Socialist Jews battled with the faithful. On 17 September there was a free fight with Jews returning from Shool and two days later, on the Monday, the Socialist Jews hired a hall opposite a Whitechapel synagogue and drove a food van through the streets. For their sins they were stoned and in turn they pelted a synagogue. The police rather took the side of the Orthodox Jews but it was not a position which found favour with Cluer, the stipendiary magistrate. Abraham Greenstone, the manager of the restaurant, was discharged on payment of the interpreter's fee and Cluer said that he hoped that next year if there was trouble the Orthodoxy would be the ones brought before him. He added that the Chief Commissioner of Police should take a strong line even if it meant 1,000 Orthodox Jews in the dock.

> [It is] disgraceful that a class of persons who for centuries have been distinguished as the victims of the fiercest persecutions should, when in the one free country of the world, turn upon those who disagreed with them upon religious points: their own co-religionists and stone and persecute them.

Later in the day he displayed something of an anti-Semitic attitude altogether when he dealt with Samuel Harris, described

[16] According to Leeson, McCoy also went to America on his release and became a successful businessman.

as an English Jew, who had robbed Esther Tobias of a watch
and chain: 'And this is the Day of Atonement. I thought they
all stopped indoors on that day.'

His comments did not pass unnoticed. A correspondent
replied:

> There are no more law abiding people in the world than
> the Orthodox Jews; but Socialists whether Jews or Gentiles
> – well they are Socialists.[17]

And it was the East End-based Socialists who, over the next
few years, would feature in a series of some of the best known
cases of the twentieth century. Their home-from-home in
London was the Anarchists Club, patronised by the Russian
nobleman Prince Kropotkin who advocated that need rather
than work was the only criterion of the distribution of
property. Hand in hand with that philosophy went the
one of expropriation – that is the taking away of property
from the individual for redistribution amongst the many.
In theory this was not a licence to steal for oneself, that
being a truly bourgeois concept. Whether in practice it was
always adopted is another matter. By the first decade of the
twentieth century there were many expropriators amongst the
immigrant community of Whitechapel.

Two of the first who came to the notice of the public
were Paul Hefeld and Jacob Lepidus who, on the morning
of 23 January 1909, carried out what became known as
the Tottenham Outrage.[18] Hefeld had for a time worked
at Schnurmann's Rubber Factory in Chestnut Road near
the police station. Lepidus had worked in a local furniture

---

[17] *ELO*, 24 September 1904.
[18] Lepidus may well not have been his name but it is used here for
convenience. If it was correct he was probably the younger brother of
Leister Lepidus who was killed in Paris on 1 May 1907 when a bomb
he was carrying exploded in his pocket.

factory. They knew the timing of the wages run to a bank in Hackney carried out by chauffeurs Joseph Wilson and Albert Keyworth, and at 10.30 as Keyworth got out of the car with a bag containing £80, the firm's wage bill for the week, Lepidus leaped on him. Wilson, who had begun to drive away, stopped the car and went to help his younger colleague. Lepidus pulled Wilson off and it was then that Hefeld shot a bystander, George Smith, in the shoulder before the pair ran into the maze of streets which would eventually take them to Tottenham Marshes.

They were chased by two constables, PC Tyler and PC Newman, who in turn were followed by a number of other off-duty policemen who had been in the nearby section house. Wilson restarted the car and collected Tyler and Newman. Now an excited crowd took up the chase. Wilson caught up with the robbers in Mitchley Road and Newman ordered him to run them down. Both held their ground and shot at the car, hitting the radiator and windscreen. Both Newman and Wilson were slightly injured. A stray bullet hit a young boy, Ralph Joscelyne, in the chest; he died almost instantly.

Now an officer was sent back to the police station to obtain guns and Tyler and Newman split up to try to head them off before they reached the Marshes. When they were twenty yards away Tyler called on Lepidus and Hefeld to surrender. Instead of obeying, Hefeld shot him in the neck. Newman borrowed a gun from one of the crowd, fired and missed. Tyler was taken to the Prince of Wales Hospital where he died.

The men made their way north-east reaching Stonebridge Lock, trading shots with their pursuers who had now been joined by footballers who had been playing on the Marshes. Generally the crowd followed at a safe distance, but when Sidney Slater came too close he was shot in the thigh for his pains. Now some men out duck-shooting shot at the pair, hitting Lepidus in the head.

The chase had lasted an hour when they shot William Roker in the leg and then saw a No. 9 tram going down the Chingford Road. This they commandeered; the driver hid under the seat and they forced the conductor to drive. Meanwhile the police had obtained a horse and cart to chase them. Hefeld shot the animal, overturning the cart and throwing the officer onto the pavement. They then jumped from the tram and took over a horsedrawn milk float, shooting the milkman in the arm and chest. They made slow progress through Walthamstow and then stole a horse-drawn grocer's van. Lepidus took the reins and Hefeld kept the police – who were now pursuing on bicycles – at a distance. The horse tired and they abandoned the van, making on foot for the River Ching, a tributary of the Lea. Hefeld, much the bigger man who in his time at Schnurmann's had been known as The Elephant, was now himself exhausted and when he reached a tall paling fence told Lepidus to go on and save himself. As the police approached he shot himself in the head; he was overpowered and also taken to the Prince of Wales Hospital.

Lepidus on his own was also tiring. He crossed into Epping Forest and occupied the Oak Cottage of Charles Relstone, a coalman. There were two young children inside but a police officer and a baker from Walthamstow, who had been in the van of the chase, broke in and took them out. Now two detectives, Charles Dixon and John Cater, climbed through a window. Another officer, a PC Eagles, borrowed a shotgun and ladder and climbed in through the back bedroom window. He saw Lepidus but could not make the shotgun fire and climbed down. Lepidus himself had almost run out of bullets by now; he had only two left and did not shoot at Eagles.

Eagles then joined Cater and Dixon and the three went up the stairs. Dixon pushed the bedroom door open and Lepidus fired. The police riddled the door with bullets and then peered through the holes. Eagles took Dixon's revolver, put his arm round the door, fired two blind shots and then crashed into the room, firing at the same time as Lepidus who shot himself in the head. He was dragged into the yard of the cottage where he died at 12.45 p.m. The chase had lasted two and a quarter hours. All that was found of the £80 was £5 in silver which Lepidus had been carrying. It was suggested but never proved that he had pushed the money up the chimney of the cottage where it was later found by the Relstones.

The chase had covered six miles, during which the robbers had fired an amazing 400 rounds of ammunition from their automatic weapons. Hefeld died on 12 February when he contracted meningitis from his injuries and shock. The only words he uttered during the whole time were shortly before he died when he whispered, 'My mother is in Riga.' He and Lepidus were buried in an unmarked grave in Walthamstow cemetery.[19]

The outrage produced another round of anti-immigrant feeling. With the successive waves of immigrants, wages had been low in the area for years and there had been rioting in 1902. Now an English shopkeeper told a reporter:

They [the immigrant community] change their homes every two weeks. If the guardians relaxed their vigilance for a single week they would go back to their old trick of

[19] PC Tyler's widow benefited from a collection of £2,000. She was, however, only to receive the income during her lifetime. She later married another police officer. The grocer whose horse had been hi-jacked claimed £2. 10s. because it had been unable to work for four days after its efforts. The owner of Oak Cottage, where at first the dying and bleeding Tyler had been taken, claimed for damage to carpets and a tablecloth. In all, apart from the robbers, three people died and fifteen of the pursuers suffered gunshot wounds. One officer, a PC Bond, 'contracted a chill through taking up the chase when only partly dressed'. Ralph Joscelyne's mother never recovered from the death of her son. She kept the shoes he was wearing when he was killed until she died nearly fifty years later. They were buried with her.

sleeping twenty-five in a room. Here and there you find
a decent, clean man or woman, but nearly all of them are
downright riff-raff. I have been here a good many years
and I have watched this and other roads go down since
they infested them.[20]

Two years after the Tottenham Outrage, two or possibly three
linked incidents once more raised a considerable amount of
anti-immigrant and therefore anti-Semitic feeling in London.
The first was the Houndsditch murders of two police officers.
The second was the siege of Sidney Street and the third the
death of Leon Beron. It is certain the first two were connected.
It is certainly possible that the third was linked as well.

Since 1906 the focal meeting point for the non-Orthodox
intellectual Jew had been the Anarchists Club opened by
Prince Kropotkin in Jubilee Street, which in previous incar-
nations had been a Methodist Free Church and a Salvation
Army depot. It could take over 800 people in the lower hall,
and in the great hall there was a stage. The second floor
held a library and reading room. It was financed through
dances and other fund-raising activities, and donations by
the sweat-shop workers. It was a hive of revolutionary talk as
well as a home for Ochrana agents of the Tsarist regime who
spent a considerable amount of time and effort persuading
the members to misbehave.[21]

One of the groups of anarchists was the Lettish Socialistic
Revolutionary Party known as Leesma – the Latvian for flame
– composed almost entirely, as its name suggests, of Letts. It
was on one of their members, Jacob Fogel, that suspicion fell
following the Tottenham shootings when it was thought that
somehow he had acquired the missing £80.

[20] Quoted in Donald Rumbelow, *The Houndsditch Murders*, p. 28.
[21] One unsuccessful attempt came in November 1909 when an Ochrana
agent persuaded four men and a young woman to throw a bomb at
the Lord Mayor's Show. Others more sensible, including the anarchist
Rudolph Rocker, discovered the plot and it was abandoned.

At the time he was living at 29 Great Garden Street in lodgings provided by Charles Perelman, a Russian photo-enlarger, sharing a room with another Lett known as 'Bifsteks' who was courting Perelman's daughter Fanny. Also in the building was a watchmaker, William Sokoloff, known as Joseph, a man whose misfortune it was regularly to work in premises that were burgled whilst he was there or very shortly afterwards. Once the police began their inquiries they were asked to leave and, in a case of fat and fire, in moved Fritz Svaars, a locksmith who shared his room with another Latvian, George Gardstein. Svaars was wanted for an American bank robbery and Gardstein for one in Germany. The back room on the ground floor was let to Fanny's friend Nina Vassilleva, who worked as a cigarette maker and became Gardstein's mistress.

The anarchists were common figures in the area. Arthur Harding recalls Gardstein as being 'the gaffer, the top man':

> The most peculiar thing about them was that they always walked in the road, never on the pavement. I can see the idea, if anyone's lying in wait for you to arrest you they wouldn't wait out in the road, they'd wait in a doorway, they could see in the road. They always marched along in the roadway with their womenfolk in the middle of the road; they numbered sometimes as many as twelve or fifteen people, men and girls – the girls were good-lookers, gypsy-style: we would have liked to be friendly with them. We knew they were crooked, but we were told they were on the run from the Russian secret police; that fact alone gained them our sympathy. They had to live, they had to pay their lodgings, and they needed the money for their politics when all's said and done. That's why they did these robberies.[22]

[22] Raphael Samuel, *East End Underworld*, pp. 136–7. Harding has it that Nina Vassilleva went mad after being beaten up by the police following the Sidney Street shooting. He is clearly wrong. It was Sara Trassjonsky who went mad, and there is no suggestion that she was beaten up.

Towards the end of 1909 Perelman and his family moved to Wellesley Street, giving Svaars and Gardstein notice to quit. Gardstein took a room and Svaars went back to Riga in a futile attempt to see his wife; he was captured by the secret police and tortured before being released. When he returned to London the following summer he decided to send for her and, if possible, emigrate to Australia. In the meantime he took up with a seamstress, Luba Milstein, and they rented two rooms at 59 Grove Street together. In the enforced absence of Fogel, Gardstein was now the effective leader of the Leesma group and he called daily, as did Peter Piaktow (known as Peter the Painter) who arrived from Paris in October 1910. They were joined in the autumn by Max Smoller, a noted jewel thief known to Sokoloff. It was Smoller who said he knew of a jeweller's shop in Houndsditch whose safe not only held a quantity of jewels but had an added attraction: it was rumoured that some of them belonged to the Tsar.

Directly behind Harris's shop in Houndsditch was a *cul-de-sac*, Exchange Buildings, and the plan was to tunnel through between the houses. Smoller rented No. 11 and Nina Vassilleva moved in. She slept downstairs on a sofa. Smoller and Sokoloff shared a bedroom upstairs. It was immediately clear that there was no way in from No. 11, but it was possible to get in through No. 9 and Svaars rented the premises saying it was for storing Christmas goods.

Work was to begin on the Jewish Sabbath, Friday 16 December, and continue throughout the weekend. The advantages were obvious. The shop would not open on the Saturday and the streets would be almost deserted. Gardstein and Smoller along with Yourka Dubof, a locksmith, and Svaar's cousin, Jacob Peters, were to begin work, with the others waiting to come in as relievers; 59 Grove Street was to be a rendezvous if things went wrong, and Piatkow stayed there so that Luba Milstein – who disliked him intensely – would stay out of the way.

The plan was doomed from the start. Despite the fact that it was a windy night, the hammering could be heard in Houndsditch. It was also heard by Max Weil who lived over the shop next to the jeweller's. About 10 p.m. he called the police at Bishopsgate Police Station and a temporary constable, Walter Piper, went to Exchange Buildings. There was a Jewish family at No. 12, the Solomons, and they told him no one was working in the yard. At No. 11, however, Gardstein opened the door and Piper simply asked whether 'the missus was in'. Told she was not he went away, apparently satisfied.

In fact a number of police were now rounded up and seven positioned themselves in Exchange Buildings. Sergeant Robert Bentley went to the building and asked Gardstein, who again opened the door, whether anyone was working inside. Gardstein half closed the door, but Bentley followed him in and suggested he should look to see if anyone was in the back. When he went into the back room he was shot in the neck at point-blank range by Peters. Sergeant Bryant, who was behind, was shot in the arm by Gardstein. Both staggered into the street where Ernest Woodhams, who went to help Bentley, was shot in the leg by Gardstein. Peters then emerged and shot Sergeant Tucker in the heart and a plain-clothes officer, Arthur Strongman, pulled his colleague away. DC James Martin took no part; he panicked and hid in a nearly house, claiming later that he had fallen, stunned, in the street.

The men now burst from Exchange Buildings and Walter Choate caught hold of Gardstein only to be shot in the leg by him. He held on and was shot a number of times, with Peters hitting him again at point-blank range. With amazing bravery he still held on to Gardstein until, as he finally fell, he left a target and one of Smoller's bullets hit Gardstein in the back.

Dubof and Peters then half carried Gardstein into Cutler Street, followed by Nina Vassilleva with Smoller behind her.

The shooting took less than a minute and twenty-two bullets were fired. The police were unarmed.

Tucker was dead on arrival at the London Hospital and Choate was taken there on a handcart; he died in the early hours of the morning. Bentley was taken to St Bartholomew's where, although he recovered consciousness, he died on 11 December.

A number of people saw the escape but the only person able to recognise any of the party was a tobacconist, Isaac Levy from Walthamstow, who had been working late. Gardstein was taken back to Grove Street and Nina Vassilleva went for a doctor who sent her away. Luba Milstein was sitting up in the back room with her friend Sara Trassjonsky, a mentally unsound hunchbacked little seamstress, and she was the one who was left to nurse Gardstein as first Smoller, Piaktow and Joseph left, followed by Milstein. When she went to see an old friend, Karl Hoffman, Svaars, Piatkow and Joseph were there already. She was persuaded to return to Grove Street to collect any incriminatory photographs or papers. At 3 a.m. a Doctor Scanlon, who had a mainly immigrant practice in the Whitechapel Road, was persuaded to come to see Gardstein who said he had been shot accidentally by a friend and adamantly refused to go to hospital. Scanlon agreed to return the next morning but, fearful that his clientele might see him as an informer, did nothing until noon when he rang Detective Inspector Wensley. It was arranged that there would be no raid until he had left the premises, but by the time he reached Grove Street Gardstein was dead and the only person in the building was Sara Trassjonsky, now thoroughly unhinged, idly throwing papers onto the fire.

Arrests followed. Sara Trassjonsky was detained on the spot and on 17 December a Russian musician, Nicolas Tomacoff, who came to Grove Street to see his friend Fritz about a Christmas play at the Anarchist Club, gave the police the names and descriptions of the men he had seen at the house.

He took them to Osip Federoff's lodgings where the man was arrested. The next down was Luba Milstein who was turned over to the police by her brothers. Nina Vassilleva fled to the country but, on her return, was interviewed by Wensley. He did not arrest her immediately in the hope that she would lead the police to the rest of the gang.

In fact it was Tomacoff who now became their main hope. He was put up in an hotel and given new clothes which cost £2.4s.6d. In fact he was something of a disappointment because although he gave them Nina Vassilleva's address they already knew it. On 22 December he did, however, lead them to Jacob Peters who promptly put the blame on Fritz Svaars. The same day Dubof was arrested in Shepherd's Bush; in turn he offered up thin pickings. He admitted he knew the house in Grove Street and that he had been there on 16 December looking for work. Now he was identified by Levy as one of the two men – Peters was the other – who had carried Gardstein away from Exchange Buildings.

Charles Perelman came forward with the information that Joseph lived with a Betty Gershon at 100 Sidney Street between the Mile End Road and the Commercial Road. Perelman was the crucial informant and told the police that Svaars would move lodgings on the evening of 3 January and that Joseph would follow when he heard that Svaars was safe.

In the early hours of 3 January, 200 police were called to Arbour Square Police Station for a briefing. All were unmarried since it was feared there would be heavy casualties – when Gardstein's room had been searched 100 rounds of assorted ammunition and a loaded pistol had been found. At 3 a.m. they had evacuated the neighbours and surrounded 100 Sidney Street. They also cleared the families from No. 100. Two men, they were told, were sleeping in the stock room. But they decided not to rush the room, since the stairs could be held against a wave of officers and the casualties would certainly be unacceptable.

The action began at 7.30 when a policeman ran across the road and threw stones at windows in the house. This brought a volley from the Anarchists and Detective Sergeant Leeson received a chest wound. He clearly thought he was dying and what were meant to be his last words were:

Mr Wensley, I am dying. They have shot me through the heart. Give my love to the children. Bury me at Putney.[23]

Fortunately, when the doctor took off Leeson's coat and shirt it was clear that the bullet had passed straight through his chest. In any event it was a signal for the police to retreat. They were hopelessly outgunned in terms of firepower and during the morning requested the help of troops stationed at the Tower of London. This required the permission of the Home Secretary and, with the regiment of Scots Guards, Winston Churchill himself came to the siege. It was estimated that from both the troops and those in the house thousands of shots were fired. It was also estimated that some 100,000 came to watch, with neighbourhood residents charging 10 shillings a head for spectators to stand on their roofs.

At 1 p.m. smoke was seen coming from the garret window and it was apparent that the second floor was alight. It was thought that the men had deliberately set fire to the house before trying to escape in the smoke and confusion, but the better thought is that a bullet had struck a gas pipe which had ignited. The troops reopened fire. Svaars leaned from the window and was shot instantly. As the wind blew the

[23] In his memoirs Wensley omits the Putney request. F. Wensley, *Detective Days*, p.172. Harding is particularly scathing of Leeson who he says '. . . was potty. He got scared and went to Australia where he imagined he met Peter the Painter on a train.' *East End Underworld*, p. 318. The story of Leeson and Peter appears in *Lost London*. Rather more likely is that these rather anodyne memoirs were bolstered for publication.

smoke away from the ground floor momentarily, the body of Joseph could be seen lying on a bed in a ground-floor room. Then part of the building collapsed.

It was then that the legends started. Although most newspapers identified the bodies as those of Joseph and Svaars, some believed that one was that of Joseph Vogel. The *Daily Mail* thought that Peter the Painter had been in the house.

The subsequent trial of the survivors was in a way both a triumph and a fiasco for British justice. The triumph was that despite the fact that three policemen had been killed there was no question of railroading the defendants. Indeed it was just the opposite. Although Sara Trassjonsky, Luba Milstein, Nina Vassilleva, Peters, Federoff, Dubof, John Rosen and Hoffman were arrested and stood trial, when it came to it not a single person was convicted.

The case for the Crown was not really handled very well. Archibald Bodkin, who later became Director of Public Prosecutions, opened the case against them by saying that Peters, Dubof and Federoff were concerned in the murder of the police officers, that the two women were accessories after the fact to murder and that all five were involved in the attempted burglary of Harris's shop. At the time they were the only ones in custody. Over a period of weeks they were joined by the others. Bodkin had taken the view that since Gardstein had opened the door of No. 11 Exchange Buildings, he was the one who had also opened fire on the police.

The first to be acquitted was Luba Milstein, who was found to have no case to answer at the Guildhall Justice Room after Bodkin accepted there was no evidence against her. She was released on 21 February. Hoffman was acquitted on 8 March and Federoff on the 15 March. The identification against him was dubious and all that could be said against Hoffman was that he was a friend of Svaars. Sara Trassjonsky was released the same day.

The trial of Peters and Dubof, accused of murder, and

Nina Vassilleva, with harbouring a felon, opened at the Central Criminal Court on 1 May before Mr Justice Grantham. There were also charges of being accessories to murder and conspiracy to break and enter. Rosen was charged only with conspiracy.

The principal witness against them was Isaac Levy, the shop manager, who said he had seen the two men with Gardstein and Vassilleva tagging behind them. He withstood a good deal of hostile cross-examination but on the second day the judge decided that, since there was no corroborative evidence of the identification, the murder charges against Peters and Dubof could not stand. Nor could it be said that Vassilleva knew a murder as opposed to a wounding had been committed. That charge must also go. This left the conspiracy case of which, at the end of the eleven-day trial, the only significant piece of evidence remaining for the jury was the fingerprints of Vassilleva. By now it was a question of humour in court and, to sycophantic laughter, the judge summed up:

> The male prisoners are aliens in this country for their own good. That is not to say it is for the good of this country.

Earlier, when Peters had given evidence that he had attended an LCC school to learn English but had in fact learned more Yiddish, Grantham had commented, 'It is a pity that the ratepayers should be called on to teach Yiddish.' Now the judge rather suggested that the lack of evidence was due to the cowardice of the unfortunate Levy in not following the quartet more closely until he came across a policeman.

The men were acquitted. Vassilleva was convicted, but the jury recommended that there be no deportation order. She was sentenced to two years imprisonment, but her conviction did not stand long. The Court of Criminal Appeal ruled that the judge had misdirected the jury and that, merely because she was living at 11 Exchange Buildings and had undoubtedly told lies, this did not constitute sufficient evidence to prove a charge of conspiracy. Her conviction was quashed on 21 June 1911.[24]

Initially Churchill did not come out of the siege too well and when he appeared in newsreels the galleries booed him roundly. He set up a commission into compensating those who had lost property as a result of the siege and it turned out that the Fleischmanns, far from living in some poverty, had (before their house was destroyed) actually owned something of an Aladdin's cave complete with fur coats, diamond rings and silver spoons let alone an evening-dress suit. The committee was not impressed and awarded Fleischmann just a quarter of his claim of £900, which of itself was half the total sought by all. There had been a £500 reward for the capture of Svaars, Peter the Painter and an unnamed woman. Since only one of the three was either arrested or killed, Charles Perelman was awarded a third of the bounty. New clothes for Tomacoff, which apart from his accommodation was all he received.

When Nina Vassilleva was released from prison her former friends had turned against her and she was looked after by the Anarchists Millie and Rudolph Rocker, who had found a solicitor, William Crocker, to act *pro bono* for her. For a time at any rate Nina believed that the whole of the Houndsditch incident had been an elaborate snare for Gardstein, deliberately murdered by Max Smoller. Throughout the rest of her life she remained in the East End, working first as a cigarette roller for Adbullah where she could be seen sitting in the shop window hand-rolling the tobacco, and then for the Soviet Trade Delegation. She died in St Bartholomew's Hospital on 24 February 1963.

The writer Richard Whittington-Egan visited her a few years before her death, finding her suffering from arthritis

---

[24] (1911) 4 Cr App R 228.

and, 'Large, run to bulk, with white hair, short and straight, and faded blue eyes'.

> I found her occupying, in poverty, a top floor front, looking out over London chimney pots, at 99 Brick Lane. It was a terrible climb for someone so disabled.
>
> The room had blue wash painted walls. Furnished with a bed, one hard chair, and a gas-ring, illuminated by a single naked bulb, it was a cheerless place. A Greek Catholic, she had a positive welter of religious objects on display, spilling over everything.

Her account was slightly different from the orthodox one:

> Nina knew Gardstein well, but denied that she had been his mistress. She told me that it was a popular canard that she had been Peter the Painter's girlfriend. She had, in fact, never known him, and her first meeting with Sara Trassjonsky was when they were both in Holloway. She told me that she was not one of those at Exchange Buildings, and denied that she had nursed the dying Gardstein.
>
> She also, most interestingly, confided that it had actually been the fire brigade who had caused the fatal blaze at 100 Sidney Street. They had deliberately set fire to the gas meter, and Churchill had forbidden any attempt to extinguish the flames.
>
> By one of those coincidences which make life bountiful, showing at that very time at a small cinema round the corner was a film 'The Siege of Sidney Street' in which Nina was magically transformed into the beautiful young woman of half a century before. It was passing strange to watch on the screen a young actress playing the part of the old lady I had just left. I had, in fact, invited her to come with me to see the film, but she did not want to. It had all been so long ago . . . and so sad.[25]

[25] Richard Whittington-Egan, 'Miss Nina and the Anarchists' in *New Law Journal*, 11 January 2000.

Sara Trassjonsky was admitted to an asylum where she died. A small present was sent to the police in 1912 by Nina Vassilleva to be forwarded to her. This they did. The enigmatic Peter the Painter may have died in Philadelphia in 1916. One version of his identity is that he was the brother of Casimir Pilenas, the interpreter at Thames Police Court who had been used to take statements in the Houndsditch trial.[26] Jacob Peters went back to Russia to become a hero of the Revolution but died in 1928, the victim of a Stalin purge. Luba Milstein, left pregnant by Svaars, gave birth and went to America in January 1912 followed by Karl Hoffman; they lived in and around New York until their deaths in 1961 and 1973 respectively. Smoller's wife had left the country with her children during her husband's trial; he had already escaped to Paris. The other defendants, Dubof, Rosen, Hoffman and Federoff, simply disappeared into anonymity.

Meanwhile the body of Leon Beron had been found on Clapham Common on 1 January 1911 whilst London and, to a lesser extent, the rest of the country was still recovering from the Houndsditch police shooting which had provoked yet another wave of anti-Semitism:

> It is doubtful if there is more than a score of English families living within a radius of 500 yards of Sidney Street. Certainly there is not a single English tradesman there; the public houses are tenanted by Jews and foreigners and foreign drinks are almost solely consumed.[27]

> . . . the borough has been inundated by a swarm of people fitly described as the scum of Central Europe.[28]

[26] See for example B. Leeson, *Lost London*, and Sir William Crocker, *Far from Humdrum*. Crocker's father represented both Trassjonsky and Vassilleva. The story is discounted by Donald Rumbelow, *The Houndsditch Murders*, pp. 184–5.

[27] *ELO*, 7 January 1911.

[28] *Morning Leader*, 12 January 1911.

Earlier in the article 'The Alien Immigrant', the leader writer of
The Times had put things clearly: '. . . the average immigrant
is insanitary in his habits: he is personally unclean.'[29]

Certainly public feeling in the area ran high, with Coun-
cillor Castle of the Stepney Bow Council urging a resolution
be passed asking that the whole of the Aliens Act be put into
effect and, as that in itself was insufficient, stronger legislation
should be passed:

> For fifteen to twenty years the Borough has been inun-
> dated with the scum of the earth driving out the native
> population. [Shouts of No.][30]

Although it lingered on until 1915, another casualty was the
Anarchist Club:

> Press agitation against the Anarchists and 'criminal aliens'
> reached a new crescendo. Police watch on the club and
> members increased. In the eyes of the local public anyone
> who walked along in a Russian blouse was considered a
> suspicious character and sometimes assaulted.[31]

It is difficult to judge who was the more unpleasant man –
Steinie Morrison or Leon Beron; possibly the latter. Beron
was born on 17 April 1863 at Gulvaki, Poland. His family
moved to France where, it was alleged, his father amassed
the fortune of £26,000. David Beron, his brother, later said
it was £60,000.[32] Again, what Leon Beron did for a living

---

[29] *The Times*, 21 December 1910.
[30] *Morning Leader*, 9 January 1911.
[31] Louis Bailey, quoted in *East End Jewish Radicals*, p. 292.
[32] David Beron, 'a miserable looking man', was charged with begging.
He was found to have on him £25. 10s. gold; 6s. 11¾d. bronze. He
told the court that at one time his father had property worth £60,000.
After a week in custody for reports he was discharged. *ELA*, 21 and 28
November 1914.

is unclear. He was probably a locksmith and almost certainly a burglar. Without doubt he was a receiver. Certainly there were no outward signs of wealth.

Arthur Harding recalls:

> We used to see Behren [sic] at the Warsaw Restaurant in Osborne Street at the bottom of Brick Lane. The watch-chains we used to pinch, we'd go there and sell them to him. With gold chains he used to pay you 27s. 6d. for 9 carat gold and 56s. for 18 carat, and about £4 for 22 carat which was very rare.[33]

Beron may have been a front man for Ruby Michaels, regarded at the time as the doyen of local receivers. If Beron could not be found in the Warsaw Restaurant then he could often be found in a shoe shop around the corner. He was always well dressed and throughout his life had a passion for jewellery, gold and women. In the early hours of a morning he was frequently seen coming out of one of the Whitechapel brothels.

He owned slum property in Russell Court, St George's in the East, which was let to prostitutes and on which he had a mortgage. He lived with his younger brother David, regarded as being of low intelligence, at 133 Jubilee Street for which he paid 2/9d. rent with David contributing the ninepence. His other brother, Solomon, who lived in Rowton House, [34] said, at the inquest that Leon had no money to speak of.

Whilst in France, Leon Beron had married a Frenchwoman, Adele, by whom he had a daughter. He later had her committed to Colney Hatch Mental Asylum in North London where

[33] Raphael Samuel, *East End Underworld*, p. 134.
[34] Montague William Cory, later Baron Rowton (1838–1903) devised the concept of hotels for working-class men, which provided lodging and catering and which had the advantages of a club at the lowest cost. Despite considerable opposition, the first of these was opened in Vauxhall in 1893. It was a great success and another five followed. The one in Whitechapel opened in 1902.

she died in May 1902 of general paralysis of the insane. She had almost certainly contracted syphilis from her husband. At the time of his death he was walking with the rounded gait which could be the sign of locomotaxia.

Steinie Morrison, a great poseur who sometimes claimed to be Australian, came to England in 1898. He was at least partly educated and had something of a gift for languages because, as Andrew Rose points out, at a time when criminals had a hard time making their mark let alone writing, he spoke Russian, Yiddish, German, French and, by the time of his trial, could write in English and speak it without the need for an interpreter.

His first traceable offence in this country was committed the year he arrived when, under the name Moses Tagger, he was given one month at Worship Street Magistrates' Court for stealing ledgers from his employer. Next, as Morrie Stein, he received two months for being found on enclosed premises; then, as Morris Jagger, it was six months at North London Quarter Sessions for burglary. In mid-April 1900, as Morris Stein again, he received 15 months. Released in the summer of 1901, almost immediately he was seen carrying property away from a domestic burglary at Cambridge Park. This time he received 5 years.

Sometime after his release from that sentence he made the acquaintance of Max Frank, a Lithuanian Jew who was a receiver and pimp operating from 116 York Road, Walworth. On 14 January 1906 he was arrested again and this time racked up 5 years plus a year and 83 days for breaking the terms of his licence. After attacking a prison officer he received 23 strokes of the cat.

On his release he lived for a time at 5 Grove Street near the headquarters of the Houndsditch gang where he paid Minnie Honigman 3/6d. rent, but returned to Frank and the prostitute Florence Dellow in York Road.

When Beron's body was found, his watch and chain and

a £5 gold piece he carried along with his day-to-day money (which could amount to £70) were gone. He had been beaten and stabbed and his skull fractured. On his forehead was carved a series of cuts which could be seen in the form of the letter 'S'. One interpretation of this was that it was the initial letter of the Russian word *spic* or double agent. A reward of £500 was offered for information leading to the conviction of his killer.

On 8 January Inspector Fred Wensley arrested Morrison but not, he said, for murder, simply for failing to report a change of address. Wensley took with him five other detectives, explaining this by saying he knew Morrison carried a gun. Morrison never left custody again.[35]

As to the murder charge which followed, the evidence against him was that he knew Beron and had been seen with him in the East End shortly before midnight on New Year's Eve. He also knew South London as he had worked in a bakery in Lavender Hill. He had given a parcel to a waiter in the Warsaw Café, saying that it contained a flute, but the waiter believed it was far too heavy for that. Morrison also had a £5 piece which the prosecution claimed was from the robbery.

There was some evidence that Beron and Morrison had

[35] Much to the annoyance of the Court of Criminal Appeal, a considerable time was spent at the trial discussing whether Morrison had mentioned the murder when he was arrested. Abinger felt that if he had not done this it was a most important point in his favour. It is difficult to see why. The whole East End must have been buzzing with the story and Morrison must have known that with his record he was a 'usual suspect'. A young officer, George Greaves, was called to give evidence to contradict Wensley and the others. He suffered very badly in a hostile cross-examination and after the case he was transferred to Ruislip. Despite appeals to be allowed to return, he remained in the country and resigned at the end of the year. *Police Review* thought he had been 'very badly treated'. He said that when he intervened he expected instant dismissal, and *John Bull* thought, 'The treatment which he has received is tantamount to dismissal'. Edward Abinger in his memoirs, *Forty Years at the Bar*, wrote that he thought the evidence should 'not have hanged a dog'.

quarrelled in the past and there were minute spots of blood on the defendant's collar. Additionally, there was identification evidence from two taxi drivers who put him at Clapham Common at the time of the murder. There was also a hotly contested 'verbal' – an allegation that Wensley, when he went to arrest Morrison, had said 'Stein, I want you for murder.' There was some allegation that at Leman Street Police Station Detective Sergeant Brogden had said to Morrison that he was being detained for murder.

The trial started on 6 March and both Morrison and his counsel, Edward Abinger, did what they could to alienate the judge and jury. It was common then for the defendant to be required to stand during his or her trial, but when the judge offered Morrison a seat in the dock he refused and stood with his hand on his hip throughout the proceedings. Worse, Abinger was continually at war with the judge, the relatively amiable (for that era at any rate) Mr Justice Darling.

Meanwhile there had been an attempt to get at some of the witnesses. Lewis James Ward, Charles Macnamara and Charles Haines, along with Lawrence Rappolt, had been charged with assaulting Alfred Stevens, one of the witnesses who put Steinie on Clapham Common. The defence argued that it was a domestic matter and that Stephens had made advances to Ward's wife, but they were convicted. When Ward came to be sentenced his counsel pleaded that he should not be sentenced to hard labour.

Mr Justice Darling: 'It will do him no harm.' (Laughter.)

The police were convinced that the instigator of the attack was Max Frank, but there was no evidence to connect him. There was, however, some evidence that Rappolt was part of a racecourse gang.[36]

[36] PRO MEPO 3 202.

The evidence against Morrison was not strong. As for the blood on the collar, he was both a fastidious man and sensible enough to have had his collar washed eight days after the murder. In fact he gave evidence that he possessed some six collars. The identification evidence was suspect and a John Greaves from the RIBA was called to point up the inadequate lighting at the Clapham Common cab rank.

Unfortunately Abinger decided to cross-examine the waiter about a period of time the man had spent in a mental hospital after a failed suicide attempt. Attempted suicide was then a felony and the introduction of this evidence entitled the prosecution to put Morrison's own convictions before the jury. If he had managed to avoid this trap Abinger had dug for Morrison, there was no possibility of escape because Abinger then accused another witness of being a brothel keeper.

Morrison also attempted to call alibi evidence from two young sisters with whom he said he had been at the Shoreditch Music Hall on New Year's Eve. Jane Brodsky gave evidence that she and her sister had gone there, had seen Morrison sitting in the same row and leaving the theatre at the end of the show. Esther Brodsky said they had paid fivepence, but Muir was able to show that to get into those seats that night a person would have had to be in the queue at 7.15 for the 9 p.m. show. The girls said they had not queued and had gone straight into the seats. When he came to give evidence Morrison said he had arrived at about a quarter to nine after spending the earlier part of the evening in the Warsaw. He thought Harry Champion and Gertie Gitana had been on the bill, along with a boy and girl acting as man and wife. Certainly Champion and Gitana had appeared, but the boy and girl act had not been on the bill until the following week. Morrison had been to the theatre on 2 January.

The jury retired a bare 35 minutes before convicting him. Morrison now told the court that money found on him had come from a bank fraud.

It was the custom for the judge to remark that he whole-heartedly agreed with the verdict of a jury in a murder case, but Darling pointedly did not do so. He had already warned the jury that merely because Morrison had called a false alibi did not mean he was guilty. Ikey Foreigner was not the same as a straightforward Englishman. Indeed he had already summed up as best he could for an acquittal.

It is possible in Scotland to return a verdict of 'not proven'. An English jury cannot do that, but for all that, if they come to the conclusion that the case is not proven . . . they give what is after all an equivalent verdict. If it is not proven then they must not say, 'Oh, it is not proven but we find him guilty'; there is only one verdict which an English jury is permitted to give.

Now he advised Morrison to say nothing more and that he should leave matters to his lawyers. When he came to pass the death sentence he used the traditional closing words, 'And may God have mercy on your soul.'

Morrison would have none of it. 'I decline such mercy. I do not believe there is a God in Heaven either,' he shouted.

He came before the newly formed Court of Criminal Appeal on 27 March and it was clear their Lordships did not like the conviction. Nevertheless they felt they could do nothing about it.

Even if every member of the Court had been of the opinion that he personally would have acquitted the prisoner the Court must yet have upheld that conviction, unless they were of the opinion that the verdict was so perverse that no reasonable jury would have given it.[37]

When canvassed by Home Secretary Winston Churchill on

[37] *Morrison* (1911) 9 Cr App R.

the question of a reprieve, Darling allowed that whilst he personally thought Morrison to have been guilty he did not think the evidence strong enough to justify a conviction. Alverstone, who led the Court of Appeal, thought he had been badly defended by Abinger. There was a consensus of opinion that had Morrison been defended by either Marshall Hall or Curtis Bennett he would have been acquitted. *The Times* was in chauvinistic mood:

> . . . the East End counts among its population, a large number of very dangerous, very reckless, and very noxious people, chiefly immigrants from the Eastern and South-Eastern countries of Europe. The second impression will be that these people add to the difficulties of the situation by their extreme untrustworthiness, since lying, especially in the witness-box, appears to be their natural language.[38]

Despite this a petition with 75,000 signatures was raised, calling for Morrison's reprieve. On 12 April it was announced that the death sentence was commuted to one of life imprisonment.

In 1912 there was an attempt to have Morrison's case reconsidered and Ethel Clayton, the woman with whom a Hugo Pool was living, went to the Home Office to give evidence and was questioned by Inspector Ward. She said that on the night of the murder Pool had left home at about 11 a.m. and had not returned for three days. When he had done so he tore up a bloodstained shirt and burned it, threatening her if she mentioned it. When Ward asked with whom the man had been that night she had replied, Steinie Morrison.

Morrison was not a good prisoner and he did his time the hard way. He constantly protested his innocence and was truculent, abusive and violent to warders and prisoners alike.

[38] *The Times*, 16 March 1911.

I never saw him laugh. He swore to me, not once but a
dozen times that he had not killed Leon Beron.[39]

In November 1913 it was thought that there might be an
attempt to free Morrison and the Governor of Parkhurst
Prison was alerted. He wrote back that the man was guarded
and there was no fear of any attempt being successful.
Nevertheless, for a time a watch was kept on Morrison's
sister and two friends, Tom O'Sullivan and Joe Collins.

Steinie had one moment of pleasure when he learned that
Inspector Ward had been killed in a Zeppelin raid during the
war: 'I had become convinced that there was no God, but I
think I shall alter my opinion after this.'[40]

Accounts vary as to the circumstances of his death. Certainly he was starving himself at the time. Some say it was
another protest of his innocence, but there is a version that
he was annoyed by a kitten kept as a pet by other prisoners
and that in a fit of temper he threw it on a furnace. He received
the No. 1 punishment of bread and water and after he had
undergone that he began to starve himself as a protest for
what he saw as another injustice.

They put him in a padded cell, but there he refused to
eat anything. Because of this a doctor ordered him out
and into the prison hospital ward where I was working
on special duty. He was too ill to be dangerous to himself
or anybody else. Poor Steinie, they put him on a mattress
on the floor and took the strait-jacket off him. One of the
screws told me to lift his head up. He looked at me, sort of
puzzled, as if he didn't know where he was. That was how
he died, in my arm peaceful as a kitten. The man who'd
murdered an old man and a cat. He died for the cat.[41]

[39] George Smithson, *Raffles in Real Life*, p. 122.
[40] Charles George Gordon, *Crooks of the Underworld*, p. 20.
[41] Wally Thompson, *Time Off My Life*, pp. 47–8.

Another version is that whilst being force-fed he accidentally choked to death. Shortly before he died he wrote:

> In this prison during the last 12 months alone about a dozen life sentence prisoners (all guilty of murder) have had their sentences reduced to 12 years or less. I am innocent. I have done close on 10 years and still I am forgotten about. Such is the justice of England.[42]

Whichever account is true, he died on 24 January 1921. It was another ten years before the Court of Appeal quashed the conviction of the Liverpudlian insurance broker William Wallace on the grounds that, whilst there was nothing wrong with the conduct of the trial or indeed the verdict of the jury, each member of the court felt a lingering doubt as to his guilt. They were right to feel doubt. It is now almost universally accepted amongst those who have studied the case that Wallace did not kill his wife.

Was the Morrison conviction a correct one, and if not why was Beron killed? Was it something more than a simple robbery? Was there a political motive? There are a number of attractive rival theories.

Assuming Morrison did kill Beron, it is highly unlikely he was alone. Wensley believed that he and the man Hugo Pool carried out the murder. Benjamin Leeson, who was a junior officer in the case, thought that Morrison was guilty but that another man was also involved. Amongst others, the writers Eric Linklater and Julian Symons both have him murdered on behalf of the Leesma anarchists who feared he was an informer.[43]

On the other hand, Andrew Rose believes he was murdered

---

[42] *Daily Mail*, 26 January 1921.
[43] Eric Linklater, *The Corpse on Clapham Common*; Julian Symons, *A Reasonable Doubt*.

simply because he was a criminal (rather than a political) informer, and there is no doubt whatsoever that he was a heavy player in crime in Whitechapel. All three, amongst many others, believe Morrison was completely innocent.

In his book of the trial Fletcher Moulton adds a fascinating afternote which gives some support to this theory.[44]

It appears that Mrs Maud Rider, an Englishwoman living in Paris, overheard a conversation on a tram about 10.15 one morning whilst travelling on the Avenue Kleber between Trocadero and the Arc de Triomphe. One of the participants was a French Jew, short, fat and bearded, with an old-fashioned curly-brimmed bowler. The second was a Frenchman who spoke poor English and the third a tall good-looking 'foreigner' who spoke fluent cockney English but with a foreign accent.

The Frenchman said in French, 'What are you doing in the affair Steinie Morrison?'

After being told to speak in English he continued, 'All right. Are you going to do anything?'

'No, Gort's (or Cort's) life is more valuable to us than his.'

'Yes, but we cannot let him hang. Can't you write a letter?'

The conversation continued. Mrs Rider watched the three men leave the tram separately, and she followed the third to the Hotel d'Amiens in the rue des Deux Gares. She reported the matter to the director of the Paris edition of the *Daily Mail* who forwarded it to the Commissioner of Police in London, who took no action. The French police were never able to identify Cort or Gort, but some other names which Mrs Rider noted down were those of a gang of international criminals. One of the difficulties Mrs Rider faced in gaining credibility was that she was a woman. She compounded this by being a writer of romantic fiction.

---

[44] H. Fletcher Moulton, *The Trial of Steinie Morrison.*

One of the most ingenious of theories is that offered by Abinger during his closing speech, that Beron had been killed by his brother Solomon. The motive could be that instead of living in Rowton House, Solomon Beron would thus acquire his brother's rooms and some of his clothes. He was undoubtedly unbalanced and in fact had attacked Abinger during the trial. He too would die in Colney Hatch. Their father was in a home at Clapham and Leon could have gone there at his brother's behest. Unfortunately there is really no evidence to support this particular flight of fancy. Given his precarious mental state, it is difficult to see how he would have had the wit to clean up his clothes and dispose of the property, let alone carve the 'S' on his brother's forehead and so divert attention. Unless of course the 'S' stood for Solomon. Another argument against this theory is that the descriptions of the other man at Clapham with Leon do not tally.

The next theory, favoured by Wensley, is that the killing was a straightforward robbery by Morrison and Hugo Pool. Despite the way that Muir opened the case against Morrison that it was a lone killing, few really thought this was the case. The marks on Beron's head had a certain symmetry. Someone surely had to hold a lantern whilst the cuts were made. One of the problems with any of the robbery theories is why they should take Beron to Clapham. There were a number of open spaces in the East End and there were any number of alleys in the area in which to kill a man. Why should Beron travel across London with Morrison anyway? One suggestion has been that Morrison knew of a brothel in Clapham and Leon Beron, always keen on prostitutes, went in search of pastures new.

In recent years the most attractive theory has been that Morrison was set up to take the fall for the gang who had murdered Beron because he was a police informer – the mutilations on the forehead were certainly similar to markings on Polish informers. The legs of the body were crossed, so signifying double crossing. If this seems fantastic, think of the practice of Mafia killers dropping three dimes by a body to show that he was an informer. The similar but older version is that Beron was killed by the Leesma anarchists either because he was a political informer or he was suspected of being one.

Lapukhin, one of the heads of the Tsarist police, who died in Paris in 1928, tied the death of Beron to the Sidney Street siege and maintained that he had Peter the Painter working as a spy keeping observation on the Houndsditch thieves:

> I never could understand why the English made the mistake of naming this man as one of the criminal gang for they must have known he only consorted with them in furtherance of his duty which was to keep me posted regarding the activities of the gang.

Lapukhin claimed that the gang were really political assassins whose real aim in life was to assassinate the Russian royal family when they visited England or France. There had been some delay in fixing the details of the tour and this caused financial problems which meant they were obliged to carry out a robbery to survive.[45]

The former policeman went on to say that when Peter the Painter disappeared he turned his duties over to Beron who had also been an agent of the Russian police. Lapukhin's version was that the nihilists were bent on killing Beron and, with the participation of Morrison, he was lured to Clapham Common on the pretext of buying stolen jewellery.

> I am equally certain that the case against Morrison was not that on which he was convicted. Morally I suppose

---

[45] Certainly they had some success in their struggle for survival. Twelve months before the Houndsditch shootings they had successfully robbed a post office in North London, carrying away the safe on a wheelbarrow. 'Peter the Painter' in *Morning Leader*, 9 January 1911.

he was guilty, but I was able afterwards to supply the English authorities information that caused them to revise their theory and I think it was this information more than any other that caused them to go back on the death sentence.[46]

---

[46] *Empire News*, 'Secrets of Sidney Street', 18 March 1928.

3

The Grizzard Gang

At the turn of the century and for the first decade of the 1900s, the great receiver of stolen goods and 'putter-up' of burglaries throughout London was Joseph 'Cammi' Grizzard. More or less every major burglary could be laid at his door or that of his subordinates who would bring the jewellery to him in Hatton Garden or to his home in the East End to fence for them.

Born in 1867, by the early 1900s he was described as being of middle height and somewhat portly build, favouring a blond moustache and diamond rings on his fingers. Sir Richard Muir KC, who would later prosecute him, thought:

> . . . [he] possessed rather a fine face with nothing in it to tell the world of the evil, intriguing brain that had been responsible for some of the most amazing coups in the whole history of crime.[1]

Christmas Humphreys took a rather different view:

---

[1] S.T. Felstead and Lady Muir, *Sir Richard Muir*, p. 130.

. . . his impudence and swaggering self-assurance served to create a personality which dominated the smaller fry who hung about the 'Garden' and turned them when required into willing if not able tools.

Like so many criminals he was a great man with a twist in his character which made him prefer to go crooked where he might go straight.[2]

Grizzard was first convicted at Thames Police Court on 1 May 1880 and received 14 days for larceny. He did not then appear before the courts for some twenty years when he was charged with a heavy burglary including 78 gold watches, 24 gold chains and 70 diamond, pearl and sapphire rings at a jeweller's in Richmond, Surrey, in which he was said to have been involved with David Jacobs, a cutter known as 'Sticks'. Despite an eyewitness who claimed to have seen him outside the shop at 5 a.m. on the night of 19 November 1902; a woman who said she had been sold a bracelet from the stolen jewellery by Grizzard; and a remark that he thought a piece of iron exhibited in court must have been his jemmy, he was acquitted.[3] Over the next few years Grizzard would come to be recognised as one of the highest quality receivers in London.

His greatest coup came six years later when he master-minded the jewel robbery at the Café Monico in Regent Street which led to the appearance of John Higgins and the former lightweight jockey Harry Grimshaw at London Sessions.

On 20 June 1909 a French dealer, Frederick Goldschmidt, left Paris and travelled to London bringing jewellery with him and staying at De Keyser's hotel. It is not clear how Grizzard came to hear of this, but he had Goldschmidt watched; almost certainly Grizzard maintained connections in Paris who would inform him of the vulnerability of certain dealers. Indeed

[2] Christmas Humphreys, *The Great Pearl Robbery of 1913*, p. 8.
[3] *The Times*, 20 January 1903.

Goldschmidt seems to have been doubly unfortunate because another gang which included the American Eddie Guerin, then still almost at the top of his form, was also seen at the hotel watching him.[4] It was really only a question of who got to him first and, past the post, it was Grimshaw.

It became clear that Goldschmidt never put his case down in public except when he washed his hands, and on 9 July he was followed to the Café Monico. When he went to the lavatory he put his bag beside him and as he reached out for the soap, he was pushed off balance and the bag was snatched by Grimshaw. As Goldschmidt chased after it his passage was blocked by Higgins. The jewels, worth some £60,000, were never found. Had the pair struck the previous day the haul would have been nearer £160,000.

Even more than today it was apparent that only a handful of people had the ability to organise such a theft and dispose of the goods. Within a matter of hours the police obtained a search warrant for Grizzard's home at 73 Parkholme Road, Dalston, and found him at dinner with his guests, three potential buyers. Grizzard and his company sat at the dinner

---

[4] In his time Eddie Guerin was one of the great safebreakers and thieves of the early twentieth century. Born in America, he worked in France and was sent to the French penal colony Devil's Island from which he escaped. He was the only survivor of the three escapers and it was said, with no evidence to support it, that not only had he killed (which he admitted) but that he had eaten his companions (which he did not). In 1906, represented by Sir Richard Muir KC, normally a senior prosecutor, he successfully fought an attempt to extradite him to France. That year Guerin was shot and wounded off the Tottenham Court Road by his former mistress 'Chicago' May Sharpe and her then companion. He was a known associate of both Grimshaw and Daniel McCarthy, and it may be that at the time of the Pearl Robbery he was in fact working for Grizzard. Over the years Guerin remained in England drifting into petty crime. In his later years he repeatedly appeared before the magistrates' courts up and down the country, usually on charges relating to shoplifting and pickpocketing His last appearance in court was in 1940 when he received six weeks' imprisonment for theft. He died in hospital on 5 December 1940 in Bury, Lancashire, where he had been sent as a war refugee. See Eddie Guerin, *The Man from Devil's Island*.

table whilst the police searched the house, but nothing was found. After they had gone, Grizzard drank his now cold pea soup and at the bottom of the bowl was a diamond necklace which was then cleaned and sold.

Higgins – defended by the talented and fashionable but dishonest solicitor Arthur Newton – ran an alibi defence that he had been with a police officer in the Old Bell public house in Holborn.[5] The officer accepted that he had been with Higgins but not at the crucial time. It was then announced that he also intended to call a character witness, a Mr Goldsmith. The cross-examination by Sir Richard Muir soon put a stop to this idea:

> Q: What other names do you know him by?
> A: Cammi, a nickname.
> Q: Did you know that he has been tried at the Old Bailey for receiving as recently as 1903?
> Silence.
> Q: And that he has been arrested for the Monico robbery?

Higgins received 15 months and Grimshaw 3 years' penal servitude to be followed by 5 years' preventive detention. It was thought that altogether six men were involved in the snatch.

But then Grizzard's fortunes began to decline. The next year he was back in the dock when he was arrested and charged with both receiving stolen jewellery from a burglary in Brighton and harbouring Samuel Barnett who had failed to appear at North London Sessions some 14 months previously. This time, unusually, the police did find a criminal to give evidence against him. Arthur Denville Sassoon Collinson, then doing 5 years on the Moor, said that for the six months prior

[5] Arthur Newton was one of the most sought after London solicitors in the period 1890 to 1912, acting in the Oscar Wilde trial as well as in the Crippen and McDougal murder cases. He was given six months for conspiracy to pervert the course of justice in the Cleveland Brothel scandal and received three years in 1913 for a land fraud. After his release he established a dubious marriage agency, and died in 1930.

to his current unhappy experience he had worked as a burglar for both men. On 8 March 1910 at the Old Bailey Grizzard received five months in the Second Division for feloniously harbouring Barnett. Barnett, wanted for burglaries around the South of England, had been given bail but had fled abroad in 1907. On his return he had been found living at Grizzard's house.

Grizzard was also behind the theft of jewellery from Vaughan Morgan, son of Sir Walter Vaughan Morgan, the City Alderman. Frank Ellis was his butler from 1904 until 1911 when he left to set up as a bookmaker. Before he left he was asked to find another footman and he obtained a man named Robinson through an agency. In the three weeks before Ellis handed over Robinson began betting with him. Ellis also knew William Bangham, one of Grizzard's men and a known jewel thief. By November 1911 Ellis's business was not going well and he was raided and heavily fined as an illegal bookmaker. He then persuaded Robinson to let him into his former master's house, and there was a successful trial run when nothing was taken. The second raid was successful, but the police dismissed the idea that there had been a break-in; so far as they were concerned it was an inside job. Robinson was arrested and discharged after naming Ellis, who was arrested but remained silent. He received 21 months' penal servitude. No amount of persuasion would make Ellis give up Grizzard.

One reason for the loyalty was that Grizzard would help friends who came to grief with the police, and their wives and children whilst they were away. He also had an unswerving loyalty to those with whom he worked. Unlike many a receiver his word was his bond; he paid what he promised. To a certain extent, to him crime was a sport. Again and again his friends tried to persuade him to settle down. He was a comparatively wealthy man and could have afforded to retire, but it was the chase that counted.

Grizzard's men included the burglar James Lockett, who

also used the names Preston, Harry Graham, Lockhart and Jim
or James Howard, who was described by ex-Superintendant
Charles Leach as 'Lockett-the-lion-hearted – the man who
never knew fear'. He had convictions in both Italy and America
and on 14 February 1906, under the name of William Preston,
he had received 5 years at Liverpool Assizes for the attempted
robbery of a man called Hutchinson, a travelling jewellery
salesman. His partner 'Long Almond' received 10 years. Along
with two others picturesquely known as 'Red Bob' and 'Shirty
Bob', they had trailed Hutchinson for some weeks and by
scraping an acquaintance with him discovered he was going
to Liverpool. They watched him leave his hotel and went to
his room to search for the jewels. Unfortunately for them he
returned to find Lockett standing holding the stones. He was
released on 15 November 1909.[6]

Long Almond's name was Arthur Norton and he was
regarded as one of the – if not *the* – finest safe-crackers of
the period. Always impeccably dressed and a resident in the
best hotels, he would cultivate the bank clerks who frequented
the hotels' bars and billiard rooms with a view to obtaining an
impression of the keys they carried. Just before the Liverpool
fiasco he had been released from another 10-year sentence
after a raid on a branch of the Bank of Sunderland in
Newcastle. This time he had persuaded a clerk to accompany
him to a Turkish bath and when the man had taken off his
clothes Norton went through his pockets for the keys. It was
something of a surprise that he had actually gone to the hotel,
and there was speculation that he had unwisely regarded it as
'a soft job'.[7]

[6] 'Shirty Bob' or 'Bobs' is mentioned in the memoirs of 'Chicago' May
Sharpe. Apparently at one time he owned a fashionable club but when
she knew him around the turn of the century he was a hotel thief
working, among other places, the Langham Hotel. Although she often
names criminals such as Dab McCarthy and Ruby Michaels, she does not
identify 'Shirty Bob'.
[7] *Morning Leader*, 15 February 1906; *The Umpire*, 18 February 1906.

Lockett had also been in the wars before the Liverpool case; the previous year he had been arrested over the theft of £10,000 of jewellery in Colmore Row, Birmingham. He and a woman had been visiting a number of jewellers where she had pawned jewels. Almost immediately after the theft she had left for America. Some of the jewels were later found in the possession of a New York pawnbroker. Almost certainly the woman was 'Blonde' Alice Smith who once fought 'Chicago' May Sharpe over the latter's lover Baby Thompson. As for Lockett, he was put on an identification parade and was not picked out.

Now in 1910 Lockett was reported to have an interest in a motor-car business in Finchley and what was rather charmingly called a 'cinematograph palace' in Golders Green purchased with the proceeds from the Birmingham theft, although according to police files he spent little time with either. Instead he was occupied as the working lieutenant of Grizzard in a series of substantial jewellers' shop burglaries in the West End during the winter of 1911–12.

Then in 1913 came Grizzard's greatest coup and most abject failure – the theft of a string of 61 pearls, one of the finest collections then assembled, with an insurance value of £130,000.

The international dealer Max Mayer had offices at 88 Hatton Garden and on 20 June 1913 sent the string to his agent in Paris, Henri Salomon, who had unfulfilled hopes of finding a buyer. On 15 July the necklace in a leather case along with two drop pearls and a round pearl, wrapped in blue paper, marked 'M.M.' and sealed by Salomon, was returned by registered post through the postal authorities in Paris.

There was nothing remarkable in this process. The standard way of sending jewellery at the time, it was regarded as far safer than having a messenger carry it around, as Goldschmidt had found to his cost a couple of years earlier. On 16 July Mayer received a letter from Salomon saying the pearls were on their way and, in fact, the box arrived in the same post.

But instead of the pearls there was only the considerably less valuable cargo of eight lumps of sugar on a bed of cotton wool, all wrapped in a piece of newspaper from *Echo de Paris* dated 2 July. There were now twin problems. First for Salomon to explain just what he had done and eliminate himself from inquiries, and secondly for the thieves to dispose of pearls which were readily identifiable. Salomon came immediately to England producing a receipt for the package. The French police and Chief Inspector Ward were able to trace the box's transfers from Paris to Calais through to the Central Sorting Office in Hatton Garden. There was, it seemed, no possibility that the box had been tampered with whilst in the hands of the postal services. The postman who had been given the box to deliver had signed for it and produced a receipt from the commissionaire at Mayer's office. He had never come under suspicion and had worked for the Post Office for over 30 years.

It was then discovered that there was an additional seal on the box to hide a cut in the paper, but this seal was also stamped 'M.M.'. Much to the wrath of the French postal authorities, the police now believed the theft had taken place on their side of the Channel, but there was no evidence of this and if the postal workers were to be believed the theft could not have occurred in transit. This left Salomon, but the police were quite willing to rule him out which left no one. A £10,000 reward was posted and an extensive description of the pearls was circulated.

Then at the beginning of August two jewel dealers in Paris, cousins Mayer Cohen Quadratstein and Samuel Brandstatter, heard that Leiser Gutwirth in Antwerp might have the secret of the whereabouts of the pearls. Brandstatter visited Gutwirth and was told the pearls were indeed available, but not for £20,000 which he was offered: he wanted double. Brandstatter said he must consult with his partner and wrote to Gutwirth, who was now in London, saying he had a buyer 'for the article'. He was immediately summoned from Paris, but the price was now £50,000.

The cousins – who throughout were only interested in the reward – met Gutwirth, Grizzard and one of Grizzard's colleagues, Simon Silverman, in a Lyons teashop in Holborn.[8] Grizzard took out a cigarette, asked an apparent stranger for a match and a box was thrown to him. When opened there were the three separate pearls. They were taken to be weighed; the box was sealed and it was agreed that only the price was in question. For amateur detectives the cousins behaved with great skill. They kept negotiations going for some 10 days whilst they contacted the assessors, the firm of Price & Gibbs, and were given 100,000 FF to use in negotiations. Unwilling to have the men caught without the pearls, the police bided their time.

On 25 August another meeting took place in Holborn, this time at the now long gone First Avenue Hotel. The cousins, joined by Spanier, a French jewel expert employed by the assessors, met Silverman and Grizzard. The necklace was produced and the three stray pearls were purchased for 100,000 FF. Over the next few days Grizzard and his team were followed and the meetings were watched by detectives in disguise.

Meanwhile Grizzard was taking some precautions himself. He had made Brandstatter and Quadratstein remain in the room in the First Avenue Hotel for five minutes while he left with the money and the necklace. He also recognised one

---

[8] Silverman, a diamond broker, lived with his mother and sister at Bow. 'Those who knew him in Hatton Garden described him as a greasy, always smiling little hunch-backed Jew. He was always apologetic and polite to everyone, too much so for the blunt and honest English mind and none too popular.' Christmas Humphreys, *The Great Pearl Robbery of 1913*, p. 21. Gutwirth was apparently a distant relation of the cousins who tracked down the pearls.

of the detectives set to watch him, and now he employed Lockett to watch the watchers. His antennae also picked up the signal that the whole thing was a trap and he arranged for the necklace to go to Amsterdam to be sold for £40,000, but Gutwirth and Silverman would not agree and Grizzard allowed himself to be overruled.

Now the police decided that the best way to follow Grizzard was not by having him tailed by a plain-clothes detective but by the simple expedient of using a uniformed constable seemingly going about his ordinary affairs, and accordingly a detective was put in uniform. On 3 September he followed Grizzard, Silverman and Lockett to a meeting at what was then the British Museum underground station. The trap was sprung and after a fight the three were arrested.

The trouble began at Bow Street where the prisoners were taken. When they were searched there was no necklace. Their houses were searched, they were charged with stealing and receiving the necklace, but by the end of the evening there were still no pearls.

Nothing was found until a fortnight later when a matchbox containing pearls was found in St Paul's Road, Islington, when a piano maker saw the box in the gutter. He thought they were imitation pearls, but nevertheless took them to the local police station where the police agreed with him and they were registered as such and sent to the Lost Property office at Scotland Yard where an officer in the case saw and recognised them as genuine. Apparently when Lockett's wife had heard of her husband's arrest she had thrown the pearls away. So Mayer received most of his jewels back.

Just how was the snatch worked? Was it done in France? In fact, as with most of the best plans, it was all deceptively simple. Grizzard knew Mayer and that he received large quantities of jewellery. What he was hoping for was not pearls but diamonds which could easily be recut and disposed of without any great difficulty. Silverman then took an office

at 101 Hatton Garden and began to chat up the postmen.
One by the name of Neville, either for money or accidentally
– and although nothing was proved it really must have been
the former – provided an opportunity for Silverman to take
an impression of the seals on a package addressed to Mayer.
From then on it was relatively simple to obtain a die, and
once the defendants were in custody a die maker named
Gordon came forward to say that he had made one for
Silverman.

On the morning of the robbery the postman making the
delivery went to 101 before 88 and – negligently, for he was
not charged either – was distracted so that the package could
be opened and the substitution made.

Prosecuted by Sir Richard Muir, Lockett and Grizzard
received 7 years' penal servitude and Silverman 5 years at
their trial in November 1913. Silverman was to be deported
after his sentence. Gutwirth was sentenced to 18 months
with hard labour. He had tried to disassociate himself from
the others.

> I was dragged into it. I have been eighteen years in Hatton
> Garden, my Lord, always straight-forward. I do not know
> what made me do it. I ought never to have done a thing
> like that. It is not my business. Mine is a straight-forward
> business.

Despite the fact that he had been in England for 25 years and
was a married man, he too was recommended for deportation:

> Mr Justice Lawrence: That may be, but he is an alien and
> we do not want such aliens here.

Their appeals were dismissed in December. After the arrests

of the four principals the police had gone looking for 82-year-old Daniel McCarthy, a long-standing member of the Grizzard and other teams. He was charged with them after admitting that he had changed some of the francs provided by Spanier, but the technicalities of proving anything more against him were too great and he was discharged.

A police report prepared after Grizzard's arrest establishes his high place in the pantheon of criminals of the time:

> He is a diamond merchant by trade, but has no established business premises. He does undoubtedly do a little business, but the greater portion of his time is taken up by organising crimes, and buying and disposing of stolen property. Much has been heard of him during the past fifteen years as having been connected with many serious crimes. A large number of statements made by prisoners are in our possession showing that they have disposed of property to him, but unfortunately we have been unable to prosecute him for a lack of corroborative evidence.

Grizzard found conditions little to his liking and he began to try to scheme his way out. Like so many thieves, he came to a long prison sentence late in life and prison, particularly in those days, takes the stuffing out of many a man. Grizzard was no exception. There is a theory that those who have received regular sentences can cope better than those who have perhaps only served a few months. Lockett knew and understood what penal servitude was all about. Grizzard did not and, while Lockett appears to have accepted his sentence and conditions stoically, Grizzard became an informer on some of his former competitors. He was in his fifties and apparently in poor health because he spent much of his time in the prison hospital. In any event Grizzard was an old man by the standards of the day. He had a heart condition and was suffering from eczema. He wanted out and now, reneging on the principles which had kept so many men loyal to him, he wrote to the authorities naming George Hanlon as a man wanted for three robberies. He was well known; he had done 3 years in Paris and 5 here. Grizzard hoped that when his wife lodged a petition for his release it would be supported.

Grizzard may have been a master crook but spelling was certainly not his long suit. On 11 October 1915 he wrote from Parkhurst giving information that an American whom he knew only as 'Yankee Johnny' and a German whose name he did not know were two of the best burglars in London. The German was kept under cover by a Jim Trott in Manchester and 'Yankee Johnny' was a great friend of Harry Snell:

> The German may have his mustarsh off – Oftern – nows. A man Rogers used to live in the Westend has a money lender.

As for his health, he was suffering from 'diebertus' and 'skin diesiese'.

Grizzard was giving good information. 'Yankee Johnny' was John Talbot, an American safe-breaker who lived in Darwin Street in the New Kent Road. The German was Max Baum. James Trott did live in Manchester and had a police record. Harry Snell lived at 83 Hungerford Road, Holloway, and was a bookmaker suspected, rather like Grizzard, of being a financier and putter-up.

The gang had been relatively quiet since the arrest of Grizzard and Lockett, but George Hanlon was indeed wanted for stealing a mailbag from St Pancras station on 24 August 1913. He lived at 14 Wroughton Road, Wandsworth, where the bag minus the contents was found. And for that matter, the house was also minus Hanlon who was now thought to be living in Streatham. Rogers was believed to be Swiss and was certainly an associate of Hanlon. He was also believed to have gone back to Switzerland. Sergeant David Goodwillie recommended that Grizzard have a reduction in his sentence, but nothing came of it.

But Grizzard was not finished and in 1917 he wrote again, informing this time on a Bernard Hedgis who was serving 3 years, alleging him to be one of the most dangerous criminals in the country. He also disclosed some of his own past. Hedgis had come from Africa at the end of the Boer War and knew a foreigner, Idleman, who lived in a boarding house in Russell Square kept by his wife. Hedgis was a dealer in stolen jewellery. Grizzard had been summoned there and later went over to buy jewellery in Paris for some £4,000. In fact this was a trick. Grizzard had been 'put out' and robbed. Hedgis, he claimed, also robbed the English in South Africa and then later went to South America living off women.

Sadly, apart from naming Hedgis and another prisoner, 0394*, he peached on his old friend Silverman saying he had been working with Lockett for some ten years. He hoped that his letter would be of assistance. The country, he thought, should be protected from the likes of Hedgis. At least he did try to row Lockett out, writing that neither he nor Lockett knew anything of the pearl necklace before it was stolen. Indeed, according to him Lockett had apparently been recruited to save the gems after they had been stolen.

Again the police made inquiries and found that Hedgis and Samuel Morris Natenson had been recommended for deportation when they were sentenced to 3 years' penal servitude on 8 December 1914. They would have been entitled to 9 months' remission. When the police checked

things out they found that the men had not yet gone to
Brixton to await their deportation, and that Natenson was
not in fact due for deportation; he was to be allowed to join
the British Army, and did indeed join the Royal Artillery.
Hedgis was to see a recuiting officer with a view to enlistment,
and on 14 April he too joined the Artillery. He denied
even knowing Grizzard, and Detective Inspector Wensley,
now having one of his most talented opponents in custody,
was implacable. Poor Cammi was to be told that in his
view the information was of no value to the police. He
would remain where he was until he had completed his
sentence.[9]

Despite his health and distaste for prison Grizzard just
could not stop. In 1922 he was charged with receiving
the proceeds of an ingenious fraud on a firm of London
jewel dealers which netted some £10,000, and again Muir
prosecuted him. Grizzard had arranged for Major Harrison
– actually ex-Major Harrison since he had been cashiered
– to purchase jewellery on approval from Bedford & Co.
in Aldersgate High Street. He advanced Harrison £3,000 to
establish a line of credit and Harrison played his part well.
The jewellery was to be shown to a Colonel who would
shortly be returning to India. It was a simple, well-established
confidence trick. The initial purchases were paid for; more
jewellery was bought and paid for and then £10,000 of
jewellery was handed over for approval. The idea was for
it to be smashed, or sold at a discount, on the Continent;
but after a quick attempt to sell it in Hatton Garden, Grizzard
and another member of the conspiracy, the American-born
Michael Spellman, received only £900 for it in Antwerp.
Foolishly he returned to England where he was found to
have another collection of stolen jewellery in his possession
and more gems were traced to Grizzard.

[9] MEPO 3 236B.

In August 1922 Grizzard was arrested and in the October received 12 months, as did Spellman. The gallant major fled to Canada where shortly afterwards he received two years for a similar fraud. Whilst awaiting trial Grizzard was found to be suffering from both tuberculosis and diabetes in an aggravated form. He was taken home where he died on 15 September 1923, aged 57. He wrote a note for Spellman leaving him 'all the spoils you have done me out of and my place in the underworld as Prince'.[10]

On his release unfortunately Spellman did not behave as well towards those from whom he bought as Grizzard had done. Operating out of Hatton Garden and Duke Street, Houndsditch, he was known to screw burglars down for the last penny. It was from an anonymous tip-off that the police arrested him in the autumn of 1925 and he received a further 12 months with hard labour for receiving.

James Lockett had been released from penal servitude in 1919. He married a second time and became a bookmaker. He had not committed – or at least had not been convicted of – any further crime in the next decade, by which time he was 67. Whilst inside there had been a curious incident over his house in Powis Gardens, Golders Green, which had been sold for £425 to a Mrs Saxby who wanted to use it as a bed-and-breakfast. Now she reported to the police that the estate agent was pestering her to buy it from her. What was the reason for this? The police did not know. They had searched the place – throughout which there was a host of electric alarms – thoroughly when Lockett was arrested, and they could not believe his family had left anything behind

---

[10] Spellman and Grizzard had worked together over a number of years. They had first met in America when Grizzard absented himself from London for a period. It was thought that Spellman had backed out of participating in the Great Pearl Robbery because his wife was ill. *Empire News*, 25 October 1925.

when they moved out. They advised Mrs Saxby to search the house again and report back. There is no record that she did.

Harry Grimshaw, who had taken the fall for the Café Monico robbery, continued an independent life of crime. Born in Bolton, in the 1890s he had been a successful jockey who could go to the scales at a pound or two over six stone, and in 1895 he won the valuable Manchester November and Liverpool Cup handicaps. Later he rode in Austria and Germany before returning to England, relinquishing his licence in 1904, and he then worked as a tic-tac man. He first appeared in court two years later when he was bound over for stealing a purse, but the same year he received three months for theft. From then it was a step up in class and he became the known associate of jewel thieves working on the Continent. October 1907 saw him receive 21 months at North London Quarter Sessions for the theft of a ring and he followed up with 3 years for a handbag snatch. In 1912 he received a total of 8 years following a conviction for theft at Marlborough Street Police Court. He was released during the war from his sentence and served well in France, but failed to report on his discharge and was returned to prison to complete his sentence. He was once more associated with a team of continental jewel thieves and in the spring of 1923 was suspected of being involved in the theft of a jewel case at Dover Harbour. It was thought he had returned to the Continent, but in fact he had gone back to the Northern racetracks and in October, described as wearing a smartly cut blue suit, he was given 21 months for receiving. At the time the police described him as one of the greatest of hotel thieves, with his speed being blinding. His colleague Frederick Johnson earned 9 months for theft at Middlesborough Quarter Sessions. Grimshaw's other colleague, Elizabeth Murray, said to be a French woman, was sentenced at Durham the following month for the theft of the jewellery worth £290. He died shortly after.[11]

There were, of course, other receivers and putters-up to replace Grizzard, although they may not have operated in the plush conditions in which he chose to work. Israel Myers was 79 when he appeared at the Old Bailey charged with receiving. Born in the East End, he went to America where he had built up a fortune before returning to Houndsditch where he bought the George and Dragon. His second, much younger wife left him and he became a receiver. By the time he had remarried and his third wife was about to give birth to their second child, he was acting as receiver of some 25 per cent of the property stolen in the Metropolitan area. He pleaded guilty to five counts; his counsel urged that this was his first lapse and emphasis was placed on his unblemished past. The *Empire News* commented sourly, 'There were indisputable facts to disprove most of this.'[12] Myers had been on remand for three months when Sir Ernest Wild sentenced him to a total of a year's imprisonment.

Another of the biggest of the receivers of the time was Joseph Betts who, at his trial for receiving stolen jewellery,

[11] Another of Grimshaw's associates was the noted woman thief 'Blonde' Alice Smith who once fought the notorious 'Chicago' May Sharpe. After Grimshaw went to prison for the Pearl Robbery in which she had been an outside decoy, she went to America where she was involved in a £20,000 blackmail scheme with Charlie Smith, May Sharpe's new lover. She also served 7 years in the States for a jewel robbery. In 1926 she served a period of 3 years for theft and was again imprisoned for another jewel robbery in December 1929. See *Empire News*, 8 December 1929.

There are many accounts of the Great Pearl Robbery including that of Christmas Humphreys. It is also given prominence in the memoirs of both Muir and ex-Superintendent G.W. Cornish who as a young officer was part of the investigating team. In *Cornish of the Yard* he gives a slightly different – and one more favourable to the Yard – account of the retrieval of the pearls.

[12] *Empire News*, 'Aged Spider Man of the Underworld', 9 September 1923.

described Duke's Place off Middlesex Street where he conducted his business:

> There are at least three or four hundred dealers there every Sunday even in a bad time like this and in summer I have seen as many as a thousand there. Dealers lay their goods out on the ground, on clothes and on stalls so that anyone who wishes to purchase anything can examine the article.

He went on to say that the Tsar of Russia's jewels had been broken down and sold in the market. His explanation did him no good; he received 5 years. After he was taken into custody, high-class burglaries were said to have ceased for a time in London.[13]

That, of course, may either have been press hype or a successful attempt by the police to put the boot in at Betts' trial, because not long after came the trial of 'the best safe-breakers in the world', one of whom was an East Ender, James Flood, whose real name was Wood. The team which consisted of him, as the putter-up and arranger, John Russell from Liverpool and two wild colonial boys – 'Daredevil' Dennis Harris, then aged 60, from Australia and a South African, John James, both of whom had in their younger days been steeplechase jockeys – were caught on 28 November 1924 *in flagrante* in a burglary in the Euston Road. Flood/Wood received 15 months and, to teach colonials not to come to England to rob safes, Harris and James were each sentenced to 3 years' penal servitude. Russell received 6 months in the Second Division.[14]

---

[13] *Empire News*, 22 February 1925.
[14] PRO MEPO 3 483, *The Star*, 30 January 1925 and see G.W. Cornish, *Cornish of the Yard*, Ch. VII. The police and press were always keen on elevating villains. Samuel Cohen, described by Detective Inspector Edward Greeno as 'a modern Fagin', received 2 years at the Old Bailey swiftly followed by 2 more for receiving and conspiracy at Winchester Assizes. He was regarded as having been behind much London crime for a number of undetected years.

4

Prostitution

It could never be said that prostitution in the East End was a way out of poverty, but it was an existence into which many young women, particularly Jewish women, were forced. Commercial prostitution was prohibited under Rabbinic laws as a form of idolatry. Part of the reason was the wish to disassociate the Jewish faith from other Middle Eastern religions in which sex played a large part. In East Europe, prostitution was almost unknown amongst the Jews until the nineteenth century.

In 1905 in Warsaw there was an *Alphonsenpogrom* in which the citizens attempted to drive out the pimps. In that city in 1889, 22 per cent of licensed prostitutes were Jewish; in 1910 in Minsk 33 per cent of official prostitutes and half the female patients in the VD ward were Jewish.

In the East End it was estimated that approximately 1,000 Jewish women a year worked in prostitution. Some 20 per cent of brothel-keeping convictions were against Jews. One reason was that young women in rural communities in Eastern Europe were effectively sold by their parents from economic necessity. Girls were also enticed away from their families with promises of marriage and jobs. It is impossible to think that the families did not at least suspect what would befall their daughters. About 1,000 unaccompanied girls a year arrived at the East End Docks alone. It is almost impossible to imagine the confusion they would feel with the bustle and with little command of English. It is no surprise therefore that many fell prey to offers of seeming kindness in the form of lodging.

The scenes at the landing stage are less idyllic. There are a few relatives and friends awaiting the arrival of the small boats filled with immigrants; but the crowd gathered in and about the gin-shop overlooking the narrow entrance of the landing stage are dock loungers of the lowest type and professional 'runners'. These latter individuals, usually of the Hebrew race, are among the most repulsive of East London parasites; boat after boat touches the landing stages; they push forward, seize hold of the bundles or baskets of the newcomers, offer bogus tickets to those who wish to travel forward to America, promise guidance and free lodging to those who hold in their hand addresses of acquaintances in Whitechapel or are friendless. A little man with an official badge (Hebrew Ladies Protective Society) fights valiantly in their midst for the conduct of unprotected females, and shouts or whispers to the others to go to the Poor Jews' Temporary Shelter in Leman Street. For a few moments it is a scene of indescribable confusion: cries and countercries; the hoarse laughter of the dock loungers at the strange garb and broken accent of the poverty-stricken foreigners; the rough swearing of the boatmen at passengers unable to pay the fee for landing. In another ten minutes eighty of the hundred newcomers are dispersed into the back slums of Whitechapel; in another few days the majority of these, robbed of the little they possess, are turned out of the 'free lodgings', destitute and friendless.[1]

All too often, however, the lodging turned out to be a brothel. The white slavers were looking for single and unaccompanied girls. Another reason for the descent into prostitution was that a married woman was unable to obtain a divorce without a 'get' from her husband and so remarry. Without financial support prostitution became a necessity. To overcome isolation from religion, some Jewish prostitutes and pimps set up their own synagogues and burial grounds in New York and Rio.

The Radcliffe Highway was known as the poor man's Regent Street because of the prostitution. In 1887, at any time there would be between 20 and 30 Jewish prostitutes at the East India Dock gates. Prostitutes' pubs included the Globe and Artichoke, the Gunboat, Malt Shovel and, the doyen of them all, the White Swan at the Shadwell end of the Highway, known as Paddy's Goose, the proprietor of which had, during the Crimean War, recruited for the Navy 'in a small steamer with a band of music and flags'.[2]

Flower and Dean Street was regarded as perhaps the roughest of streets of the East End and ones notorious for prostitution. In the early 1870s the Reverend Samuel Barnett gave notice to the Guardians to have the area demolished under the so-called Cross Act; the Artisans and Labourers' Act which had been passed thirty years earlier and which was designed as an answer to the challenge presented by criminal

[1] Charles Booth (ed.), *Life and Labour of the People in London*, vol. 1, pp. 582–3. It is of course no different today with girls and boys being importuned at major railway termini in London, and the Port Authority bus terminal on 8th Avenue being a favourite recruiting point for pimps as young girls from the Mid-West arrive in New York.

[2] Quoted in Kellow Chesney, *The Victorian Underworld*, p. 381. Chesney remarks that despite this apparently wholly successful display of patriotism the proprietor soon fell out with the authorities.

slums. The notice followed a severe outbreak of cholera in the street. Although the improvement scheme was signed in 1877 nothing was done because the authorities fought shy of making 13,000 people homeless in a time of severe depression. It was not until 1883 that part of Flower and Dean Street was demolished and the Charlotte de Rothschild Buildings were constructed. This now created quite separate communities in the street.

In October 1885 efforts were being made to clear out brothels from Lady Lake's Grove and Oxford Street leading into Bedford Street. Messrs F.N. Charrington and E.H. Kerwin went round the houses with a black book. As parishioners, if they gave notice to the police of the keeping of a disorderly house, on conviction the overseers of the street would pay them £10 under the Act of 25 Geo II c 36 s.5. They were attacked with fish and other filth and the next day they were stoned. One feature of the attack was the 'extreme scarcity' of the police. They had watched a police officer visit the brothel of a Mrs Hart in Canal Street.

Indigenous prostitutes suffered from the Jewish immigrants:

> Also, Jews had moved into those houses where certain rooms had been used for vice. Initially they would occupy one room, and persist in staying, notwithstanding the insults and provocations by the bordello operators. Eventually the Jew would take over a second room, and, in the long run, tough Jewish puritanism proved formidable against its more permissive antagonist. The demi-monde could see no profit or pleasure in remaining, and eventually took off to more lucrative areas.[3]

At the turn of the century, Sol Cohen ran the Jewish Association for the Protection of Girls and Women. His research

---

[3] W. J. Fishman, *East End Jewish Radicals*, p. 58.

into the White Slave trade showed that many of the girls had
been prostitutes before going to South America but, indeed, in
many cases there had been no coercion. The Association was
involved in 125 cases in 1900, 128 in 1901, and there was a
massive leap in 1902 when 206 girls who had disappeared
were thought to have been abducted or exported to South
America.

His experiences were rather different from those described
in a Metropolitan Police report of 1906 which recorded that
cases of procuring innocent girls for immoral purposes were
few and far between. There were perhaps half a dozen genuine
instances, but they were mostly French and Belgian girls
brought to work here before being sent to South America
or South Africa.[4]

However, the Home Office was not wholly deaf to the
worries of the vigilance groups and on 17 October 1912 a
small White Slave Traffic Squad was launched. It consisted
of one CID inspector, one CID constable, two uniformed
constables in each of C, D and H divisions and one constable
in E and L. The constables were to be given seven shillings
a week to enable them to perform their duties in plain
clothes.

Thirteen months later, on 7 November 1913, John Curry,
the Detective Inspector in charge of the squad, reported:

At the time of the formation of the Branch the country

[4] PRO MEPO 2 558. An interesting case of a Jewish procurer was that
of Matthew Gammersbach of Hertford Road, Dalston, who was deported
in 1906 following a conviction for living off the proceeds of prostitution.
He had been sentenced to three months hard labour and ordered to
pay £22. 6s. 0d. costs. He was found back in the country when he
should, at the very least, have been in Belgium. His story was that he
was obliged to defend an action brought by one of the girls, a Miss
Montyai, who was claiming the not inconsiderable sum of £1,110 from
him. He was allowed to stay for the action, which he lost, but he was
shadowed throughout by police officers who found him talking to other
undesirables in disreputable public houses. PRO MEPO 2 1006.

was being aroused by a number of alarming statements
made by religious, social and other workers who spread
the belief that there was a highly organised gang of White
Slave Traffickers with agents in every part of the civilised
world, kidnapping and otherwise carrying off women and
girls from their homes to lead them to their ruin in foreign
lands, and were thereby reaping huge harvests of gold.

I have to state that there has been an utter absence of
evidence to justify these alarming statements, the effect
of which was to cause a large shoal of complaints and
allegations [many contained in anonymous letters] to be
received by police, against persons of all classes.

The year's work had produced a total of fifty-one arrests.
Two were for procuring; and two for attempting to procure.
Forty-four were living on immoral earnings and the three who
were aliens and who were suspected slavers were deported.[5]

The Inspector thought that 'the Criminal Law Amendment
Act 1912 has had a salutary effect on foreign ponces'. Happily,
there was 'No case of unwilling or innocent girl' being
recruited into white slavery and anyway, 'Mostly [they are]
Jewesses of Russian or Polish origin [who] go to Argentina
and Brazil.'

The size of the squad was accordingly reduced.[6]

He was probably correct when he said that most were
Jewesses, but note the anti-Semitic tone. With the pogroms,
poverty and the forcing of the Jewish community in Russia

---

[5] There were, however, undoubtedly gangs with international connections.
One such was headed in London by Aldo Antonious Celli (alias Carvelli,
Shanks, Cortini, Ferrari and Leonora) who had convictions in Australia
and was said to be of Swiss origin. Girls recruited in Belgium were told
they would be taken to Wellington, New Zealand. On 30 November
1910 he and a Frenchman, Alexander Nicolini, pleaded guilty to a
general conspiracy to procure women within the King's Dominions
and he was sentenced to 6 months' hard labour and deportation. PRO
MEPO 3 197.
[6] PRO MEPO 3 184.

away from rural communities into the city, there was undoubtedly a trade in young Jewesses.[7]

One such case where the victims escaped was followed by
the prosecution of Joseph Karmeler and Sam Scheffer who
had prepared mock marriage certificates in Hebrew and who
were trying to lure young girls on board a ship bound for
South America. The girls very sensibly went to their parents,
as a result of which, in an unsuccessful effort to save himself
from the inevitability of prison, Karmeler, who was known to
have a direct link to a brothel in Rio, was obliged to hand in
a written statement:

> Dear Judges
> I am innocent of these charges . . . This is written not
> with ink but with the blood and tears of my eyes.

He received 15 months imprisonment and Scheffer 3 months
more. Each also received 12 strokes of the cat.[8]

In fact, possibly because there was no money around,
prostitution was not that much of a problem in all parts of
the East End and it was confined largely to the Pennyfields,
Limehouse and Aldgate areas. Nor, of course, were all prostitutes Jewish.

> The brides were mostly down the other end of Brick Lane
> where the lodging houses were in Flowery Dean Street. The
> 'Seven Stars' next to Christ Church School was mostly used
> by the ladies of the town, and the 'Frying Pan' on the corner
> of Thrawl Street and Brick Lane was famous for being the
> centre of the red light district.[9]

[7] See Edward J. Bristow, *Prostitution and Prejudice: The Jewish Fight Against White Slavery 1870–1939*.
[8] *East London Advertiser* (*ELA*), 11 August 1915.
[9] Raphael Samuel, *East End Underworld*, p. 109.

The lodging houses charged fourpence, sixpence and a shilling, and some allowed 'husbands and wives'. In 1902 a survey of some 23 prostitutes found that their average age was 27 and that they stayed in the same lodging house for weeks rather than for long periods. Set again this were Elizabeth Stride and Catherine Eddowes, both of whom were Ripper victims and who lived in the same lodging house for years. Common lodging houses were allowed to accommodate a maximum of 323 people and one of the principal owners was the very popular Jimmy Smith of Bancroft Road who was regarded as the governor about Brick Lane.[10]

Smith was a man of all trades who had started life selling coal in Flower and Dean Street. He would deliver it at a price for those who could not carry it home and, with the money earned, he invested in the common lodging houses. He was also a liaison between the police and street bookmakers.

There was an echo of Jack shortly after the turn of the century when, at about 7.30 a.m. on 26 May 1901, 28-year-old Annie Austin was heard moaning in a cubicle in a lodging house at 35 Dorset Street, Spitalfields, London. She had been separated from her husband for about ten days. When she was examined by a doctor it was found that she had been stabbed in both the anus and the vagina. When he asked her if she knew who had done it, she said it was by the man who had come in with her the previous night but whose name she did not know.

She died in the London Hospital on 27 May. She was somewhat unfortunate because, through a series of administrative blunders, she was not examined for some 12 hours. The police

---

[10] Stepney MoH Report 1902, p. 28. At the time of the Ripper murders it was estimated there were at least 63 brothels and 1,200 prostitutes operating in 'W' Division. The Home Secretary wished to close down the East End brothels, but Sir Charles Warren rather pragmatically thought they should remain in place. Driving away brothel keepers would simply demoralise the rest of London. See D.G. Browne, *The Rise of Scotland Yard*, p. 207.

had been called but did not arrive in time to interview her and instead she had told the doctor her story. She said she had slept with the man and then, as he was getting up to leave in the early hours, she felt a sharp pain as if a knife had been run inside her. She described her attacker as short, with dark hair and moustache and a Jewish appearance.

The hostel was managed by a Henry Moore and his wife. His brother-in-law, Daniel Sullivan, sometimes acted as his deputy, and it was he who took her to hospital. The lodging-house rules, observed in their breach, were that only married couples should share a cubicle. The manager said that customers were insulted if they were asked whether they were married.

On 30 May, Austin's husband was arrested and charged with her murder. At the inquest the pathologist reported no signs of a struggle and that, somewhat ironically, Annie Austin was healthy but for long-standing syphilis. Moore said that he had allowed the man and woman into the premises and that it was he who, the next morning, had sent for Dr Dale and had called a cab for her to go to the hospital. His wife, Maria Moore, said she had been up and about all that night but had heard no screams. One of the unanswered questions was when had the man slipped away, or if indeed he was part of the hostel staff.

Both Sullivan and Moore came under suspicion because for some reason they gave the wrong cubicle number to the police. At first they said Austin had been in cubicle 44 rather than the correct number 15. Was the street door unlocked before her screams were heard? If so, it would indicate that the man had left. If it was still bolted, it would almost certainly be that the killer had remained on the premises.

Maria Moore seems to have made some effort to divert attention. She made a positive identification of Austin's estranged husband, but he was able to give a cast-iron alibi. There was also some suggestion that Daniel Sullivan had been the man with Annie Austin that night, but he provided an alibi that he had shared a bed with a man named Timothy Batty at 10 Paternoster Row. The coroner, once again Wynne E. Baxter, took the view that the alibi was not conclusive but in the absence of any contradictory evidence the jury should give weight to it. Discharging Austin, he said he regarded the whole of Mrs Moore's evidence as perjured. If the Director wished to bring a prosecution on new evidence that would be up to him. The Director did not.

As the final police report reads, they felt the man was known to the lodging-house habituées and was being protected by them. Clearly they had a hard time during their investigations.

> From the first to the last we have to deal with a class of witnesses that are as low as they can well possibly be and it is difficult to know when they are speaking the truth. In some instances they lie without any apparent motive.
>
> Although we never despair I fear that nothing further can be done to elucidate this mystery and the perpetrator of this crime unfortunately goes unpunished as a result of the scandalous conduct of nearly the whole of the witnesses in this case. Thomas Divall (Inspector).

Apart from anything else the police were not happy that they had had to pay out the then not inconsiderable sum of £5 to sober people to round up the witnesses and make them keep their appointments.

Certainly, whilst prostitution down in the East End at the turn of the century was rife it could not necessarily be called a lucrative trade:

> There were two kinds of girl. Those who went up West and mixed with the toffs. They would get as much as ten shillings a time or even £1 and they would ride home in hansom cabs . . . The girls who stayed at Spitalfields were

very poor. That was what you called a 'fourpenny touch'
or a 'knee trembler' – they wouldn't stay with you all night
. . . Even if you stayed all night with the girls like that it
was only a couple of shillings.[11]

Dock prostitutes were known as trippers-up. Three or four
would band together when ships docked and it became a
battle of wits to separate a sailor from his money. The sailors'
defences included pads in which they kept their money which
they wore in their shoes; pouches sewn in waistbands, and
leather bags under shields attached to belts.[12]

[11] Raphael Samuel, *East End Underworld*, p. 109.
[12] For an account of some of the schemes and counterschemes see James
Berrett, *When I Was at Scotland Yard*, Chapter 3.

5

Mobs – 1

As with other cities, each area of London had its own gangs each of which occupied a certain amount of territory even if only a street. Sometimes they expanded into the territory of others in the locality, and in the case of the bigger organisations such as the Sabinis and the Krays into completely different areas such as Soho. The East End was no exception and, given that until well after the Second World War the area was almost a series of villages, there was a proliferation of gangs who at the beginning were named simply after streets rather than areas.

One of the earliest of this period was the Green Gate Gang, from the road of the same name, which seems to have been principally a fighting gang but whose members were quite capable of straying out of their area to take on rivals.

In the spring of 1882, Thomas Galliers and James Casey stood trial at the Old Bailey for the murder of Frederick Willmore who was beaten up on the Sunday before Christmas 1881 and died from his injuries on 14 January the next year. There were about 20 in the Green Gate Gang who attacked

Willmore and another man from the Dover Road or Lambeth Boys. Encountering the pair on the Embankment, they had asked where they came from. On being told, they said 'we pay (meaning hit) the Lambeth chaps' and 'trashed them with square brass buckled belts'.

Thomas Galliers was said to have had a public house door-strap with a large brass buckle on which was engraved a gate, which he wore as a belt. He received 10 years for manslaughter but the jury disagreed over Casey, who had made a self-serving statement whilst awaiting trial. Many of the remainder of the gang had been involved in a riot in Bethnal Green the previous month and received between 12 and 18 months' hard labour.[1]

Twenty years later the problem was just as acute.

The shortening of the hours of labour, together with the absence of any guidance in the use of the leisure hours is the cause of many of the social problems of the day. The young people have the whole of the evening to themselves. From seven till bed-time they can do what they please. We practically make them a free gift of one-third of the working year. But we offer nothing in the place of work except the street. Their own idea of employing their idle time is to do nothing to amuse themselves, and as the street is the only place where they can find amusement for nothing, they go into the street.[2]

Outside fighting gangs there were layers of criminal activity on a semi-organised basis. The lowest status was called the kinchin lay, or stealing from children who were delivering washing for their mothers. There was also the organisation of children to beg. In 1902 Jane Kelly, also known as Steele,

---

[1] PRO CRIM 1/13/6.
[2] Sir Walter Besant, *The East End and Its People.*

was sentenced to 5 years' imprisonment for kidnapping an 8-year-old boy, Willie Crawford, and forcing him to beg. She had lured him away from outside his home in the Bethnal Green Road with the promise of cakes and sweets and had then toured the neighbourhood getting him to offer vestas (matches) to passers-by. The child had finally tired of the game and had tried to run away in the Costers' Market in Whitecross Street, but she had held on to him. A crowd gathered and a policeman came; she told him the child was hers. She had earlier served 18 months and 7 years for previous similar offences, and 15 months from an unexpired sentence was added to the 5 she received at the Old Bailey.[3]

One of the senior indigenous gangs to flourish was the Blind Beggar Gang – a team of skilled pickpockets who were not averse to roughing up their victims if they complained. They took their name from the Blind Beggar public house in the Mile End Road. One story about them – concerning an attack on a travelling salesman in which an umbrella ferrule was pushed through the victim's eye by a man named Wallis – relates that, acquitted of murder, he was driven back from the Old Bailey in triumph in a phaeton drawn by a pair of bays. This whole story, like so many tales of these early gangs, is probably apocryphal and is based on the true story of Paul Vaughan (who went under the name of Ellis) who was charged with manslaughter following the death of a perfectly respectable man named Frederick Klein in 1891 when he and his wife had been subject to a series of anti-Semitic taunts. There is no record of his acquittal and so the gang broke up.[4]

The early gangs seem to have been relatively informal associations, something which continued throughout the century. One, led by the engagingly named One-Eyed Charlie,

---

[3] *ELA*, 9 and 16 August 1902.
[4] In some accounts the Wallis story is attributed to a Tottenham-based gang.

hung out around Clark's coffee shop near a railway arch in Brick Lane. According to Arthur Harding, a major villain of the time and later chronicler of the East End, they do not seem to have acted much in concert. The leader, Charlie Walker, had tuberculosis and, true to his name, had also lost an eye. Another of the gang, Edward Spencer, seems to have been the only 'complete all-round criminal'. A well-built man who took a great pride in his appearance and was known as 'the Count', he was a thief and robber. Most of the others were pickpockets and 'tappers', van draggers, watch chain or handbag snatchers, or petty blackmailers. The Walker team flourished, if that is the right word, until about 1904 when Charlie Walker died in a prison hospital, and re-formed some years later with some younger men, of whom Arthur Harding was one and he became the leader. Although he did not regard his loose 'connection of youngsters' as a gang, it was a much more cohesive organisation than in Walker's time:

> We were a collection of small-time thieves ripe for any mischief . . . We were ready to steal anything. Sometimes we went in couples, sometimes alone – it was only when there was a big fight on that we went as a gang.[5]

Whether the local residents actually agreed with Harding's definition is a different matter entirely. Harding caused a great deal of nuisance at the evidential hearings of the Royal Commission into the Metropolitan Police by alleging that Inspector Wensley, after failing to have him convicted on a series of robberies, had framed him for an assault on an officer, something Wensley strenuously denied. Various local shopkeepers were brought along to give evidence of the activities of Harding and his definition of going in couples. One of the witnesses, William Southey, a hosier with two

[5] Raphael Samuel, *East End Underworld*, p. 148.

shops in the neighbourhood, thought the Harding team was some 30-strong.

> There is a gang of lads and young men that hang about the corners of Brick Lane and my corner is unfortunately a very convenient corner for these young men because they can see four ways. They are a regiment of soldiers; they do not talk to each other. They use dumb motions. If they were going to rob a man and they saw it was convenient to take his watch they would use their fingers, their head and the movements of their body. Harding is the captain of the gang and has been for many, many years . . . Whilst he was doing 20 months it was paradise.

A publican, Frank Rayner, manager of the Old Crown off Brick Lane, said that another of their activities was tapping local shopkeepers to pay their fines: 'As soon as the thieves "fall" as they call it they terrorise the neighbourhood with a paper for something to help him pay the fine.'[6]

Sixpence was apparently the going rate.

It was their activities as a gang that earned them the name the Vendetta Mob, but it was largely a question of what was in a name. One of Harding's ventures, along with his friends Dido Gilbert, Tommy Taylor and Danny Isaacs, whether as the Vendetta or an independent gang, was the holding-up of card games in the Jewish spielers and taking the proceeds, often as little as £3 or £4 a time. Harding justifies the activity by claiming the victims were all crooked men who regarded the raids as little more than a minor inconvenience: 'Yiddisher

[6] See evidence of William Southey and Frank Rayner, questions 23,123 *et seq*, Royal Commission into the Metropolitan Police 1908, PRO HO 45/10523/140292.

people make a laugh of it. They said, "Give them a few bob and get rid of them."[7]

Eventually, however, the cardplayers became bored with these raids in which they were made to stand with their hands in the air and they recruited some of their own to deal with Harding and the others. A meeting at Mother Woolf's public house in Whitechapel saw the Vendettas badly beaten. Finally Ruby Michaels, fearing there would actually be fatalities if the raids escalated, explained the facts of life to Harding through his henchman Tommy Hoy.[8]

> Ruby Michaels was the most noted receiver of stolen property. He was the biggest buyer of stolen jewellery in East London. His headquarters was the Three Tuns in Aldgate. He had several front men – Leon Behren [sic], the man who got killed in 1911, was one of them. They picked the stuff up from the daylight screwsmen at the spielers and took it to Ruby at the pub. Anyone who had any diamond rings to sell, they took it to him, and the buyers came from all over the world. In Portland I met a crook who had come all the way from America to buy something off Ruby.[9]

Michaels had a long and successful career. He was friendly with 'Chicago' May Churchill Sharpe, and it was she who tipped him off that Tim Oakes, who was regarded as King of the Panel Workers and who owned an antique shop in the

[7] Raphael Samuel, *East End Underworld*, p. 120. Gilbert was killed in the First World War, Taylor became a ponce and, according to Harding, died of syphilis in 1915. Harding later fell out with Isaacs over a girl they both knew and whom, so Harding believed, he was beating.

[8] From reports in the local papers Hoy was clearly a man with whom to be reckoned. At least twice he was charged with shootings. He was friendly with Billy Chandler of the bookmaking family and was an expert dealer at faro. See *ELO*, 9 January 1909, 28 January, 11 February 1911.

[9] ibid, p. 134.

City Road, was unfortunately also a police informer.[10]

In 1907 shortly before Sharpe was arrested for shooting at Eddie Guerin, her former lover, Michaels put up a jewel robbery for her in the Strand. A young Italian thief, Louis Lorenzano, who worked with Sharpe and her then partner Charlie Smith, was to be the coachman and drive her in an open barouche (on which had been placed a temporary coat of arms) to the jeweller's not far from Charing Cross. Usually the jeweller was left on his own during the lunch period. Lorenzano, fine in livery and with a birthmark painted on his cheek, was then to go into the shop and ask the jeweller to come to the carriage as his mistress was an invalid. Smith was then to snatch a tray of diamonds which were on display. Unfortunately the jeweller noticed Smith working on the hasp and staple which secured the jewels and ran after him. To maintain her cover, Sharpe found herself obliged to buy a solid gold collar button. As she remarks, Michaels was 'out his expenses'.[11]

However Michaels generally kept a low profile, surfacing in court only in 1915 when he and Aaron Lechenstein – who, in his salad days, had been a police court interpreter – pleaded guilty at the Old Bailey to trying to bribe a police officer to allow them to conduct illegal gaming in East End clubs. The payment was to be £10 a week for each of three clubs totalling £1,500 a year, and an amber cigarette holder was delivered to the officer as a mark of esteem. The proposal had followed a raid in the previous June when a club owner had been fined £500, and Michaels thought that prevention was the best cure.

Under the direction of his superiors the officer played along with them, and the pair were arrested at a meeting

---

[10] A panel was a brothel or low boarding house in which theft from the customers was rife.
[11] May Churchill Sharpe, *Chicago May – Her Story*, pp. 116–17.

to which they had brought a document for him to sign. There was clearly money about because Michaels had Sir Edward Marshall Hall KC to defend him. The receiver was, he said, now paralysed and prison would be a death sentence. Chief Inspector Wensley put his oar in, saying he had known Michaels as a gambler and receiver for some 24 years, but Marshall Hall won through. Michaels was fined £100 and Lechenstein, said to be in a poor financial way, a mere £10.[12]

Another crime of the period which was prevalent in the East End and was viewed by judges with extreme disfavour was organised horse-stealing. On 12 April 1913 three members of a gang specialising in stealing the animals for sale as food received lengthy periods of imprisonment, with the leader Schofield drawing 6 years. He had been selling meat for consumption for 15 years, but it was not clear whether this was horse or ox. The others received 12 and 9 months.[13]

A more long-lasting organised gang which came from the very rough area of Nile Street, a market street off Shepherdess Walk near the City Road police station, was the Titanic Mob, so called (in tribute to the liner) because they were always well dressed. Their specialities were robbery and pickpocketing at race meetings, railway stations and at the theatre, although they do not seem to have been averse to burglary either. They were highly regarded in the trade, partly because they only robbed men. Harding recalls that in 1908 his gang fought the Titanics following an argument over the protection of a coffee stall in Brick Lane. The Titanics seem to have been much the smarter of the sides:

[12] *ELO*, 18 September 1915. It was around this time that it was decided that, as a sufficient number of immigrants now spoke English, the services of a full-time Yiddish interpreter could be dispensed with at Thames Magistrates' Court.
[13] *ELO*, 14 April 1913. They were defended by the West Ham solicitor, Charles Sharman.

What they done was crafty. They set a trap for us. They
was well in with the police and directly the fight started
the police were there. They got hold of us – including
Cooper who had a loaded gun on him. It wasn't an
offence to carry a gun, but we got a week's remand for
causing an affray. I always had it in for them afterwards.
I thought, 'You twisters – you always have the bogies on
your side.'

They survived until the early 1920s when they were broken
up by the Flying Squad after raids on them following a
pickpocketing expedition at a North London derby football
match.[14] Five members of the gang were caught at Euston
Square station picking pockets in something which sounds
more like robbery. Their ages showed that pickpocketing
was not necessarily a young man's game. They appeared
at Marlborough Street on 10 September 1921 when Alfred
Mclennan (53), James Parrott (46) and Richard Canter (44)
were committed to the Sessions for sentence. Dominic Mack
(56) and George M. Measures (39) each received 12 months
hard labour. One member of the gang had been holding
the iron supports on either side of the door of the trains,
so preventing passengers from getting on or off, whilst the
others picked pockets. This and further arrests signalled the
end of the Titanics.

Guns were easily obtainable and their possession was not
unduly punished. Arthur Harding bought his first in about

---

[14] There is mention of them in the memoirs of a number of police officers
of the period. George Ingram gives a fictionalised account of a fight in Nile
Street with the 'Sabatis', who are clearly the Sabinis, in *Cockney Cavalcade*.
Edward T. Hart also fictionalises the fight in *Britain's Godfather*, although
he names some of the combatants who were undoubtedly Sabini men of
the period. He suggests that at one time Fred Gilbert was a member of the
Sabinis and they only split apart after the Nile Street fight. Some writers,
however, say the fight was a complete fiction. See also S. Felstead, *The
Underworld of London*.

1904. A Royal Ulster Constabulary revolver cost 2/6d. in Brick Lane, others four or five shillings.[15]

Nor were shooting incidents regarded by the courts with the gravity of today. Three years earlier Charles Callaghan had been convicted of the wounding of John Bailey who had been shot in the thigh at his home. Callaghan's counsel pleaded that his client should be bound over to come up for judgment and when Warburton (prosecuting) suggested it was nearly an attempted murder, crossly remarked, 'You've had your pound of flesh.' A police officer giving evidence thought Callaghan was a 'Good employee during the day but at night he associates with thieves and rogues'. Judge Rentoul KC did actually consider a bind out. He adjourned the case until he had spoken with other judges, after which he sentenced Callaghan to the modest 6 months' hard labour.

What appears to have happened is that the members of the Bailey family had attacked him in the White Hart in Shoreditch, hitting him on the head with a hammer. Nothing daunted, he had collected some friends and visited the Baileys' home. Later Callaghan would be sentenced along with Harding for his part in the Old Street affray.[16]

John Bailey was one of a family who came out of the Nichol, an area in Hoxton. Although one was a burglar, Harding did

---

[15] Donald Rumbelow records the 1905 case of a Russian stopped at Dover Harbour on his way to London with enough arms to start a small war. He had in his luggage 47 automatic pistols and nearly 5,000 rounds of ammunition. None was confiscated. That year a firearm could be purchased over the counter for 16 shillings. If the buyer was caught the maximum penalty was £5. *The Houndsditch Murders and the Siege of Sidney Street*, p. 41. In fact offences involving firearms rarely merited much more than a paragraph in the local paper and days rather than weeks in prison. In August 1914 William Voase and other members of the Bow Road Gang attacked Frederick Alvin, all armed with belts and one with a revolver. Voase received 14 days' hard labour. The member locked up for the most time in a year became the gang's captain. *ELA*, 28 August 1914.

[16] *The Times*, 19 September 1905.

not regard them as thieves but more as fighting men – the father Alf being a particularly vicious man.

Perhaps, as today, it depended on the quality of the defence for in 1908 George Askew, a member of the Globe Bridge Gang, shot George Etherington of the Bow Road Gang and received a relatively lengthy 15 months' hard labour for his pains.[17]

Even immediately after the First World War the possession of firearms was not regarded as anything much out of the ordinary. On 15 February 1919 Edward Joyce, described as a commission agent, struck Joe Palmer, the referee at The Ring, with the butt of a pistol after Palmer had disqualified Con Houghton in the ninth round for persistent holding in his contest with Dick Moss. Later 'Gossip of the Game' thought that 'if one or two other gentlemen had been attacked there was a sort of rough justice but not Palmer.'[18]

However, Arthur Harding was very much more than a villain pure and simple. He was a great baiter of the police and as such fell seriously foul of Wensley. Before that happened he had played a considerable part in the Royal Commission into the Metropolitan Police 1908, and had assisted in the prosecution of a number of officers for assault.

The catalyst that sparked the Commission was one of those cases which need never have happened. However, once it was in the public domain a great deal of capital was made of it to the general discomfort of all concerned.

On 1 May 1905 Eva D'Angeley was arrested in Regent Street for 'riotous and indecent behaviour' or, in plain language, prostitution. The charge was dismissed after a Mr D'Angeley told the magistrate that he was married to the lady and that she was merely waiting for him, something she had done

---

[17] Raphael Samuel, *East End Underworld*, p. 109.
[18] *The Mirror of Life and Boxing World*; 15 February and 1 March 1919. For more of Palmer's career in which he does not figure quite so well, see Chapter 19.

on a regular basis. Better still, the Sub-Divisional Inspector MacKay told the court he believed the D'Angeleys to be a respectable couple.

The experienced Marlborough Street magistrate, Denman, dismissed the charges and so another desert storm blew up with allegations of harassment, bribery and corruption. A Royal Commission was set up to inquire into methods and discipline in the force.[19]

The case was not the only one before the Commission, however. Another was that of a PC Rolls who, it was alleged, had planted a hammer on a cabinet maker sleeping on a bench at London Fields and had then arrested him. The case was dismissed at the North London Police Court by the eccentric magistrate Edward Snow Fordham, who was continually at loggerheads with the police and who was not invited to give evidence to the Royal Commission. Rolls was later prosecuted at the Central Criminal Court and received 5 years' penal servitude. Another officer was allowed to resign.

This led to the formation of the Public Vigilance Society, and such success as the public had in establishing any misconduct by the police was largely due to it and to Earl Russell, who appeared for the Society and who later wrote modestly:

I was instructed by a curious body called the Police and

---

[19] As for the D'Angeleys, McKay had conducted further inquiries and now came to the conclusion he had been mistaken in his assessment of the pair. How could he have been deceived in the first place? Did not he or his colleagues know the French girls who worked his area? Could he not tell D'Angeley was a pimp? Why did he not ask for a short adjournment to make proper inquiries? Meanwhile both the D'Angeleys had retreated to Paris and sensibly stayed there, despite the requests of the police who offered to pay the lady's fare back so that she could give evidence to the Commission. Sadly from the point of view of Anglo-French relations, their return to France had been hasty. When they caught the Dover packet they had not had time to pay for their lodgings, and had left behind a few empty trunks.

Public Vigilance Society run by a fanatic called Timewell. He was prepared always to believe anything he was told against the police and to resent with some indignation the demand for proof which a lawyer always makes. However, we selected about twelve of the likeliest cases, and in spite of the extreme poverty on our side and the whole force of the Treasury and the police against us on the other we succeeded in getting home seven of them, largely on my cross-examination of the police.[20]

One of the cases which they 'succeeded in getting home' was that of PC Ashford, who is described by Arthur Harding as having a nice wife 'but always after the women. He wasn't intelligent enough to catch a thief, but he was good at perjury and he could do a man an injury by strength.'[21]

In August 1906, Ashford came across a young man named Gamble out walking with a prostitute, Ethel Griffiths. It appears he wanted the girl for himself and told Gamble to clear off. In turn Mrs Griffiths told Ashford she did not want him and the officer then knocked Gamble down and kicked him. A police sergeant, Sheedy, came up and told Gamble to get up and fight like a man. Then when he saw how badly the man was injured, he told Ashford to go away as he had done enough. Gamble was in hospital for four months and was operated on four times; he later spent nearly a month in a convalescent home. One member of the Commission compared his injuries with those which would have been sustained by falling on a railing.

This was one of the cases in which the Public Vigilance Society was aided and abetted by Harding, who discovered two witnesses and arranged for the Commission's investigator to take statements from them. Later another witness was produced. The Commission found that PC Ashford was guilty

---

[20] Earl Russell, *My Life and Adventures*, pp. 304–5.
[21] Raphael Samuel, *East End Underworld*, p. 191.

of the misconduct alleged, that is kicking Gamble, but that he did not intend to do him the serious injury which resulted. In Sergeant Sheedy's case, it was found that he had not stopped the assault and that he had failed to make a report to his superiors. So far as the investigation of the incident by an Inspector Hewison was concerned, this had aborted when he found no trace of Gamble's name at the London Hospital – he had been wrongly listed under the name Pearce. The Commission found that Hewison had done 'all that could be reasonably expected'.

The aftermath was the prosecution of Ashford. Proceedings were commenced immediately after the Royal Commission published its findings and, at the Old Bailey in September 1908, the jury was instructed to disregard the evidence of Ethel Griffiths because she was a prostitute. The defence also claimed that there had been no proper identification of Ashford as the kicking officer. After a retirement of two hours by the jury, he was found guilty and sentenced to 9 months' hard labour. Leave to appeal was refused.

Within days of the appointment of the Commission its members had been inundated with letters and postcards alleging corruption, perjury and bribery, often in language 'foul and intemperate'. From these, 19 cases, including that of Mme D'Angeley, were closely scrutinised and a variety of witnesses came before the Commissioners, who sat on 64 occasions over a period of 11 months.

Unsurprisingly, the Commission became increasingly bored with the East End evidence, exonerated the police and declared that, far from harassing street offenders, they were kind and conciliatory to them. True, in some nine cases there had been reprehensible conduct but, by and large, the Commission found, 'The Metropolitan Police is entitled to the confidence of all classes of the community.'

The Times for one was enchanted.

We have no hesitation in saying that the Metropolitan
police as a whole discharge their duties with honesty,
discretion and efficiency.

The Hoxton Mob was the generic name given to a succession
of gangs from around Hoxton Street over the next 40 years.
One of the early versions had its headquarters at the Spread
Eagle public house and, amongst other interests, they were
into the protection of the local clubs and spielers such as
Sunshine's, a card and billiard club in an alley off Shoreditch
High Street. Harding is dismissive of them:

> They weren't such good-class thieves as the Titanics. They
> were more hooligans than thieves. They worked ten- or
> twelve-handed. They all finished up on the poor law, or
> cadging. Their leader died a pauper, whereas the leader
> of the Titanics ended up owning a dog-track.[22]

Another local gang leader of the time was Isaac Bogard,
known as Darky the Coon. Although he was Jewish he
was so dark-skinned that some references to him are as a
coloured man and his mob was accordingly known as the
Coons. Although when giving evidence he described himself
as an actor, Bogard had a long criminal record which included
a flogging for living off immoral earnings. On 10 September
1911 at about 8.30 in the evening, he was set upon by Harding
and the Vendetta Mob in the Blue Coat Boy in Bishopsgate.
Bogard and his team ran a string of prostitutes in Whitechapel
High Street and the quarrel had been about their ownership
and the protection of a stall in Walthamstow Street market.
Harding describes the fight:

> As it was we did a lot of damage. The Coon had a face like

---

[22] ibid, pp. 147 et seq.

the map of England. He was knocked about terrible. I hit
him with a broken glass, made a terrible mess of his face.
I knew I'd hurt him a lot, but not anything that could be
serious.[23]

Bogard, who in evidence at the subsequent trial said his throat
had been cut, was taken to the London Hospital where after
he had been stitched he discharged himself. But the next
weekend there was more of the same for him when he was
attacked once again by Harding and friends on the Sunday
evening.

The outcome was dramatic. The police arrived and arrested
both Bogard and George King on charges of disorderly
conduct, to appear at Old Street Magistrates' Court on the
Monday. Meanwhile Harding – then known as Tresidern – and
his Vendettas met at Clark's, the coffee shop in Brick Lane, to
rally support against the Coons who were about to commit the
one really unforgivable crime: they asked for police protection.

Accounts vary as to exactly what happened, as they do to the
precise lead-up to the earlier battle and the arrest of Bogard,
but there is no doubt whatsoever that Bogard and King were
besieged at Old Street by Harding and the Vendetta Mob until
Wensley arrived from Scotland Yard in a horse-drawn vehicle
to restore order.[24]

Money was again found from somewhere, because Harding
and the others were defended privately, Harding by the
well-known barrister Eustace Fulton.[25] It did him little good,

---

[23] ibid, p. 154.
[24] Bogard maintained in court that he had once been a member of the
Vendettas but had left and tried to become respectable. This was what
had done for him. For the competing accounts of just who was the most
heroic see Raphael Samuel, *East End Underworld*, p. 154 *et seq.*; Chartres
Biron, *Without Prejudice*, pp. 251–3; and Fred Wensley, *Detective Days*,
pp. 103–6.
[25] Harding says the Sabinis from Clerkenwell put up funds for the defence
which, if he is correct, means that the family was operating many years
before they are usually credited. ibid, p. 120.

for in December 1911 the team appeared at the Old Bailey in front of Mr Justice Avory who, when passing sentence, gave this little homily:

> This riot was one of the most serious riots which can be dealt with by law, for it was a riot in which some, at least, of the accused were armed with revolvers, and it took place within the precincts of a court of justice.
>
> I wish to say that the condition of things disclosed by the evidence – that a portion of London should be infested by a number of criminal ruffians, armed with loaded revolvers – ought not to be tolerated further, and if the existing law is not strong enough to put a stop to it some remedial legislation is necessary.

Harding received 21 months' hard labour to be followed by 3 years' penal servitude. His career was sketched by Wensley when giving the antecedents of the convicted men before sentence:

> When he was fourteen – he is now only twenty-five – he was bound over for disorderly conduct and being in possession of a revolver.
>
> At the age of seventeen he became a terror to Bethnal Green, and captained a band of desperadoes. In all he has been convicted fourteen times, yet he was one of the complaining witnesses before the Police Commission.
>
> He has developed into a cunning and plausible criminal of a dangerous type. I have never known him do any work.[26]

---

[26] *Illustrated Police News*, 23 December 1911. Dido Gilbert, part of the spieler robbing team, received 15 months. Charlie Callaghan, who after his brush with the Baileys became both a thief and also a thieves' ponce, received a prison sentence. He had an unfortunate record of being hit over the head; his antipathy to Bogard had resulted from his being hit over the head following a quarrel in the Horns in Shoreditch High Street. Later he worked for a bookmaker.

Wensley records that after Harding's imprisonment peace returned to the East End – for a little while anyway. Bogard certainly functioned until the 1920s when he was then what was euphemistically described as the 'governor' of the market stall-holders in Petticoat Lane and Wentworth Street. During the War he had served with gallantry and was awarded the Military Medal.

Associations were formed and broken. For example, the 'top man of the Jews', Edward Emmanuel, at one time had a working arrangement with Harding, then broke with him and joined up with the Sabinis, in turn broke with them and in the 1920s, working almost as an independent, was regarded as a great fixer with the police.[27]

Nor was it impossible for uneasy truces to be established with the police. Another of Harding's *bêtes-noires* was an officer he called 'Jew Boy' Stevens, yet at one time he and Emmanuel were going out with two sisters and Stevens with the third.[28]

The Old Street siege was undoubtedly the pinnacle of Harding's career, but he served another 5 year sentence in 1915. From then on he seems to have had the sense to be an employer and manipulator rather than a front man. Two of the men he employed were destined to become East End legends and links with the present and they, along with Charles Horrickey, made as fine a trio as could be wished. The pair were Jack 'Dodger' Mullins and Timmy Hayes, known in the early part of his career at least as Dick Turpin.

[27] Others in the Emmanuel gang included Jacky and Moey Levy and Bobby Nark who would also go on to work for the Sabinis.
[28] Jack 'Jew Boy' Stevens in fact came from Hampshire where he had been a groom and gardener before he came to London and joined the police. A swarthy man, he grew a beard and so could pass as Jewish. He rarely appeared in court and once when, after some undercover work, he did, he appeared clean-shaven. The next day he was back in his beard which a wig-maker had furnished. On his retirement he bought and ran the White Horse in Harlow. See *Reynolds' News*, 31 May 1925.

The best known of the three, Jack 'Dodger' Mullins, was born probably about 1892 – there is no record of his birth at St Catherine's House – into a respectable family. The belief in the Underworld is that, as with many of the families, he had a half-Irish, partly Jewish or even gypsy background, but according to his family they had been in England since at least the beginning of the nineteenth century and there was no Jewish blood.

He was a small man, about 5′ 6″ tall, slightly built, with dark curly hair and a scarred face. Albert Appelby, his nephew, recalls him as a quiet man with a dry sense of humour who 'never brought any of his activities near the family' to whom he was close; as close that is as his prison record would allow. Every Christmas he would send Fred, his driver, to collect his sister Louise for a Christmas get-together:

> One year Fred did not arrive.
> 'You're a new face,' said Louise. 'Where's Fred?'
> 'In hospital.'
> 'Nothing serious, I hope.'
> 'No, someone threw some flowers at him.'
> 'Well, he shouldn't have to go to hospital for that.'
> 'Trouble was, they were still in the pot at the time.'

Mullins may have been fearless on the streets, and in the First World War when he received the Military Medal, but like so many others he was terrified of his common-law wife, Minnie Dore, a big woman and East End matriarch of the old school. Louise kept a spare room vacant for him when Minnie was on the warpath:

> 'Hiding from the police again?' the neighbours would ask.
> 'No, from Minnie,' his sister would reply.

Mullins' great friend was Timmy Hayes, who was even smaller

than he was but just as violent. Ex-Detective Chief Superintendent Ted Greeno describes them in his memoirs:

> When there was no racing Dodger and Tim once tried
> to earn a little protection money in London's East End.
> There the tradesmen paid tribute to the local hoodlums
> to 'protect' them and Dodger told the owner of a billiards
> hall, 'You don't want to pay that Yiddisher mob of yours.
> I could eat the lot of them. Now what are you coming
> across with?'
>
> 'Nothing,' said the billiards man.
>
> Dodger gave him a day or two to think it over, then he
> tore down the racks and smashed the tables and chairs,
> snapped the cues and threw billiard balls at the lights.
> It didn't take long and I didn't need telling who had
> done it.[29]

On 2 July 1926, Mullins received 4 years and Hayes 9 years
at the Old Bailey after being found guilty of blackmail and
assault. The police described the pair as 'pioneers of gang
warfare in East London and on the racecourses'. Mullins said
he could prove the case had been got up by the Sabinis and
'some of the Yiddisher people' in order to get him and Hayes
out of the way.

What really did for Hayes was that since 1908 he had
served twenty terms of imprisonment and one of penal
servitude. He had also been charged with being a habitual
criminal. By 1910 he had three convictions for wounding.
At the Old Bailey, in his defence to that second charge, he
claimed that after he came out of prison on 2 May he had
been a volunteer railway worker for eight days during the
General Strike before committing the offence on 17 May.
This, it was argued, showed that he had exhibited 'a desire

[29] Ted Greeno, *News of the World*, 15 November 1959.

for work inconsistent with the habit of crime'.

Once again money was found to pay for Hayes' appeal. He was represented this time by J.D. Cassels KC who cannot have appeared cheaply. His solicitor on that occasion was George Edjali, the Parsee who had been wrongly convicted of horse mutilation and whose case had been championed by Sir Arthur Conan Doyle.

The formidable Mr Justice Avory, who had been prosecuting counsel in the case of Adolph Beck and who was now regarded as a hanging judge, would have none of this sort of specious argument about work.

> [But] this Court has said over and over again that the mere fact that a man has done some honest work after he has served the sentence for the offence last before that with which he is now charged, is not by itself a reason why the jury should not find him to be a habitual criminal.[30]

Arthur Harding claimed the success of Mullins' light sentence for himself, saying he had used him and Hayes in conjunction with some of the Watney Streeters as strike-breakers in the General Strike of 1926 and continued to work with him over the next few years. He is a bit ambiguous about Mullins' level of violence:

> Dodger lived by tapping people for money. They gave it him because they were frightened. I once watched him kick a little white dog to death. 'It bit me,' he said.

And on another occasion he wrote, 'He was a thief but not a

[30] (1926) 19 CAR 157. For more of Hayes' career see also *ELA*, 9 April 1910. Edjali was the son of a Parsee clergyman who was sentenced to 7 years' penal servitude after five horses, three cows and a number of sheep were killed or mutilated in Staffordshire where his father was a parson. After three years and a substantial campaign, in 1906 he was released on ticket of leave. The following year he was granted a free pardon. For an account of the case see Richard and Molly Whittington-Egan, *Mr George Edjali*.

violent type.' And yet again he described him as 'one of the biggest terrors in London at the time'.

Mullins probably worked as an enforcer on the increasingly popular dog tracks and was certainly having a violent time in 1930 because, along with George and Charles Steadman and Henry Barton, he was arrested for demanding with menaces and assault at the Argus Club in Greek Street. The quartet had first asked for drinks which were served and then demanded to know whether there were any 'Raddies' on the premises. Unfortunately for a man named Costognetti there was one; he received a beating and a woman who tried to protect him had her blouse torn. Eventually the charges were dropped.

Harding seems to have finally fallen out with Mullins around that time when Mullins came round for a loan. Harding was now married with four children and his wife shouted from the bedroom window for them to go away:

> They foully abused her, using the most filthy language that I had ever heard even from the prostitutes of Dorset Street.

Now, Harding did what he had found most reprehensible in the conduct of Bogard some twenty years earlier: he involved the police. Not that he was averse to a little dealing on the side.

> Mullins got six years for demanding with menaces. The other chap got less. His people straightened me up – they gave my wife £50 or £60 so I was lenient in my evidence. It was the best thing I ever done when I put Dodger Mullins where he belonged. I should have been at everybody's beck and call when there was a fight on if I hadn't done so.

The quarrel with Mullins effectively ended Harding's association with crime; he was now no longer regarded as one of the fraternity. Perhaps he feared for himself and his family when Mullins was released because 'it became like a craze with us to get away'. In 1932 Harding moved from Brick Lane to a flat in Leyton and then bought a house in Canterbury Road for which he paid £675. His last court appearance seems to have been when he was acquitted of being a suspected person in 1932.[31]

Meanwhile Mullins was in Dartmoor prison at the time of the celebrated mutiny on 26 January 1932 when fighting broke out in the chapel and, with the mutineers in control, the officers' mess was attacked and the prison set alight. The Army were called in and a number of prisoners were shot and injured. Mullins went into his cell and shut his door. The prisoners opened it and he shut it again.

His release brought no fortune to his friend Wally Challis who collected him from Dartmoor. On the way back he knocked someone down in the motor car he was driving and received 5 years himself.

In later life Dodger maintained his low profile. Albert Appelby recalls:

> When my mother died my son and I went looking for Dodger with whom we'd lost touch. We'd heard he'd been over Dalston way and we went and asked people in the area. No, no one knew him, never heard of him at all. Then we asked a newspaper man and this time I said it was to tell him his sister had died. The man said he thought we should ask in the butcher's shop on the corner. They didn't want to know at first. They'd never heard of him either but I said again it was about Dodger's sister. The man called up the stairs, 'Jackie, get your Dad, your Auntie's died.'

Mullins attended his sister's funeral, but that was the last time the Appelbys spoke to him. His final conviction seems to have been in August 1956, when his age was given as 64 and he was sentenced to 12 months' imprisonment for theft at

[31] Raphael Samuel, *East End Underworld*, pp. 132, 148, 185, 218–19, 235, 245.

Inner London Sessions. He had by this time racked up 51 convictions. Equipped with a stick, he would barge into his intended victim entering a tube train while his co-defendant, a man named Simmonds, would be standing behind ready to pick the pockets at the moment of impact. Then, as the train doors closed, they would jump clear and move off down the platform. His barrister, Neil McElligott, later the fearsome stipendiary magistrate at Old Street, said that Simmonds was the 'dip' and Mullins was simply playing the lad to the artful dodger. He received 12 months' imprisonment.[32]

Frank Fraser recalls him in 1948 in his later years:

> The last time I saw Dodger Mullins was in 1948 when he was on a J.R.[33] in Wandsworth. He was standing at the end of A wing. Little did I know that forty years later I'd be on the same spot as Dodger and I could see people looking at me knowing I'd been there forty years previous. Between us we went back eighty prison years.

> I liked him. What he really was a thieves' ponce. I knew him in 1943 when I was just out of Chelmsford. We were in the Queen's Club in Queen's Road, Peckham. It was a licensed afternoon drinker for when the pubs shut at 3.30. Bertie Wymah had a row with Lennie Garrett and smashed a glass in his face, then Lennie chinned him and a couple of Canadian soldiers got involved and we all steamed into them. I remember Dodger saying, 'Get out of here quick, son.'[34]

He did not always take his own advice and suffered for it. The previous year he had been badly knocked about by two men, Johnny Dove and Mickey Harris, in an Old Compton Street

---

[32] *The Star*, 28 August 1956. I am very grateful to Albert Appelby and his family for their recollections of Mullins and for allowing me to use the family archives.
[33] Judge's Remand when a man was held for reports prior to sentence.
[34] F. Fraser, *Mad Frank and Friends*, p. 13.

club after he had remonstrated with them in the lavatory for cat-calling during a performance by Billy Hill's sister, Maggie. He was saved from further punishment by Billy Hill himself who 'cut them to pieces'.[35]

In old age he still maintained a presence. In the last years of his life he was a close friend of the Krays and once when Johnny Nash and Joey Pyle walked into the Kentucky Club in Stoke Newington he took Reggie Kray aside and said that if there was trouble he was on their side, producing a Beretta to prove it. Kray explained that while he was most grateful there was no need – they were all on the same side.[36]

He died following a car accident after a tour of drinking spots in the East End. Taken to hospital, he contracted pneumonia some days later.

Dodger Mullins' son was Jackie Dore. Again Fraser recalls:

> He brought the boy up as his own but his wife had the boy by someone else before she met Dodger. How do I know this? Jimmy Brindle was driving past Sadler's Wells in Rosebery Avenue in one car and Jackie in another. We'd left Aggie Hill's Cabinet Club and were on our way to the Duchess of Kent. We're all nicked and when Jimmy said something about, 'My friend Jackie Mullins,' the copper said, 'No, you mean John Dore.' After that I asked Jackie and he told me.

By November 1914 Timmy Hayes had racked up ten previous convictions. Then he recorded his eleventh and his co-defendant William Driscoll his ninth when they received 3 months' hard labour apiece for pickpocketing. He would later live in Essex and is popularly supposed to have been the father of Lilian Goldstein, known as the Bobbed-Haired Bandit. His son Jimmy would keep up his father's good work.[37]

[35] F. Fraser, *Mad Frank*, p. 52.
[36] Reggie Kray, *Villains We Have Known*, p. 20.
[37] *ELO*, 14 November 1914.

The third of the trio, Charlie Horrickey, 'another typical half-breed' – by which Harding means half-Jewish, half-Irish, 'as ignorant as hell' – was charged with grievous bodily harm, together with Harding, after cutting Moey Levy's throat in the Whitechapel Road in 1926.

Moey Levy, one of a family of seven, along with his brother Bobby was one of the big names in the East End at the time. He began life working for the Jewish gaming clubs and married an English girl, Polly Cash. He then worked as a bookmaker in Brick Lane where the Jewish kept to one side of the street and the English to the other. Later he and a man called Gardiner kept a club over a confectioner's shop on the corner of Middlesex Street.

When, around the turn of the century, police courts sprang up over London, they also spawned a kind of second division solicitor, seemingly neither as trustworthy nor quite as well regarded as his colleagues. '"A Police Court solicitor" being used to denote advocates of a less exalted type,' wrote Sir Travers Humphreys, later the High Court judge, while accepting that fine examples of solicitor advocates who practised in police courts could be found.[38]

One man who was not tarnished with his words was Charles Crank Sharman. Then as now what the villains needed was a good and sympathetic solicitor, and there was none better or more sympathetic than he. Sharman practised in Stratford police court where there was a lay bench, whilst neighbouring West and East Ham had a metropolitan and a stipendiary magistrate respectively. Sharman appeared before all and earned Humphreys' sincere admiration, striking him as one of the few natural lawyers he had encountered.

I never had a brief from him, but we were on many occasions opposed to one another. He never talked non-sense and seldom repeated himself with the result that the

[38] Sir Travers Humphreys, *A Book of Trials*, p. 134.

magistrates always listened with respect to his arguments.
So far as I knew, no breath of scandal had ever attached
itself to his name in his professional or his domestic
life . . .[39]

So it was with something approaching horror that Humphreys
learned that his old court adversary, now in his middle
seventies, had been charged with receiving a share certificate
stolen from a post office mailbag and with the forgery of a
cheque stolen from the same bag.

Humphreys was briefed by the Director of Public Prosecutions and, to his further amazement, discovered that
this kindly and courteous old man – who had defended
Frederick Bywaters in the celebrated Bywaters–Thompson
murder case – had for many years been suspected of heading a
gang of international thieves specialising in stealing mailbags.
Sharman's part had been to assist in the disposal abroad of
the stolen bonds and certificates.

In around 1922 a mailbag had been stolen on a train
somewhere between Liverpool and London. The contents
included £50 Bonds addressed to the Bank of England, some
of which were then cashed in Antwerp and Brussels by an
elderly gentleman giving the name of Johnson but who had
been identified by a bank clerk as Sharman.

Given the reputation of Sharman, the matter was left on
the file despite the fact that a month later another mailbag
disappeared on the Birmingham to London run. This time a
transfer of £900 Quebec Railway Stock went with it, only to
end up at Sharman's, who was now interviewed. He explained
that a poor man had picked it up in the street and brought it
to his office. It was the sort of explanation one would expect
to hear from a common-or-garden criminal on a receiving
charge at Quarter Sessions, but apparently the Director of

[39] ibid.

Public Prosecutions thought there was not sufficient evidence to prefer a charge.

In 1924 a mailbag disappeared between Bristol and Paddington. One of the stolen letters contained a £50 Mexican Oil share which was sold by someone closely resembling Sharman in Manchester. He provided an alibi to the effect that he was home all day. However, he failed to convince the police that nine people were wrong when they identified him that summer as selling War Bonds in Canada which had been stolen from the same bag.

He appeared at the Old Bailey on 25 June 1925 charged with conspiracy to steal and receive mailbags, receiving War Loan coupons and forging and uttering a receipt, before Mr Justice Salter. He was then 75.

Opening the case, the prosecution had said that:

> Inquiries have been made by the police into a number of other matters, and the result of those inquiries can be placed before the court. But as those matters have never been the subject of any charge and it is not proposed they should do so, your Lordship may decide that he does not want to hear about them.

Unfortunately his Lordship did decide that he did not want to hear about them, and so a deal of interesting information was lost to the public. Defended by Sir Henry Curtis Bennett KC, Sharman's mitigation was that he had fallen into the hands of thieves who had been blackmailing him. He had, said his counsel, that very week completed sixty years in the law.

> For a considerable period at least Mr Sharman has been the victim of continuous blackmail from those who knew what he had done. It is not difficult to appreciate the state of mind of a man in fear from day to day, week to week,

month to month, that at any moment he might be arrested on charges and tried.

Salter would have little of this.

So far as you are concerned this is a most scandalous offence .... I am satisfied that you as an experienced solicitor of the High Court of Justice have made yourself an associate of a gang of very daring and very dangerous thieves – mailbag robbers. These men robbed the mails and thereby acquired a mass of valuable securities which were of very little use – most of them – to them unless it had been for your assistance. They required a man of your standing and knowledge of business to dispose of the booty for them.

They robbed the mails and you sold the securities for them all over Europe and America in false names and not hesitating at forgery where forgery was necessary. No one in his senses can doubt you shared the booty. I hear that you have been blackmailed. Thieves often blackmail one another. If you had been a younger man I would have sent you to penal servitude for seven years. Having regard to your age and the professional ruin in which you are involved, I direct that you be sent to penal servitude for three years and that you must pay the costs of the prosecution.

Penal servitude in the 1920s meant Dartmoor, where the conditions were dreadful. Apart from the diet the walls of the prison, built for prisoners from the Napoleonic wars, ran with water. It was not a situation in which any man, let alone a 75-year-old, would wish to find himself. Yet, perhaps against the odds, Sharman survived the sentence, dying on 5 December 1933. His elaborate will left gifts to various members of the judiciary but, if he had indeed been the head of a successful gang, he had either squandered or hidden his assets. Probate was granted to an Annie Tharp two months later. His estate was worth the relatively modest £2,568. 9s. 3d. It was estimated that the bonds involved in the thefts had been worth over £1,500,000.

In fact Sharman was another who deceived many people for years on end. He had begun his career in Chelmsford as a clerk to a solicitor – an unfortunate start because this Bible quoter had been involved with a young woman and had been railroaded from the town. He later obtained articles and in 1888 was acquitted of misappropriation of funds but was suspended by the Law Society for two years. About the same time he was made bankrupt and was not discharged until 1901. It seems he had been in a criminal partnership with the malevolent clerk, William Hobbs, before they fell out and Hobbs went on to blackmail 'Mr A.'. Apparently Sharman had begun receiving in a small way, taking articles from those whom he defended and, it was said, enriching himself in the winding-up of estates in lunacy.

Just which was the international gang into whose clutches he claimed to have fallen is not known, but he certainly acted for the Sabinis and their allies. When in August 1922 Alfred White was accused of the attempted murder of Fred Gilbert, the Camden Town gangleader, Sharman instructed J.D. Cassels to act on the man's behalf. On appeal Cassels again appeared, this time with Cecil Whitely KC, when the conviction was quashed.[40]

Traditionally the Sabinis are thought of as simply race-course hooligans and club owners, but there was a good deal more to them than that. It is not impossible that Sharman was more than simply their solicitor. Other suggestions as to his associates include a mysterious 'international gang of gentlemen crooks'.[41]

---

[40] *Reynolds' News*, 28 June 1925.
[41] *Empire News*, 28 June 1925.

6

The Sabinis

Although they operated principally from Saffron Hill, Clerken-well, any account of East End crime between the Wars without including the Sabini family would be sadly lacking. Over two decades they and their Hoxton and Hackney allies and opponents dominated street and racecourse crime until, at the beginning of the Second World War, the brothers – along with their formidable friend Papa Pasquale, known as Bert Marsh – were interned as enemy aliens, appropriately enough at Ascot racecourse.

They are mentioned regularly enough, but writers have not always been clear about how many brothers there actually were. For example, Charles and Darby Sabini are often referred to as the same man when in fact Charles was an older brother. Darby Sabini, when it suited him, was quite prepared to be known as Fred Sabini who was in fact the eldest.

In all there were six brothers beginning with Frederick born in 1881, who according to police files traded as Bob Wilson at the Harringay Greyhound Stadium and took no part in

the other brothers' affairs. There is no note on the files as
to what he did before greyhound racing became popular at
the end of the 1920s. Next came Charles, who was two years
younger and was a list supplier working for the bookmaker
Joe Levy in what the police saw as a protection racket. He
owned shares in West Ham Stadium and was thought to be
'slightly mentally deranged'; certainly by 1940 he had spent
some time in mental hospitals. Then came Joseph who on
paper was the villain of the family. He had served in the
First World War in the Royal Welsh Fusiliers and then the
Cheshire Regiment, and had been wounded in France. He
had then been invalided out and received a 12 shillings a
week pension. On 12 October 1922 he was given 3 years'
penal servitude for his part in the shooting of Fred Gilbert
in Mornington Crescent. The police thought, however, that
after that he had split from his brothers and there was no
evidence that he was operating behind the scenes. He traded
as Harry Lake at Harringay. George Sabini was the youngest
of the brothers – there was a sister who was a cripple – who
had no convictions and worked at both Harringay and White
City. He was not regarded as being any part of the gang, but
it was noted that his name alone would provide him with
protection. Of the brothers it was principally Darby and Harry
who provided what was euphemistically called protection and
what, in reality, was demanding money with menaces from
the bookmakers.[1]

   Ullano, better known as Darby Sabini, was born in 1889
in Saffron Hill, Little Italy. His Italian father died when he
was two and the family was raised by their Irish mother.
Sabini left school at the age of 13 and joined Dan Sullivan,
a small-time boxing promoter and bookmaker who later
worked for Bella Burge at The Ring at Blackfriars. At one
time it was thought that Sabini could, in the words of Marlon

[1] PRO HO 45/25720.

Brando, 'have been a contender'. Whilst still in his teens he had knocked out the fancied middleweight, Fred Sutton, in the first round. Unfortunately he did not like the training required and instead became a strong-arm man for Sullivan's promotions at the Hoxton Baths.[2] Later he was employed by George Harris, a leading bookmaker of the time, again as a strong-arm man.

Harry, always known as Harryboy, was educated at St Peter's Roman Catholic School in Clerkenwell and then went to work for an optician. During the First World War he worked in a munitions factory. He then became a bookmaker's clerk, working first for Gus Hall and later for Walter Beresford. When the latter died he became a commission agent. By 1940 he was a wealthy man with money in bonds for his children's education, bank accounts and a number of properties. His solicitors regarded him as a 'conveyancing client'. He was also a Life Governor of the Northern Hospital.

After the First World War attendance at racecourses boomed, particularly at the Southern tracks at which trotting was also a popular spectacle. Before the war the Birmingham gangs had established a hold on racecourse protection and now they sought to advance their empire. Under the leadership of Billy Kimber from Bordesley in Birmingham, who described himself as a bookmaker and punter, and the heavy gambler Andrew Townie, they metamorphosed as the Brummagen Boys despite the fact that most of the members came from the Elephant and Castle area of London. They had a fearsome reputation, being said to be willing and able to kill rats by

---

[2] There is no trace in boxing records of this bout. It is, however, possible that the contest took place at a fairground booth. Until the 1960s, when it was banned by the British Boxing Board of Control, it was common for licensed boxers to take on all comers at booths. Sullivan was himself part Italian and on one occasion broke up a fight at The Ring between the Sabinis and the Hoxton element.

biting them. Their organised racecourse protection began in around 1910 and for a time Kimber's mob took control of Southern racecourses such as Newbury, Epsom, Earls Park and Kempton. There were also other gangs operating from Leeds, Uttoxeter and Cardiff, with links throughout the country. Later Kimber's men also had a loose alliance with one of the metamorphoses of the Hoxton Mob. In fact Kimber was not a layer but instead controlled the best pitches on the courses, leasing them out on a half profit but no loss-sharing basis. Kimber, according to some accounts, was well regarded and it was looser elements out of his control who terrorised the mainly Jewish bookmakers in the cheaper rings at the Southern courses. The Southern bookmakers accepted the imposition fairly philosophically.

Racecourse protection worked in a number of ways. First, there was the question of the pitches themselves. The Sabinis, and their rivals simply bullied the hapless bookmakers away from their spots and then sold or let them to their cronies. One way of preventing a bookmaker from attracting any business was to surround his stand with thugs so that the punters could not get to it to place their bets. Then there was the bucket drop. If a bookmaker wished to avoid this trouble he would drop 2/6d. in a bucket containing water and a sponge carried up and down the line between races. The sponge was also used to wipe out the odds next to the printed sheet of runners on the board. If the tribute was not paid, then the odds would be wiped at inappropriate and totally inconvenient times. The sheets of runners had themselves to be purchased; costing about a farthing to produce, they were retailed by the Sabinis to the bookmakers for another half a crown (2/6d). Chalk had to be purchased, and a stool cost ten shillings to hire for the day. Other manoeuvres included starting fights near a bookmaker's pitch, claiming a non-existent winning bet, and having other pitches put so close to the non-paying bookmaker that he physically could not operate. Quite apart from that there was the straightforward demand for a non-repayable loan of £5 or £10. The sums may seem small, but added up it came to big money and the racecourse business was a profitable one. When a gang went to a course like Brighton they could clear £4,000 or £5,000. At Epsom on Derby Day, it could be £15,000 to £20,000.[3]

Now the Sabini brothers, 'The Italian Mob', who were said to import gangsters from Sicily, began to put together their organisation. The fact that 'there wasn't an Englishman among them'[4] did not mean they could speak anything but English. Once when Mr Justice Darling, who fancied himself as a linguist, addressed one of them in Italian the man stared in amazement.[5]

The Sabinis may have had no great command of Italian, but they had command of the police:

> Darby Sabini got in with the Flying Squad which had been formed about 1908 or 1909; they got in with the racecourse police, the special police, and so they had the police on their side protecting them. Directly there was any fighting it was always the Birmingham mob who got pinched. They was always getting time, five year sentences and that.[6]

With the arrival of the Sabinis and their superior relationship with the police, Billy Kimber and his gang retreated to the

---

[3] Raphael Samuel, *East End Underworld*, p. 184.
[4] ibid, p. 182.
[5] Apparently until this moment in the Cortesi case Darling had been taking a close interest. Now he confined his remarks to the jury to the effect that the witness must be descended from the Sabinis and went on to tell the story of the Sabine women.
[6] Raphael Samuel, *East End Underworld*, p. 183.

Midlands. For some time the factions lived in an uneasy relationship. Kimber and Co. worked the Midlands and Northern tracks; the Sabinis, along with a gang called the East End Jews, the London and Southern ones.[7]

In some versions of the legend the meteoric rise of Darby Sabini can be traced back to a fight he had in 1920 with 'Monkey' Benneyworth, a leader of the Elephant Gang, when Benneyworth deliberately tore the dress of an Italian girl serving behind the bar of the Griffin public house in Saffron Hill. Benneyworth was knocked out and humiliated by Sabini. When his broken jaw had mended he returned with members of the Elephant Gang, but they were driven out of Little Italy by Sabini with the help of young Italians who looked on him as their leader.[8] Now, with them behind him, he saw the opportunity to muscle in on some of the smaller gangs who were providing protection around the racetracks. Although the big gangs such as the Broad Mob from Camden Town, the mainly Jewish Aldgate Mob and the Hoxton Mob could boast a membership of up to sixty, they could be spread thinly because they were obliged to operate several tracks a day. The Sabinis moved in in force.

The next five years saw a long-running battle over control of on-course bookmakers. On the one side were the Sabinis, allied to the Jewish bookmakers from Aldgate. On the other were Billy Kimber, George 'Brummy' Sage and Fred Gilbert from Camden Town. Kimber's Brummagen Boys did not give in easily and the fighting continued throughout the year. The file on the Mornington Crescent shooting appeal against

[7] There were numerous tracks in the South, many of which such as Gatwick, Lewes, Alexandra Park and Hurst Park have now closed down. In addition trotting was popular, with courses at such places as Greenford and Hendon.

[8] Benneyworth is something of a shadowy and unsung figure who reappears over the years. On 8 August 1935 he was involved in the beating of a pickpocket by the name of Flatman in the Waterloo Road.

internment provides a good, although probably incomplete, list of the major bursts of violence.[9]

A bookmaker under the Sabinis' protection was threatened at Sandown Park and was beaten up when he refused to pay a £25 pitch fee. Darby Sabini sent a retaliatory force to Hoxton. He himself was caught at Greenford trotting track on 23 March 1921 and escaped a bad beating from the Brummagen Mob by shooting his way out of trouble.[10] It was one of the few occasions when he was arrested. Charged with unlawfully and maliciously endangering life, he was acquitted after arguing self-defence, fined £10 and bound over to keep the peace on a charge of possessing a five-chamber revolver without a certificate. Inspector Heaps told the court that about 20 Brummagen people tried to get at Sabini, shouting, 'Come on, we've got them on the run. The police are frightened of us too.' Sandy Rice and Fred Gilbert were charged with being suspicious persons, but since they could not be linked to the Sabini incident they were discharged the following week.[11]

On 26 March, Robert Harvey was beaten at London Bridge Station. He had been suspected of welshing at Greenford. The next day there was a serious piece of violence. Billy Kimber, 'accompanied by a number of other roughs' who may, or more likely may not, have been trying to pour oil on the troubled waters, was found shot on the pavement outside Sabini's house in King's Cross. He had apparently gone to 70 Colliers Street to remonstrate with Alfie Solomon and produced a revolver. Solomon took it away from him and Kimber was shot with his own weapon. On 27 April 1921 Solomon was acquitted of attempted murder when the jury accepted his claim that it was an accident.

Reprisals for the Greenford incident came quickly. On 4

9 PRO MEPO 3 158.
10 *Glasgow Herald*, 25 March 1921.
11 PRO MEPO 3 366.

April at 'The Ascot of North London', Alexandra Park, a small frying-pan-shaped track which closed in the 1960s and which was known as Ally-Pally, the police were informed of a likely showdown. By one o'clock, all they had found were two Birmingham bookmakers' touts who had been beaten up. Later, however, two Jewish taxi-drivers, chauffeurs to the Sabinis, were caught in the Silver Ring by the Birmingham men. One was shot twice as he lay on the ground; he too could not identify his shooter. A further reprisal came later that spring at Bath when Billy Kimber and his men attacked the East End Jews found in the Two Shillings Ring.

The quarrel between Sabini and the Jewish element in his contingent and outsiders continued throughout the summer. Fallers included David Levy of Bethnal Green who went to prison for 3 months at one of the magistrates' courts which were specially commissioned at the Derby meeting. He had been found carrying a pistol with soft-nosed bullets. His explanation was that he had been told that if he and his brother Moses went to Epsom they would be shot by 'The Sunderland Kid'. Nothing daunted, they had gone to the course. Levy had 18 previous convictions for assault and two for larceny.[12]

This was clearly a small part of the celebrated battle on Derby Day. It appears to have been engineered by Reuben Bigland, the Birmingham tycoon known as 'Telephone Jack', following a complaint by the publisher and later convicted swindler Horatio Bottomley. He complained that it was wrong that Italians such as the Sabinis should be depriving 'our boys' of a living, particularly after the latter's gallant fight in the First World War. The outcome was a punitive expedition by the Brummagen Boys, who were fuelled by the knowledge that the previous evening one of their men had been attacked in Covent Garden and had needed 70 stitches in his legs alone.

After the Derby itself, won by Steve Donoghue on the

[12] *The Star*, 1 June 1921.

ill-fated Humorist, the Birmingham Boys left the course and
blocked the road with their charabanc to lie in wait for
Sabini and his friends. Unfortunately for them the Sabinis
had already left the scene and the first cab in sight – which
was duly attacked – contained their allies from Leeds. In the
ensuing fracas one man lost three fingers. Twenty-eight men
were arrested by a Sergeant Dawson, who at first thought the
affray was a Sinn Fein riot and removed the sparking plugs
from the charabanc. He then held the men at gunpoint until
help arrived.[13]

It is curious how throughout the history of organised
crime the victims will align themselves with their oppres-
sors who, in turn, through that alliance somehow gain a
quasi-respectability. After bookmakers at Salisbury races had
been forced at gunpoint to pay a levy for the privilege of
having a pitch, in 1921 they formed themselves into the
Bookmakers and Backers Racecourse Protection Association,
today a highly respected organisation. Eight stewards were
appointed at a wage of £6 per week, including Darby Sabini,
Alf White and Philip Emmanuel (son of Edward) who became
the association's vice-president. Another curious steward was
Fred Gilbert.[14] It is said that at the time Darby was earning
£20,000 a year. This may be an exaggeration but, taken at the
lowest level, 60 sheets sold at 2/6d. made a working man's
wage for the week and there is no doubt the brothers did far
better than that. It did not last long for it was soon apparent
that the stewards had reverted to their old ways and were
demanding a shilling for every list sold.

[13] PRO MEPO 3 346. It is often suggested that Jack 'Dodger' Mullins was
one of those involved in the attack. If so he escaped arrest. Humorist
began to haemorrhage after the race and died within a few weeks. A
post-mortem showed he had won with only one sound lung.
[14] The Bookmakers and Backers Racecourse Protection Association, *What
It Has Done and What It Can Do with YOUR Help* (NAB File, 'History'
1921); The Bookmakers and Backers Racecourse Protection Association
General Committee, Minutes, 12 September 1921.

Emmanuel senior also set up a company providing layers with tickets for the punters. There is also a suggestion that in 1922 he was now controlling the Sabinis. In September of that year their services were dispensed with by the BBRPA.[15]

Violence may have spread away from the racecourses, but 1922 was a vintage year in the battle for supremacy on them. On 23 February 1922 Michael Sullivan and Archie Douglas, both of them Brummagen Boys, were slashed in Coventry Street by a Sabini team consisting of Alfred Solomon and his brother Harry, Alfred White, James Wood and a man named Mansfield.

On Good Friday Fred Gilbert was slashed about the legs in the New Raleigh Club in Jermyn Street by the Italians led by Alfie Solomon. He declined to bring charges. The Derby meeting that year, when Captain Cuttle won after spreading a plate on the way to the start, passed off quietly. But two months later, the Sabinis were back in the dock charged after a fight in Mornington Crescent, Camden Town, during which shots were fired at Fred Gilbert who had been out walking with his wife and some friends when he was ambushed. For once the Birmingham men were able to give the names of their attackers to the police, but by the time the case was heard they had forgotten them.

Things did not stop there and real consideration was given by the Jockey Club to shutting down the courses on which there was trouble. There had been persistent stories that a son of the boxer George Moore, a Gilbert man from West London, was stabbed to death in a club off the Strand, or perhaps in Tottenham, but the police report specifically denies this. What is clear is that the Sabinis and their rivals fought for supremacy on street corners, on trains, on the roads and at the racecourses.

[15] South PA Folio 47, 15 May 1933, 'Printing of Lists', The Bookmakers and Backers Racecourse Protection Association General Committee, Minutes, 15 May, 12 June, 4 September 1922.

On 29 July 1922 there was an affray just outside the Red Bull in Gray's Inn Road. William John Beland said that he had heard shots fired from a public house. He went to the scene but was stopped by Fred who said, 'Go the other way or I shall blow your fucking brains out.'

Beland had also been down at the canal bank off Caledonian Road at the beginning of 1920 when Gilbert and George Droy were fighting. When Gilbert was getting the worst of it he took a razor and slashed Droy across the shoulder. Trixie Droy, a manufacturing optician, came to his brother's assistance and for his pains Gilbert shot him in the shoulder.

On 22 August 1922 Jewish bookmakers actually went to the police complaining that George 'Brummy' Sage and Gilbert had demanded £10 from them as they waited for a train to the races. Samuel Samuels said that he was at Waterloo Station on 19 August when George Sage came up to him and said, 'You Jew bastard. You're one of the cunts we're going to do. You're a fucking bastard Jew and we are going to do you and the Italians and stop you going racing. I want to be the governor here.'

Jack Delew from Yorkton Street, Hackney, said he had been in the Rising Sun at Waterloo on the same day when Sage, Jim Brett and Gilbert approached. Sage caught hold of Harry Margolis and said, 'This is one of the bastards, do him Fred, through the guts.' Gilbert then pressed a large service revolver into Margolis' body and said, 'Give us a tenner and you can go.' Jim Brett, aka Stevens, pulled a butcher's knife on Delew and asked, 'Shall I do him?' when a man, Sullivan, entered and said, 'Let them alone. They'll do later.' He then said there were 50 of them and the Sabinis and Alf White would be done in for certain.

Earlier that same day the Sabinis, including Alf White – now Chief Steward of the Racecourse Protection Association – Joseph Sabini, George West aka Dai Thomas, Paul Boffa and Tommy Mack, arrived at Mornington Crescent in a fleet of taxis and shot at Gilbert.

There was a good deal of ducking and diving by friends of the Sage and Brett contingent in respect of their bit of bother, as a result of which on 24 November John Gilbert, Joseph Smith, Thomas Ackroyd and George Moore were found not guilty of perverting the course of justice by getting Margolis to give false evidence. It had been alleged that on 12 October, when Margolis went to the Old Bailey to give evidence, he was met by George Moore whom he knew from the races. Moore said he was ashamed of him giving evidence. Margolis went with him across to the Wellington Coffee Shop and there saw Joe Smith and John Gilbert. Later he went with Gilbert and met Fred Kimberley who had offered money to change his story. Overall neither of the cases could be seen as noted successes by the prosecution. On 1 November, Gilbert, Jim Brett and Sage had all been found not guilty of demanding with menaces. No one bothered about the shooting of George Droy.[16]

Meanwhile most of the Sabini gang involved had been acquitted of the Gilbert shooting in Camden Town. Alf White was convicted but acquitted on appeal. 'The sooner the Bookmakers Protection Agency is disbanded the better,' said Mr Justice Roche. Joseph Sabini was not so fortunate. He received 3 years which he was serving in Maidstone when Alf White, together with George Drake and another unidentified man, decided his conditions should be improved. To this end they approached a warder Matthew Frygh and offered him £2 to deliver letters for him. Frygh reported the matter and the recently released White found himself back in the dock along with Drake. The police wanted to charge George Sabini but there was no evidence against him. It had been thought he had masterminded the whole thing but, on closer inspection, it turned out that the 'George Sabini' who had visited his brother in prison had been another of White's men. This time

16 PRO MEPO 3 366.

White received 18 months and Drake 6 months more. They appealed and because White had an arguable point of law he lost no remission when his appeal was dismissed. Drake apparently had a good service record, being the batman to an RSM in the British Expeditionary Force in France. Now Lord Justice Swift had a little judicial fun at his expense.

> It is clear that society is not safe unless Drake is in the army or in prison and as the court cannot send him into the army what are we to do? One thing is certain. If the sentence stands he will not be able to bribe another warder from outside.

The unfortunate Drake lost his appeal and with it his remission.

At the Doncaster St Leger meeting the Brummagen team sent word that no bookmakers or their employees would be allowed to attend Town Moor. As a result, in open defiance, Sabini and his men 'protected' the London bookie, Walter Beresford, putting him safely on the train to Doncaster where it was met by Kimber's men who then allowed only him and his staff to go to the racecourse. It is often suggested that this was an act of generosity by the Sabinis. Beresford had employed Harry Sabini – or was it the other way around? – for years.

The next trouble spot was at the Yarmouth autumn meeting, a course claimed by the Sabinis as theirs. They arrived the day before the meeting to search the public houses in the town to see if the Brummagen men had arrived. They had not. Instead they were met by Tom Divall, an ex-Chief Inspector of the CID and a superior of Wensley and Leeson down in Whitechapel, but now working for Wetherbys. Divall, something of a supporter of the Midland team, calmed things down.

Divall wrote of Kimber that he 'was one of the best' and of another incident:

Just to show what generous and brave fellows the aforesaid Sage and Kimber were, they would not give any evidence or information against their antagonists, and stated that they would sooner die than send those men to prison.[17]

One explanation of the Sabinis' success and longevity comes from Billy Hill:

There were more crooked policemen about than there are today. The Sabinis received protection from certain elements of the law. If a thief or pickpocket was seen on a course, a Sabini man would whiten the palm of his hand with chalk and greet the thief with a supposed-to-be 'Hello'. In doing so he would slap the thief on the shoulder, just like a long-lost friend. The whitened hand-mark would identify him to the law. Then they knew without doubt that this man was safe to be nicked for being a suspected person.[18]

According to Divall it was Beresford who in 1923:

. . . brought the two sides together, he is still continuing in the good work, and I am very pleased to see the two crews are associating together, and, in addition, to have their principals assuring me that no such troubles will ever occur again.

The Sabinis and Kimber did agree to divide the racecourses between them and the racecourse wars died down. Now, with the Sabinis controlling the south, where there were more meetings, and Kimber and his friends the rest, the bookmakers were firmly in their hands.

But if by then Darby Sabini had made his peace with that

---

[17] Tom Divall, *Scoundrels and Scallywags*, p. 200.
[18] Billy Hill, *Boss of the Underworld*, p. 4.

fine fellow Billy Kimber, for some time he had been under threat
from other sources inside his own organisation. Some of the
troops decided to seek a higher percentage of the takings. The
four Cortesi brothers (Augustus, George, Paul and Enrico, also
known as the Frenchies) were deputed to act as shop stewards
to put the case. Almost immediately afterwards part of the Jewish
element in the gang, to become known as the Yiddishers, also
formed a breakaway group. In true business fashion the Sabinis
negotiated. The Cortesis would be given a greater percentage.
The Yiddishers were given permission to lean on one, but only
one, of the bookmakers under protection.[19]

However, peace did not last long. The Yiddishers began
to side with the Cortesis and with defections amongst the
troops to the Frenchies, the Sabini position was substantially
weakened. In the autumn of 1922 the new team had effectively
hi-jacked the Sabini protection money from the bookmakers
at Kempton Park. Retribution was swift. As a result of the
reprisals, Harry Sabini was convicted at Marylebone Magistrates' Court of an assault on George Cortesi. More seriously,
one of the other leaders of the breakaway group was attacked,
for which five of the Sabini troops were sentenced to terms of
imprisonment for attempted murder.

Then on 19 November 1922, just before midnight, Darby
and Harry Sabini were trapped in the Fratellanza Club in
Great Bath Street, Clerkenwell. Darby was punched and hit
with bottles whilst Harry was shot in the stomach by Augustus
and Enrico (Harry) Cortesi. Darby suffered a greater indignity.
As he told the magistrates' court, his false teeth were broken
as a result of the blows from the bottles. He was also able to
confirm his respectability:

> I am a quiet peaceable man. I never begin a fight. I've
> only once been attacked. I've never attacked anyone . . .

[19] Arthur Tietjen, *Soho*.

> I do a little bit of work as a commission agent sometimes
> for myself and sometimes for someone else. I'm always
> honest. The last day's work I did was two years' ago. I
> live by my brains.

He had only once carried a revolver and that was the time
when he was attacked at Greenford Park. Indeed he turned
out his pockets in confirmation that he was not carrying a
gun.

The Cortesi brothers, who lived only five doors from the
Fratellanza Club, had been arrested the same night and, at
the Old Bailey on 18 January 1923, Augustus and Enrico
each received a sentence of 3 years' penal servitude. George
was found not guilty, as were Paul and Alexander Tomasso,
the latter known as Sandy Rice. A recommendation by the
Grand Jury that the Cortesi brothers should be deported was
not followed by Mr Justice Darling.

> I look upon this as part of a faction fight which has raged
> between you and other Italians in consequence of some
> difference which the police do not entirely understand.
> You appear to be two lawless bands – the Sabinis and
> the Cortesis. Sometimes you are employed against the
> Birmingham people, and sometimes you are employed
> against each other. On this occasion you were carrying
> out a feud between you and the Sabinis. I have the
> power to recommend an order for your deportation. I
> am not going to do it. I can see no reason to suppose
> that you two men are worse than others who have been
> convicted in these feuds and have not been recommended
> for deportation.

A rather sour note on the Home Office file reads: 'It is a pity
that the Cortesis were not charged with the murder of the
Sabinis'.

Meanwhile anonymous letters to the police detailed a series
of incidents for which the Sabinis were said to be responsible.

The principal correspondent was 'Tommy Atkins' who said he had been victimised and, if the police cared to contact him by putting an advertisement in the *Daily Express*, he would reveal all. Meanwhile he alleged that Edward Emmanuel and a Girchan Harris were financing the Sabinis and that they had a number of members of the Flying Squad in their pay as well. The police inserted the advertisement suggesting a meeting, which was declined by 'Atkins' who, nevertheless, did supply details of some 12 incidents including an attack by James Ford and George Langham (also known as Angelo Giancoli) on bookmaker John Thomas Phillips in Brighton. He also reported the story that the brother of George Moore had been killed and that the *Evening News* racing correspondent J.M.D. had been attacked at Newmarket. There was a suggestion that Billy Westbury had been injured so badly that he was now 'mentally insane'.

The police could find no trace of the death of Moore's brother and reported that poor Billy Westbury had suffered 'minor injuries'. It was correct, however, that J.M.D. had indeed been attacked.

In June 1923 Darby and Harry Sabini, along with George Dido, were arrested at Epsom races and charged with wounding Jack Levine, known also as Maurice Fireman. The allegation was that they had used knuckledusters on the unhappy bookmaker. They were fortunate in that the incident had been witnessed by Sgt-Major Michael O'Rorke VC, a resident of a local veterans' hospital, who saw no knuckledusters and Fireman as the aggressor. Dido gave evidence that he had been wearing a ring which might have seemed at a glance to be a knuckleduster. Asked where it was, he said rather piteously that he had pawned it to pay for the defence. Not Guilty.[20]

One of the most serious incidents came in 1924 when Alfie

[20] *News of the World*, 24 June 1923.

Solomon stood trial for the murder of Barney Blitz, known as Buck Emden, who had nine convictions for wounding and assaults on the police including one at Old Street Magistrates' Court when, on 20 July 1916, he had been ordered to pay £20 compensation for striking an officer with a bayonet.

The police only managed to persuade a bare half-dozen of the 40-odd present in the club to come to give evidence. One defaulter was the fishmonger, soon to be boxing promoter, Jack Solomons. He wished he could help, but since he had been drinking all evening he could not give an accurate recollection even though he had been sober enough to play faro when he arrived at the premises.

The story is that Darby Sabini arrived at the flat of Sir Edward Marshall Hall KC brandishing a bundle of white £5 notes in an endeavour to persuade the great man to appear for Solomons. He was sent to see Hall's clerk and Sir Edward accepted the brief. Solomons' defence was that he had seen Edward Emmanuel being assaulted and struck a blow with a knife to save his dear old friend. As for his part, Emmanuel, who had now left behind his East End upbringing and was living in Golders Green, wished he could cut off his own hand if the act would bring Emden back to life.

Some felt that the real villain of the piece and the person who had set it all up was indeed Emmanuel, who was alleged to have controlled things from the Tichbourne Club in Paddington, and Scotland Yard received another anonymous letter.

I feel (rec 25 Sept) I must write and tell you something about the poor man that was stabbed in the Eden Street Club. The man who started the row was Edward Emmanuel who I know went there with Solomons. He is making his brags all over the East End that his money will keep him out of this affair. I know him and know he paid this man Solomons to do this poor man some injury. The police must know this Emmanuel he has had gambling houses all over London and it was because he had a previous row with this poor man that took him there with Solomons who is also a villain and this is not the first one he has stabbed. Make Solomons say who he went to the club with and who broke the glass and hit the poor man on the head. Please take notice of this letter and make this Emmanuel come forward. I only wish I had curage (sic) to come and see you and tell you more you will find out this is true. He professes to be a very good man by helping poor jews and that is why they will never say anything about him you have got his photo at Scotland Yard if you look it up I am a poor woman who has suffered through these gambling dens.[21]

Without their leaders the Cortesi faction had folded, but 1925 was a vintage year for gang fighting in London. The list of incidents is formidable. According to the newspapers, on 15 February there was a razor slashing in Aldgate High Street, and another slashing took place at Euston Station on 24 April. On 21 May ten armed men raided a club in Maiden Lane looking for the Sabinis or their men. Later that night shots were fired in the Harrow Road. On 30 July, three men were wounded in a club in Brighton. There was an incident when men fought on Hampstead Heath on 3 August. Five days later a man was attacked in the Marshalsea Road in the Borough, and on 16 August 24 men fought in Shaftesbury

[21] The Solomons referred to is obviously Alfred rather than Jack. On his release from prison he went bent on his former associates and supporters, writing to the police asking for protection as he had been going straight and working the racetracks when he was threatened at Clapton by a gang headed by Dodger Mullins. The police thought differently, saying that Alfred Solomons was 'a dangerous rascal and his enemies are far more in need of protection than he is'. The whole saga appears in the file PRO MEPO 3 373.

Avenue. Four days after that there was a pitched battle when 50 men fought with razors on the corner of Aldgate and Middlesex Street.

The police, asked for their comments, were dismissive, saying that the fight at Middlesex Street had been a minor incident and the fight in Shaftesbury Avenue was total invention. They accepted the Maiden Lane incident and that Monkey Benneyworth had been involved. In connection with the Hampstead Heath fight, there was no evidence that race gangs were involved. As for allegations that Flying Squad officers were standing by watching some of the incidents, this was totally incorrect; indeed the newspapers should be ashamed of themselves for such irresponsible reporting. However, in the House of Commons the Home Secretary, William Joynson Hicks, vowed to stamp out the race gangs.

And just as swiftly as they had arisen so did the street fights die away. Darby Sabini moved to Brighton where, in October 1929, he was fined £5 for assaulting bookmaker David Isaacs. After an incident at Hove Greyhound Stadium, he had attacked him in the Ship Hotel and then in a billiard saloon. When Isaacs was asked why he had not brought witnesses he replied, 'How can I get witnesses against a man like this, when everyone goes in fear of their life of him?'

It was not until the 1930s, by which time the Sabinis had expanded their territory into greyhound racing, that they again came under serious threat from another team.[22] This time it was from their former ally Alf White whose family and friends had been getting stronger over the years and were now set to challenge their previous allies. Trouble had been brewing for some time and Sabini had not been able to control the disparate interests of the Jewish and the Whites, the more right-wing arm of the organisation. There was also

---

[22] In February the faithful James Ford received two months' hard labour for an attack on William Farmer who was said to be taking control of Belle Vue Greyhounds. *The Times*, 25 February 1929.

the small matter of the pitches on the open courses at Epsom and Brighton which were outside the control of the racecourse stewards, as well as bookmaking at point-to-points, let alone the dog tracks where, according to the son of a man who ran a pitch, 'they terrorised the bookmakers'.

Meanwhile, from the 1920s onwards the Sabinis had been branching out, taking interests in the West End drinking and gambling clubs and installing and running slot machines. They were also extending their protection to criminals. If a burglary took place the Sabinis would send round for their share.

Burglars and thieves had no chance. If they wandered 'Up West' they had to go mob-handed. And they had to be prepared to pay out if they were met by any of the Sabinis. If they went into a club it was drinks all round. The prices were usually doubled especially for their benefit. If they did go into a spieler they never won; they knew better than to try to leave while they were showing even a margin of profit. If one word was spoken out of place, it was all off. The Sabinis, who could rustle up 20 or 30 tearaways at a moment's notice anywhere 'Up West', stood for no liberties, although they were always taking them.[23]

The family was also undoubtedly behind one of the best of the bullion robberies of the 1930s, the very carefully planned gold snatch at Croydon Airport. Gold used to be shipped from the airport and, on 6 March 1936, three boxes of gold bars, sovereigns and dollars intended to be sent by Imperial Airways to Brussels and Paris disappeared. The boxes had been placed in a safe room and amazingly only one man, Francis Johnson, remained at the aerodrome overnight. He had to leave the actual building at 4.15 in the morning to receive a German airliner which was landing. An impression had been made of the keys to the safe

[23] Billy Hill, *Boss of the Underworld*, p. 5.

room and, while Johnson was on the tarmac, the gold was stolen.

A cab had been hired from King's Cross and driven to the airport where the boxes were loaded and brought back to Harringay. Cecil Swanland, John O'Brien and Silvio Mazzardo (known as Shonk) and a Sabini man who lived off Saffron Hill were arrested. The police found wrappers and seals from the gold in Swanland's room but there wasn't a trace of the gold itself. The evidence included identification and, since it was clearly not strong, the mandatory confession to a cellmate. Mazzardo and O'Brien were acquitted. Swanland's defence was that by the time the boxes arrived at his home they were empty. He had a number of old convictions mainly for forgery, and had already served 7, 5 and 6 years' penal servitude. This time he received a 7-year term. None of the gold was recovered. Bert Marsh, who had earlier been acquitted of the murder of a Monte Colombo brother at Wandsworth Greyhound Stadium, was suspected of being the actual mastermind.[24]

But the Sabinis and the Whites were not without rivals. In 1937 the crime writer and novelist Peter Cheyney wrote in the *Sunday Dispatch* that there were five major London gang districts: Hackney, Hoxton, North East London, North London, and the West End, this last being 'worked over' by a loose alliance of the Hoxton, Elephant and Castle Boys and the Hackney Gang as well as the West End Boys.

Until 1927, wrote Cheyney:

. . . the Hackney Gang was supreme in the West End. Then came the battle of Ham Yard when the gang suffered

---

[24] Just as bookmakers' pitches on the racetracks had been controlled so it was with the new sport of greyhound racing. Marsh and Bert Wilkins were involved in a fight over who should work at the pitches and Massimino Monte Colombo was stabbed to death on 1 September 1936. They were acquitted of murder and received short sentences for manslaughter. See James Morton, *Gangland*, pp. 20–21.

a severe reversal in terms both of blood spilled and prestige lost.[25]

Apart from the gangs which ran their areas there would be splinter teams such as the squad of pickpockets from Aldgate who worked the nearby City.

After his unfortunate incident at Maidstone prison White had maintained a low profile as far as the courts were concerned until in July 1935 he and his sons William and Alfred jnr each received 12 months' hard labour for assaulting John McCarthy Defferary, the licensee of the Yorkshire Stingo in the Marylebone Road, at the Wharncliffe Rooms on 17 April that year. The fight had been at a dance in aid of St Mary's Hospital and Defferary lost the sight of his left eye. There was a suggestion that Carrie White, Alf's daughter, had been given £12 taken from the victim.[26]

On 28 April that year, Frederick Ambrose had written to the police alleging that Alf White was 'one of the Worse Race Course Pests and blackmailers that ever put foot on

[25] Reprinted in *Making Crime Pay*. Cheyney was writing a decade later and in fact the battle took place at the end of 1923. The following January George West (43) and James Ford (30) had wrecked the New Avenue Club in Ham Yard for which they went to prison. West had a long record beginning in 1898 when he served two months for larceny, interrupted by a career when he boxed as Dai Thomas. In October 1922 he had been acquitted of the attempted murder of Fred Gilbert in the Mornington Crescent shooting. This time West received nine months and Ford six.

In February 1927 Freddy Ford (no relation of James), who ran the Musicians and Artists Club, an *alter ego* for the New Avenue, went to prison for receiving along with a man named Chandler. The club was described by Inspector Wensley as patronised almost exclusively by thieves – male and female. If, by mistake, a genuine patron stumbled into the club it was rare that he left with his money. *Empire News*, 13 February 1927.

[26] The White appeal against his conviction in the Gilbert incident appears in the Law Reports under (1922) CR App R. 60 and also in PRO MEPO 3 910.

a racecourse' and the file contains another series of letters suggesting White had the police in his pay.

Now when the Whites appeared at the Old Bailey they were supported by some 40 members of the gang and fighting broke out. There were no arrests. The guilty verdict was thought to be very much against the weight of the evidence and the writer of an internal Scotland Yard memo said 'success in such an appeal would, in the matter of Law and Order, be a catastrophe'. There had been a threat against prosecuting counsel, Horace Fenton, and for a time he was given police protection.

As for the racecourses, the last major pre-war fight took place when, at Lewes racecourse on 8 June 1936, the Bethnal Green Gang in alliance with the Hoxton Mob and probably sponsored by Alf White, ran riot. In retaliation for an incident at Liverpool Street when a member of the Whites had his throat cut, 30 members of that firm went to the races with the specific intention of injuring two of the Sabinis. They did not find them and instead set upon the bookmaker Arthur Solomons and his clerk, Mark Frater, known to be friendly towards the family. After a running battle 16 men were arrested. As always serious money was available and they were defended privately at Lewes Assizes by the very fashionable J.D. Cassels KC and G.L. Hardy, but on pleas of guilty the ringleaders who included Jimmy Spinks, and other Hoxton men, drew 5 years' penal servitude from Mr Justice Hilbery who imposed a total of 53½ years on the defendants.[27]

It was after that that an accommodation was reached. The Sabinis should have the West End, the Whites the King's Cross area. They became known as the King's Cross Gang and Alf White would hold court in the Bell public house or

---

[27] For an account of the battle, see Edward Greeno, *War on the Underworld*, Chapter 4. Greeno, on whose recollections it is not always safe to rely, gives credence to the story that a Sabini man was killed in the Benneyworth raid on Maiden Lane.

Hennekeys in the Pentonville Road exercising strict discipline amongst his followers. 'No bad language was allowed,' says John Vaughan, a former police officer from King's Cross. 'First time you were warned. The next time – out.' It had been the same with Darby Sabini; women were to be treated properly; Italian youths could not drink before they were twenty. His had been a reasonably benevolent dictatorship.

Darby Sabini lost another battle when, following a series of unfavourable articles, he sued D.C. Thomson, the proprietors of the offending *Topical Times*, for libel. On the day of the action he failed to appear and costs of £775 were awarded against him. He did not pay and bankruptcy proceedings were commenced.[28]

The Sabini empire was effectively destroyed by their internment at the outbreak of the Second World War. Darby Sabini had moved to Brighton with, according to Saffron Hill legend, two sacks of gold, where his daughters were educated locally – again Saffron Hill legend said it was at Roedean, but there are no records of the girls there – and where he had a penthouse flat in the Grand Hotel. Harryboy, who escaped internment, was sentenced in 1942 to 9 months' imprisonment for perjury when attempting to prevent that fate. Their business interests were now up for grabs. For a time their West End interests were shared by the Whites, Jack Spot and the Elephant Gang, with the Whites increasingly the dominant force.

Another old Sabini man to gravitate to Brighton was Patrick Daley who in August 1937 received six months in the local magistrates' court. He had been leaning on bookmakers at Brighton races, demanding two shillings from each of them. When arrested he hit a detective and it had taken a further six policemen to get him to the station. Up until 1926 he had 20 convictions for assaults and thefts but had then given up drink and become a bookmaker. He had, he told the court,

[28] *The Times*, 16 December 1925.

lost his money some 18 months previously which accounted for his present actions. In return the chairman told him he was a 'dangerous man'.[29]

Just what were Darby Sabini and his brothers like? A picture taken of the Cortesis and the Sabinis before the Fratellanza shooting shows Enrico Cortesi in a straw hat sitting in the middle of the group like the captain of a cricket team. To his left is Darby, less than middle height, with the flat cap he always wore and a shirt with no collar. He wore a dark brown suit with a high-buttoned waistcoat, a black silk stock and the light checked cap; he had selected this outfit when he was twenty and wore it for the rest of his life – indoors, outdoors and, so it is said, sometimes in bed. To Cortesi's right and in the background is handsome Harryboy Sabini who wore highly polished springsided boots. Brother Joe liked cherry checks, whilst George wore a grey fedora.

On 17 June 1943, Darby Sabini, under the name Fred and having by then been released from internment, was convicted of receiving wine and silver worth £383 which had been stolen by soldiers from the Uckfield house of a retired Sussex magistrate. The jury had rejected his defence that he thought that he was buying goods from an hotel which was being sold up. The Recorder Gilbert Paull, passing sentence, told him in the time-honoured words judges love to use to receivers: 'It is men like you who lay temptation before soldiers. If there were none like you there would be no temptation to steal.' Sabini, who was said to have no previous convictions, received 3 years' imprisonment.

After the war Harry joined his brother in Brighton. Darby's son had joined the RAF and was killed in action. In the late 1940s he functioned as a small-time bookmaker with a pitch on the free course at Ascot – a danger to no one, certainly not the up-and-coming Jack Spot and Billy Hill.

[29] *Empire News*, 8 August 1937.

When he died in Hove in 1951 his family and friends were surprised that he apparently had so little money. Yet the man who had been his clerk, Jimmy Napoletano, was stopped when leaving the country on his way to Italy with £36,000. Sabini's wife returned to live in Gray's Inn Road, Clerkenwell.

Sabini also lives on in fiction and film as the Brighton gangleader Colleoni in Graham Greene's *Brighton Rock*. One of the key scenes in both book and film is the meeting between him and Pinky in the Brighton hotel. The slashing of Pinky at the race meeting is based on the Lewes battle of 1936.

7

Chinatown, my Chinatown

I was glad when I was through Pennyfields. It was
the only street in the miles of East London that I
traversed day and night that inspired me with any
real fear.

East of Aldgate, p. 141.

Until my visit to the Asiatic Sailors' Home I had always
considered some of the Jewish inhabitants of Whitechapel
to be the worst type of humanity I had ever seen.[1]

---

[1] Health Inspector in *Chambers Journal* 81 (1904), pp. 193–5. At the end
of the eighteenth century most of the Chinese population had been
discharged from vessels and were living in poverty until the ships were
ready to sail again. In 1814 the East India Company was required to
provide food, clothing and lodging for them (Report on Lascars and
other Asiatic Seamen 1814–15). They were mainly employed through
the East India Company and it was only at the turn of the century that
Chinatowns began to develop. The 1851 Census for England and Wales
showed there were 110 London residents born in China of whom 32
were British subjects and 78 foreigners. Ten years later the number was
almost double and in 1901 had reached 545, most living in Stepney and
Poplar where over 20 per cent worked in the laundry industry.

There were anti-Chinese riots in the East End in 1908 caused by the fear
of sailors that with the companies using more Asiatics their jobs would be
lost. Several Chinese boarding-houses were ransacked. (continued)

It is difficult to know just how accurate were the tales in books such as *Women and Crime*, but they certainly enthralled the readers and added to the mystery of Limehouse. In this autobiographical episode Bishop, the Scotland Yard officer turned private detective, is asked by J.W., 'a well-known London man', to find his young wife who has disappeared. It was thought that she would be found 'in some East End Joss House'.

> I received information that the girl was in a particularly unsavoury den in Limehouse. I visited the place with J.W. We were received by a Chinaman whom I persuaded to show me the women addicts then in his house. One of the women answered the description of the girl for whom I was searching. She was largely undressed, as it so often happens that proprietors of opium dens will remove the clothes of sleeping clients so that they may not leave the den until all their money is spent. I told the Chinaman that I should take the woman away with me, and when he heard that I was an ex-Scotland Yard officer he consented. Some Chinese clothes were found and we returned to J.W.'s house in the West End. But no sooner had I placed the girl on a couch than my companion groaned and told me that we had brought the wrong woman.

Unfortunately Mr Bishop does not disclose what he did with the unfortunate girl, but he returns to the den saying that he

---

The Chinese were not the only targets. As early as 1736 there were anti-Irish riots in Spitalfields when cane weavers protested about undercutting. Two Irish heavers, Murphy and Duggan, were hanged after an affray between sailors and coal-heavers in 1768 at Wapping (Annual Register, 25 May 1768). This time the Irish had been in revolt about their own poor conditions of employment. After the disturbances in the spring of 1768 five Irishmen were hanged in Sun Tavern Fields off the Ratcliffe Highway in front of a crowd said to number 50,000. Then in 1786 seven Irishmen were hanged after an affray at Shadwell (Annual Register, 26 July 1786).

wishes to find a girl who took morphine. The Chinaman explains that he only sells opium and recommends him to another den. Because the proprietor of the second establishment knows and loathes the detective, Bishop puts on a disguise, one of the key features of which is a wooden leg – rather, it seems, like Tony Hancock playing Robert Newton playing Long John Silver. He visits his own wife who fails to recognise him and so, satisfied with the disguise, off he goes back to the East End where he buys the girl for £50, the price the Chinaman tells him he would receive from white slavers. He gets a nearby labourer to help him carry the girl out, but all does not go smoothly.

> [We were] halfway down the short flight of stairs, the labourer carrying the girl, when the floor collapsed and we were precipitated into the cellar. In the fall most of my disguise came off and the Chinaman recognising me, drew his knife and rushed me.

Now follows a bit of verisimilitude and instruction for those readers who might venture into Pennyfields.

> A Chinaman has a peculiar way of stabbing. He rushes at his enemy with a knife held on a level with his hip. He then slashes low down, once right and once left. It is seldom that more is needed. One does not observe the Queensberry rules on these occasions, so I kicked my Chinaman with my wooden leg and he collapsed. We got the woman away safely, but shortly after arriving home she died. The effects of the fall had been too much for her drug-weakened heart.[2]

---

[2] Cecil Bishop, *Women and Crime*, pp. 155–7. Bishop also gives Wu On and Tu Sen as major drug dealers of the period. Because of the various spellings of Chinese names the latter may have been Tung-Tse-Ana-Tse, known as Mr Johnson or Mr King, who was regarded as one of the major financiers of the trade. 'Secret Chief' in *Empire News*, 10 October 1920.

One of the first and certainly the best known of the major
Chinese drug dealers was Brilliant Chang, a stocky figure
scarcely 5 feet tall with patent leather shoes and a fur-collared
melton cloth coat who described himself as a general merchant and an Admiralty contractor and was described as,
'the unemotional yellow man, his narrow slit eyes blank,
his face a mask. He had a Chinese wife and three yellow
children.'³ Chang, gap-toothed with dark hair swept back,
was apparently the son of a well-to-do Chinese businessman
sent to England in 1913 to pursue a commercial career or
study medicine; accounts vary. Instead he opened a restaurant
in Regent Street and started drug-trafficking on the side from
his private suite. In a short time he was looked on as the leader
of drug-traffickers in the West End. White women fascinated
him and he trafficked in them. Those who attracted him would
receive a note via a waiter.

> Dear Unknown,
> Please don't regard this as a liberty that I write to you.
> I am really unable to resist the temptation after having
> seen you so many times. I should extremely like to know
> you better and should be glad if you would do me the
> honour of meeting me one evening when we could have
> a little dinner or supper together. I do hope you will
> consent to this as it will give me great pleasure indeed,
> and in any case do not be cross with me for having
> written to you. Yours hopefully, Chang.⁴

Curiously, since these were clearly pre-printed and their
recipients could not possibly think they had suddenly induced
an irresistible urge for Mr Chang to write to them, he had a

³ *Daily Express*, 11 April 1924.
⁴ One of the letters is in a file on the Chinese and the drug trade, PRO
MEPO 3 469.

high success rate. From there it was often a short step to drugs and degradation.

In 1917 several men in Birmingham were arrested with correspondence showing that Chang was a leader in the drug business, but although there was a period of police surveillance nothing came of it. Chang was almost certainly the supplier of the drugs which led to two well-publicised deaths. After the Victory Ball held in aid of the Nation's Fund for Nurses at the Albert Hall, Billie Carleton, a pretty young actress who had been been addicted to drugs for a number of years, collapsed and died. Born in 1886, the illegitimate daughter of a chorus singer Margaret Stewart, she was described as:

> a frail beauty and delicate . . . all of that perishable, moth like substance that does not last long in the wear and tear of this rough and ready world.[5]

In fact she was a tough young woman who had been one of Cochran's young ladies and appeared with Gertrude Lawrence and Bea Lillie in the revue *Some* at the Vaudeville Theatre in 1916. Along with the sinister Reggie de Veulle, she took parties to Limehouse where she was supplied with drugs by a Chinese, Lau Ping You and his Scottish wife Ada, who had a house at the eastern end of Limehouse Causeway under the railway bridge which leads to the Isle of Dogs.

The inquest showed she had died of cocaine poisoning and was addicted to opium smoking. It was common knowledge that Chang had been a close friend but although her companion of the night before, Reggie de Veulle, was charged with manslaughter nothing was ever proved against Chang. De Veulle, prosecuted by Sir Richard Muir, was lucky to be acquitted of manslaughter but received 8 months' hard labour for supplying Billie Carleton. Ada Lau Ping

[5] *Sunday Pictorial*, 1 December 1918.

received five months also for supply, whilst her husband was altogether more fortunate. Liable for deportation, he appeared in front of one of the few magistrates who thought that a little smoking was no worse than a glass or two of whisky and was fined £10.[6]

Also attending the Carleton inquest was Sui Fong, later described as the Yellow Snake of the Underworld when he, Yong Yu and Long Chenk all received three months and were recommended for deportation at Marlborough Street. Fong's wife was described as an Austrian Jewess and Yong Yu had married an English girl. Fong had come over at the turn of the century as a steward on a liner and had been linked with one of the most spectacular gambling dens where after the gaming had finished orgies took place. He had been seen near the White Swan (known as Paddy's Goose), the celebrated public house on Radcliffe Highway, and was a marriage broker between the Chinese and English girls.

Then on 6 March 1922 Freda Kempton, a dancing instructress, was found dead also from an overdose of cocaine.[7] This time Chang did feature; he had been with Freda the night before and faced a hostile series of questions at her inquest. 'She was a friend of mine, but I know nothing about the

---

[6] De Veulle, described as having an 'effeminate face and mincing little smile', had designed Billie Carleton's gown for the ball. The son of a former British Vice Consul at Le Mans, he was part of a scheme to blackmail William Cronshaw, a well-known homosexual of the time. See *The Times*, 13 December 1918; *News of the World*, 15 December 1918. Earlier that same year Walter Gibson, a West End shipping merchant, died from an overdose of morphine, and Gow the Limehouse dealer received one month's hard labour.

[7] A note in the *News of the World* has it that Freda Kempton was to have married a Manchester businessman the Monday after her death. A friend recalled that she had promised to give up dancing and the man had sent her money for clothes. *News of the World*, 30 April 1922. Other demi-mondaines of the period who died through drugs included Audrey Harrison and Vacera Steane. In April 1926 Violet Kempton, Freda's sister, alleged that her sister had been deliberately poisoned. 'Queer disclosures in Drug Tragedy' in *Empire News*, 4 April 1926.

cocaine,' he told the coroner. He had given her money but not drugs. 'It is all a mystery to me.'

> There was no mistaking the thrill that passed through the court room as the Chinaman in his matter-of-fact fashion referred to the bedroom incident and went on to speak of the present of £5 which he gave to the erring girl on that occasion.[8]

The coroner ruled that there was not sufficient evidence to link Chang with the death of Freda Kempton, but not before he had taken the opportunity of delivering a little homily:

> [It is] disgraceful that such a dangerous drug as cocaine should be handed about London helping to ruin the bodies and souls of inexperienced girls.

The jury recorded a verdict of 'suicide during temporary insanity'.

> When the jury returned the verdict Chang smiled broadly and quickly left the court. As he passed out several well-dressed girls patted his shoulder while one ran her fingers through his hair.[9]

In the flurry of unwelcome publicity after Freda Kempton's death, the police used two out-of-work dressmakers, Gertrude Lewis and Mabel Smith, to whom they paid £3 to act as undercover agents. Chang's premises at 107 Regent Street were frequently raided, and in one which netted six Chinese in West London four were found to be waiters at his restaurant. Eventually he sold his restaurant and, to the annoyance of the formidable Mrs Kate Meyrick – who had her own club at

---

8 'The White Girl and the Chinaman' in *Empire News*, 30 April 1922.
9 *News of the World*, 30 April 1922.

No. 43 and who certainly did not want police attention –
became a partner in the Palm Court Club in Gerrard Street.[10]
He then moved to live and conduct his operations at 13
Limehouse Causeway. The premises were almost derelict, with
an unoccupied shop on the ground floor, and he let out the
second floor to Chinese seamen. It was the middle floor which
Chang used for himself and which excited the public. The great
bed was a 'divan of luxury'. Silver dragons were everywhere, as
was costly furniture all derived – so the press and police said
– through drug-dealing. 'This man would only sell drugs to a
white girl if she gave herself to him as well as paying.'

The method of dealing from there was simple. Couriers
such as Violet Payne, euphemistically described as a failed
actress, who had a number of aliases, bought the drugs in
Limehouse and took a taxi to the West End to sell them on. At
the end of May 1923 a Paddington chemist James Burnby and
his wife Mary were convicted of supplying heroin to Payne.
According to the statement she had made to the police, over
a period of years she had taken stolen property to Mrs Burnby
who had supplied her with heroin and had allowed her to fix
in the kitchen behind the shop. One one occasion blood had
sprayed all over the cooker and Mrs Burnby had cried out,
'Don't die here.' When arrested she is alleged to have said,
'Oh, do overlook it this time for the sake of my poor dear
husband.'[11] She received six months and he a mere two.

Brilliant Chang was arrested on 23 February 1924. The
police had been keeping watch on the Commercial Tavern
public house in Pennyfields and 15 Limehouse Causeway
which was a Chinese restaurant. Violet Payne had been seen to

[10] Kate Meyrick was one of the most notorious night-club owners of
the period. She served a number of terms of imprisonment and was
a partner of the corrupt police sergeant George Goddard who would
warn her of impending raids and who in 1929 received 2 years for
conspiracy to pervert the course of justice. Mrs Meyrick becomes 'Ma'
Mayfield in Evelyn Waugh's *Brideshead Revisited*.
[11] *Empire News*, 27 May 1923.

flit from one to the other and when stopped she was found to be once more in possession of drugs. When pressure was put on her, she mentioned his name. A small packet containing cocaine was found under a loose board in Chang's kitchen cupboard. Since he did not wish to alienate the Old Bailey jury and more particularly the judge, he ran the defence that it had been put there without his knowledge rather than that the police had planted it. The jury did not leave the box before convicting and he was sentenced to 14 months in the Second Division and recommended for deportation. During his imprisonment he continued to be something of a thorn in the flesh of the authorities because although he could write in English perfectly well he insisted on writing in Chinese. Since none of the warders could read Mandarin and so censor his letters, they had to be sent to the Home Office for translation.

He was deported in April 1925, taken by cab to the Royal Albert Docks where his family had reserved him a suite on the boat. Whilst in prison he had been sent numerous letters from women friends, and he was allowed these but not to speak for long with the well-wishers. He left to calls of, 'Come back soon, Chang.' During his six-year reign in England it is estimated he made over £1 million from drugs trafficking, most of which he had remitted home.

It was thought he might indeed be back.

Chinese physiognomy is practically a blank page to the average Englishman. They all seem alike. Chang may return as Han Fat Sang, his appearance slightly altered.[12]

---

[12] *Empire News*, 5 April 1925. Shortly after his imprisonment Lily Brentano, whose real name was Rumble, said to have been living with him in Pennyfields, received six months' hard labour for dealing. No cocaine was found on her but she had been heard talking ambiguously with two women described as Big K and Brixton Peggy. *East End News*, 6 May 1924.

Now there were reports that he had disappeared when the ship docked at Marseilles, Port Said and again when it finally reached China. At Marseilles a number of Chinese had gone on board when the ship docked and Chang had left with them, only to be spotted by a detective. In Port Said he disappeared completely.

After a spell in the East or Middle East he returned to Europe. There were then rumours that he had gone blind and that he had died, but it is thought that some of these were cover stories put about by himself. There were also reports that he had gone to Zurich, and was controlling the London drug traffic through his old accomplices, intending to flood the Thames Valley area. According to one source he was visiting a South Coast town on a monthly basis aided by a new lieutenant, the Dutchman Henri Boom, who had been deported only a matter of weeks previously. He was certainly in Paris in the summer of 1927 because in September that year he was arrested after allegations that he was dealing in drugs and had been responsible for the disappearance of girls in the Latin Quarter. He was also suspected of setting up the rolling of clients by prostitutes. He was finally given bail in the sum of 200,000 francs and absconded along with a young woman Suzanne Fichet with whom he had been living. In 1929 there were reports that he was wanted concerning the death of Minna Spermel, a German cabaret singer. He was also linked to the addiction of another actress, Marie Orska, who had been confined to a mental hospital after attacking her understudy with a knife.[13]

The British authorities had been convinced that with the compulsory retirement of Chang they had struck a major blow against cocaine and opium dealing and, if statistics do

[13] See *World's Pictorial News*, 19 April 1924; *Empire News*, 14 November 1926; 22 May, 11, 15 September 1927; 8 September 1929; *John Bull*, 13 February 1926.

not lie, they were correct. Between 1921 and 1923 there were 65 cocaine prosecutions a year. The figure had dropped to five between 1927 and 1929. Over the same periods the opium prosecutions had declined from 148 to 36.

Almost immediately after the conviction of Chang, down went one of his successors. Ah Wong had been his factotum when Chang was running the West End and after his master and mentor had been driven to the East End he took over. It was thought that at the time of his conviction in June that year he was making £100 a week.

The next month the opium den of Chong Sing in Limehouse was raided. When the police burst through the door bells began to ring and the only two people in the house, described as 'such as might have been fashioned for the opium den of a mandarin', were Chong Sing and his brother New Mok Sing. There were a number of warm pipes and the other smokers had disappeared through a series of secret passages. Chong Sing received three months' hard labour and was recommended for deportation. It was thought that his brother was not involved in dealing and he was fined £3 or 21 days. The fine was paid. The police believed they had finished another major dealer.

The public galleries of the magistrates' courts were invariably packed with members of the Chinese community when the drug and gaming cases were heard. Reports often speak of stoic English women, forever outcasts from their own society, watching the sentencing of their husbands. In his book of reminiscences of his life as a London magistrate Horace Cancellor, who spent much of his time sitting at Thames Magistrates' Court before and after the First World War, wrote in his chapter 'The Heathen Chinee':

Distasteful as such unions seem to our Western minds, the magistrates seldom receive complaints against husbands from white wives. On the other hand the women often give evidence to screen their yellow spouses and show in court that they have taken lessons in the art of lying from their lords and masters. They appeared laden with jewellery. They were treated well unless they were perceived to fancy another man.

He was not alone in his dislike of mixed marriages. The Rev. W.H. Lax, who had a parish in Limehouse, displayed a singularly un-Christian attitude to some of his parishioners.

There is something inherently revolting about this union of European girls with black men or Asiatics, and by entering into such unions and marriages girls are fomenting a danger which, I am convinced, will give rise to a great conflagration in the future.

The Chinaman is a gregarious creature. He will not live alone. When an English girl takes on the responsibilities of a Chinaman's household she finds that he will bring ten or twenty men to the house.

He lives in a crowd. The crowd will probably live with him, and while it is not my desire to indulge in wild charges I am certain that these girls suffer a moral degradation which, in many cases, ends in their becoming the hireling of any Chinaman who happens to desire her.

The streets abound with little, slant-eyed babies with the high cheek-bones of the Celestial, yet possessing the pink-and-white colouring of their European mothers. This combination of Asiatic and European qualities is a grave menace to the peace and well-being of the community.[14]

---

[14] Rev. W.H. Lax, 'The Lure of Gambling' in *Empire News*, 3 October 1920. On the other hand Cyril Demarne writes, 'They seemed to be happy marriages and Chinamen could be seen playing with their children in the street on warm summer evenings.' 'The way it was – the recollections of a Poplar boy' in *East End – Then and Now*, p. 99. Annie Lai says that there were only three Chinese married women in Limehouse in the late 1920s.

But the magistrate Cancellor seems to have been fascinated by one particular man:

> In the centre of the space a tall thin Chinaman always stood in the front row . . . I felt sure that he was there for the set purpose of exerting will power on my mind.

He turned out to be the treasurer of the community, who came to pay the fines, but this did not satisfy Cancellor: 'No doubt he was trying to hypnotise me into making the penalties light.'

He nearly obtained his revenge when the man appeared in the dock on gaming charges and Cancellor saw it as the opportunity to send him to prison. Unfortunately he was only present and not taking part in the gaming, so the kindly magistrate was thwarted.[15]

All sorts of excuses were offered for possessing opium, mostly that it was used by the Chinese as an alleviation of consumption; but one of the most ingenious, if ultimately unsuccessful, was that of James David Jackson, a commission agent, who said his wife had picked up the bottle at Goodwood Races and after winning three bets decided it was a lucky charm and to keep it as a mascot. Six months.[16]

That same month in 1923 the police struck another blow to drug operations in the East End.

> The negro rolled, struck, kicked and bit like a savage. He looked like a beast of prey and almost foamed at

---

[15] H.L. Cancellor, 'The Heathen Chinee' in *The Life of a London Beak*, pp. 61 et seq.
[16] *Empire News*, 29 July 1923.

the mouth . . . the raving maniacal nigger was brace-
leted.[17]

This dispassionate account was of the arrest of Jack Kelson
after buying cocaine from a Chinese café on Limehouse
Causeway. At the time he was almost certainly operating for
his superior, Eddie Manning. Kelson, who had been looked on
as one of the safest runners between Limehouse and the West
End, like Manning also dabbled in the White Slave trade.

Eddie Manning is often regarded as a successor to the
Chang dynasty but in reality he was a contemporary. He
was considered to be one of the Big Four dealers in the West
End, obtaining his supplies from Limehouse. Born in Jamaica,
his real name was McManning and he came to England in
around 1914, working as a labourer until 1916 when he was
discharged for ill-health. He was then a jazz drummer, and an
actor in small-time touring reviews, at the same time running
prostitutes and selling drugs from his flat in Lisle Street. The
other three in the quartet were Alexander Iassonides, his wife
Zenovia and his nephew Leonidhas. Unfortunately for the

---

[17] *Empire News*, 29 July 1923. This was fairly typical reporting of the
time. In the issue of 9 September that year, 'In black clutches at seaport
towns', Rosie Sherella, who had drifted into Limehouse and bigamously
married a series of men, concluded her story of degradation with the
words, 'I am safe from the black man now forever.' Overall the popular
papers offered an almost undilutedly hostile and racist approach. For
example girls were forever telling of their ordeals in Chinese laundries;
e.g. 'In a Chinaman's House' in *Empire News*, 17 October 1920, 'Drugging
Mystery of Chinese Laundry' in *Empire News*, 26 November 1922 and
Lily Siddall, 'My Experiences in a Chinese Laundry' in *Empire News*, 3
December 1922. Miss Siddall had the misfortune to be employed in the
Sheffield laundry in which Lee Doon killed the owner Sing Lee. In fact
it was her worries over the disappearance of her employer which caused
the police to make serious inquiries. For an account of the case see J.P.
Bean, *Crime in Sheffield*. Even when the girls did not tell their stories but
merely appeared in court to support their husbands and lovers, they were
described in terms such as 'Vice was written plainly in their dimming
eyes and whitened cheeks' in 'Menace of Darkness' in *Empire News*, 12
September 1920.

quartet Manning became fascinated by Madame Iassonides, by all accounts a striking woman who, much to the fury of her husband, eventually went to live with him.

In September 1920 Manning received a sentence of 16 months for shooting at three men in a fracas at Cambridge Circus. If the witnesses can be relied on, Manning had been in Mrs Fox's Restaurant in Little Compton Street when 'American' Frank Miller – who was a pimp, and had just been acquitted at the Old Bailey of receiving – tried to abstract, extort probably being too strong a word, £1 from him and insulted a girl by throwing a lighted cigar in her face. Manning chased after and shot at him and the others.

It was his first conviction and Mr Justice Greer took the view that he had been more sinned against than sinning, saying how much he regretted having to sentence a man of respectable character but that foreigners had to be taught that guns could not be discharged on London streets. Even then the police were not totally fooled. There was much more in the matter than met the eye, said the officer in the case. It may be that the men had been turned on Manning by the jealous Iassonides. Certainly that was suggested later. Two of the 'victims', Miller and Charles Turnick, said to be his brother, disappeared after giving evidence in the police court. Manning cannot have been doing too well at the time. He was living with a prostitute, Doreen Taylor, and some fifteen pawn tickets were found when her premises were searched.

On his release he went to live with Madame Iassonides, and now cocaine injections at ten shillings each and lessons in how to apply the drug were available at the Berwick Street cellar café owned by the pair. On the side Manning ran prostitutes and also illegal and crooked roulette parties, as well as '. . . dope orgies [at his flat in Lisson Street] at which scenes of the wildest debauchery were witnessed'.[18]

[18] *Empire News*, 'The Dark Tempter of Chorus Girls', 22 July 1923.

He had also come to notice over the death of Freda Kempton and now a former army officer, Eric Goodwin, died from a drug overdose at Manning's new flat in Hallam Street, Marylebone. He gave evidence at the inquest to the effect that he had never known Goodwin take drugs, but Manning was now well in the frame.

A successful police raid on Mrs Iassonides' flat at 33 Regent's Park Road in April 1922 resulted in her receiving six months and her deportation. She was followed in quick succession by her nephew in the September and the estranged Alexander the following March. He had survived one case when drugs were found beneath the stair carpet of the Soho café run by his nephew. A tame doctor appeared to give evidence, saying that Alexander was a kind man whom he could not conceive being involved in drugs. The magistrate said it would be unsafe to convict.[19]

Manning also received six months for the Regent's Park raid, but since he was British he could not be deported. After their release Madame I. and her nephew retreated to Paris from where she maintained a steady correspondence with Manning.

Just before the downfall of Kelson, Manning received 3 years' penal servitude for possession of opium, but he continued to survive if not to flourish for some years more. In 1927 he was fined for harbouring prostitutes and given six months for possessing cocaine. Then in 1929 he received what would be his final sentence. By now he too had been chased out of the drug-dealing world and was into receiving. Property worth £2,000, the result of a number of burglaries, was found at his flat. He was sentenced to another 3 years' penal servitude and died in E2 Ward at Parkhurst on the Isle of Wight, apparently from the ravages of syphilis. One of his great fears was of owls and when dying he heard one hoot.

[19] *News of the World*, 15 October 1922.

'His body shook and his eyes rolled in abject terror.'[20]

Part of both the Manning and Chang empires passed into the control of William Allan Porter, who had been another pair of safe hands on the Limehouse run until, in December 1924, he was found with the equivalent of 2,000 doses of morphine on him and he received 12 months. He tried to bribe his co-defendant – a young Irishman, John Mason – to take the blame, and when the offer was turned down threatened to attack him in the dock. Porter had apparently always been a lieutenant rather than a captain and after his sentence he, too, faded into oblivion.

The so-called White Queen of Limehouse, May Roberts, was arrested at the end of December 1922 and charged with being in possession of black opium. She and an Albert Ellis were arrested at Ludgate Circus after a dramatic car chase through Trafalgar Square and along the Strand and Fleet Street. She had been followed since leaving her home in Limehouse. Ellis, a man of good character, appeared at Marlborough Street Police Court where conveniently at the back of the court he apparently said to the arresting officer, in the sort of remark which might well be regarded by the cynical as a 'verbal':

> I have been a mug. I had best get it over. Can I be dealt with here? I don't mind getting a fine.

No doubt he did mind, however, when he received six months' imprisonment, as did the lady herself. In fact, Ellis had not been a mere mug. He had been actively engaged in the dope trade for several years along with his brother David Ernest Ellis and the sinister Max Faber, who eventually swindled the Ellis brothers and his Chinese partner with whom he ran a brothel in Hamburg, before retreating to

---

[20] 'Black Dope King's Spell over White Women' in *Empire News*, 15 September 1929. Val Davis, *Phenomena in Crime*, p. 90. For an account of the Cambridge Circus shooting see also PRO MEPO 3 424.

Montreal where he was an associate of some seriously big-time players. David Ellis had been convicted and fined in December 1915 on charges of illegally exporting opium.[21]

May Roberts was born and married in Liverpool. Before her marriage she had met Wun Loo, an assistant doctor on a ship, and after he had shown her Liverpool's Chinatown she became enamoured with him and left her husband. He died in a drug-dealer's fight, and her next amour was killed in Rotterdam either in a quarrel over drugs or possibly over her charms. She seems to have been a woman of immense character and some physical strength because she survived several attacks from other women and once when she had been swindled out of a drug deal went in search of her robbers with a gun. She is also credited with stopping the drug wars in Liverpool and putting together some sort of peace amongst the various gangs. At one stage it was suggested by the police that the distribution of the entire opium traffic out of England for consumption by the Chinese abroad was in her hands. Eventually she came to London where the newspapers referred to her as either the White Queen of Limehouse or the Queen of the Yellow Men.

In a reply which has all the hallmarks of the hand of an experienced journalist composing it, when asked about her predilection she said:

> Whatever may be his faults the Chinaman has the power of fascinating a woman and of holding her in a way the White man cannot do. There is a subtle charm, a romance and a

[21] Max Faber or Farber, known as Sheba Max and Big M, was the head of Maxie's Gang in Montreal, a friend of William Mack, alias Paul Webster, and Harry Stone who was shot by guards and left to die in a failed wages snatch in Montreal on 1 April 1924. 'He [Farber] usually dresses rather poorly, may have a fur hat [Mink]. He bears all the appearance of a Jew . . . He is an exceptionally cunning scoundrel. In the drug traffic his part usually has been the handling of the money, leaving the passing of the poison to be performed by others.' PRO MEPO 3 469. For an account of Stone's part in the early days of crime in Montreal see James Morton, *Gangland International*.

poetry about his lovemaking that makes the efforts of the average Westerner seem ridiculous. I have been told again and again that I ought not to have anything to do with Chinamen; that they have a degrading effect. I cannot see it. I prefer Chinamen to the Englishmen or other white men I have known. This preference may have its origin in some wild primitive instinct that may or may not be a reversion to a barbaric past as I have been told by a missionary, but the fact is that the preference is deeply ingrained in my soul and I cannot get away from it no matter how much I try . . . I am not going to alter in this respect for anyone.[22]

When she was released from prison in the summer of 1923 she went to live back in Limehouse with another woman from Liverpool, Julia An Kitt, who had also married a Chinese, Choy An Kitt. It was all of five months before she in turn was arrested, claiming the drug had been planted. For a period she was regarded as the chief figure in running between the East and West Ends. She also had been born in Liverpool and . . .

. . . for many years her worst fault was a flighty disposition and an insatiable thirst for the fleeting pleasures of life. No matter how carefully she chose her course, the moth that plays constantly near the flames of human passion must some day pay the penalty of scorched wings. And so it was with Julia.

A man robbed her of her honour and then cast her aside like an old glove . . . Presently she cut loose definitely from home ties and became a 'woman of the town'. She did not

[22] 'White Queen of Yellow Dope Smugglers: Mystery of Woman's Strange Choice' in *Reynolds' News*, 14 January 1923. See also *Empire News*, 31 December 1922 and *Reynolds' News*, 7 January 1923. Another girl involved in the trade and who began her career as a lure for seamen so they could be robbed was Lily Ellis, who in October 1920 received 5 years for burglary and was regarded as one of the best thieves of the period. *Empire News*, 3 October 1920.

like any of the Chinese and Japanese seamen with whom she mixed, only accepting their admiration because it was profitable and with a secret feeling of contempt. But fate tricked her, for the lure of the Eastern character was stronger than her own will.[23]

She and Choy An Kitt had two children, and at first she acted as a runner for her husband before branching out on her own. Dressed as a poor Chinese woman, she would move around the Limehouse restaurants before changing into fashionable clothes for her visits to the West End.

Not long after that, Choy An Kitt left for Hamburg to conduct that end of operations as agent for Choy Loy with whose underling, Lum Chung, May Roberts now took up. An Kitt and Julia remained on good terms and he also supplied her with cocaine obtained from Germany which was much cheaper and on which she was able to make a profit of £10 an ounce. On a good evening she could handle 1 lb. Along with Ellis, Julia An Kitt also received six months.

Running parallel with Brilliant Chang and Manning was the altogether more structured operation of the Japanese, Yasukichi 'Sess' Miyagawa. One account of his career has him as initially the tool of an international syndicate, ensnared by his fascination for white women which had led him into debt and so their clutches. He and his family had an import and export business on Ludgate Hill and this provided excellent cover for the repackaging of the drug. Miyagawa took over the English end of the business, importing from Germany and Switzerland and exporting to France, Japan and India, and again reimporting for consumption here. It was estimated that the contents of a 100 lb consignment could be disposed of within the hour. Given today's huge drug imports Miyagawa's efforts may seem puny, but he was exporting 500 lb of morphine on a regular basis when the average quantity used

[23] 'Snow Queen from East to West End' in *Empire News*, 2 December 1923.

per patient at the London Hospital was 8 ounces a year.

During October 1923 Miyagawa paid £37,000 to a Hamburg-based firm for heroin. He was also receiving substantial amounts of morphine from Switzerland and his monthly profits were thought to be in excess of £25,000, 'most of which was dissipated on a life of excess in the West End'.[24] Eventually morphine was seized at his premises in Ludgate Hill and he received 4 years, coupled with a recommendation that he be deported, at the Old Bailey. His appeal was dismissed on 21 January 1924.

He is described as:

> [an] unassuming little Oriental, boots cracked and down at heel, a threadbare suit, and battered bowler hat, shuffling his melancholy way along the gutters of the East End. Spending but a few coppers on his meals in carmen's pull-ups, sleeping in cheap lodgings, and sometimes in doss-houses – not a detail overlooked in the part he so ably played, that of a down and out.
>
> Yet Sess Miyagawa was a millionaire! Through a pair of horn-rimmed glasses a pair of soft brown eyes peered sadly and timidly. Who would have suspected that such a non-entity was a master criminal, the head and fount of a colossal narcotic trade employing hundreds of lesser crooks.[25]

The last of the old school to go was To Yit who lived at 32 Pennyfields. He had been around since the early 1920s and

[24] *Reynolds' News*, 16 December 1923.
[25] Val Davis, *Phenomena in Crime*, p. 92. Davis met Miyagawa during his sentence in Dartmoor. See also 'Evil Negro Caught' in *News of the World*, 22 July 1923. According to Davis, Miyagawa was succeeded by the German Loffenholtz Brandstaetter. If so Brandstaetter had a long run. He was found hanged in his cabin whilst being extradited to New York in the summer of 1936. This followed information given by Marie de Wendt or Marie Wenn, daughter of a German father and Chinese mother, after she had been picked up by the San Francisco police trying to import opium and had escaped to New York where she was arrested trying to impersonate a passenger on an English liner. See *New York Times*, 11, 14, 30 August; 5 September 1936.

had been associated with practically every Chinese national who had been deported over the years. He had an English wife, Maud Alexandra, in Cane Hill Mental Hospital – admitted, it was said, as a result of his cruelty to her – and two sons.

In September 1929 he racked up the sixth of his convictions for drug and gaming offences but, because of his wife, the magistrate declined to deport him. The police raided his premises again in February 1930 and found nothing, but they then received a letter suggesting that they would find opium if they searched his other premises at 51 Pennyfields. Sunday around 4 p.m. was suggested as the optimum time. This time they struck lucky but, defended by a local solicitor, Edward Fail, To Yit was acquitted. The police agreed that the front door was always kept open and To Yit suggested that the drugs had been planted by the man downstairs who not only disliked him but wanted to take over the whole house. To add insult to injury the man, he said, ran English prostitutes from the basement.[26]

The magistrate may have had doubts but the Home Office had none. 'He is a worthless and particularly crafty type of Chinaman,' wrote an official, suggesting he be deported. What particularly worried them was not so much the opium smoking, although he was forever in clubs in the West End, but the fact that he ran a Fan Tan game at which the English lost their money at great speed.[27]

[26] There was often a good deal of money available to be spent on defence. For example, on 5 August 1921 J.G. Jones KC MP appeared on behalf of a Low Ping You accused of frequenting rather than running an opium den.
[27] Fan Tan, a game played at enormous speed, depends on the total number of buttons or counters left in a jar after a series of withdrawals of four at a time. Another game played at the time in Chinese gambling clubs, and about which the kindly Reverend Lax complained, was Peccapur or Puk-a-pu, meaning plucking pigeons, which was a form of lottery. Stakes were sixpence upwards and prizes of £25 were not uncommon. Cyril Demarne recalls that as a boy he would be sent to place bets in Puk-a-pu gambling shops. See 'The way it was – the recollections of a Poplar boy' in *East End – Then and Now*, pp. 98–9.

A. Maxwell, a Home Office official, wrote in a memorandum of 10 January 1933:

> Is To Yit the organising spirit, and are the people in the West End, his tools? Or is To Yit a tool for more important persons? If so, what are we doing about the more important persons?[28]

Clearly someone thought he was a mover and shaker for, after a short inquiry, along with his sons Edward and Alexander he was put on the SS *Glenamoy*, bound for Hong Kong, at 1 p.m. on 22 April at King George V Docks. Even then there were fears that To Yit might escape deportation. The boat was in a collision as it sailed down the Thames and had to return to the dock. Could the crafty Chinaman possibly have engineered this to effect his escape? The police hurried to the dock to make sure he stayed on board until the boat sailed the following Wednesday. After it did, a note was sent to the authorities in Hong Kong warning them of the impending arrival of this thoroughly unsavoury character.[29]

Not all Chinese kept their front doors open to welcome customers. When Lai Chi (Chee)'s house at 17 Limehouse Causeway was raided in November 1929 the police had some trouble getting in. At the foot of the stairs there was

[28] In fact, in one of its less anti-Celestial moods, the *Empire News* had posed this question thirteen years earlier: '. . . the men who control the traffic are not Chinese, they are Jew and Gentile scum.' 'Brain of the Secret "Dope" Traffic' in *Empire News*, 3 October 1920. It may have been Faber and the Ellis brothers to whom they were referring. Another East Ender Monty Cohen was a candidate for being behind the trade. A known associate of Manning and Madame Iassonides, in September 1923 he received 4 years' penal servitude, the longest sentence so far handed out for trafficking. Instead of solely preying on women he had used unemployed former servicemen, paying them £1 a day to distribute the drugs. See 'Women Slaves of Snow King' in *Empire News*, 16 September 1923.
[29] PRO MEPO 3 1049.

an electric bell-push concealed under the linoleum. On the first floor there was a stout plank door across the staircase, locked and bolted. A trapdoor had been lowered over the staircase top and bolted with iron bolts. He received the standard six months and was deported. The police were well pleased; they considered him to have been running a major opium den.[30]

But by now the authorities had cleared most of the large-scale Chinese dealers from the East End – that, or they had moved to other cities. For instance, one of the old Pennyfields school was found in Cardiff with 1½ lb of raw opium strapped in each armpit.

It may seem from the six-month sentences handed out at the time as compared with those convicted of drug-trafficking today that the courts dealt leniently with the inhabitants of Chinatown. But it was the deportation order which accompanied them rather than the almost tariff six months' hard labour which was the real penalty. In financial terms the price of an ounce of cocaine was the annual wage of a girl in service, and those at the upper end of the trade such as Chang and Miyagawa made fortunes.

By the 1930s much of the drug trade in Europe was in the hands of the Eliopoulos family, Greeks from Alexandria of whom Elie was reputed to be the head and whose London offices seemed to be the Hellenic Club in Notting Hill. He was said to have been the chief accountant of the Constantinople Gasworks which he had defrauded. They had connections throughout Europe not only with the East End dealers but with Paul Carbone in Marseilles and with the French concession in Shanghai, as well as links with the United States and Canada. The substantial hold of the Chinese on the East

---

[30] PRO MEPO 3 434. For other accounts of devices to keep the police at bay see *Evening Standard*, 15 November 1929; *Daily Express*, 16 November 1929 and *The Star*, 18 February 1930.

End drug trade had effectively been broken.[31]

One of the last survivors, Annie Lai, lived to feature in a television documentary. She had married Yuen Sing Lai in 1923 after arriving in Limehouse two years earlier. When he was deported to America following a conviction for wounding she took up dealing, turned to the drug herself, became hooked and became a prostitute to support her habit. Apparently, her husband died in Hollywood in another fight shortly after his arrival. She maintained that there were prostitutes at Charlie Brown's pub, the Railway Tavern, but never in Chinatown. Many of her problems, she said, came from officials who expected her to repay their lack of interest in her dealing with sexual favours.[32]

Throughout the period there was an unhealthy trade in smuggling Chinese into the country. By the end of the 1920s the price was £50 a head.[33] By the end of the Second World War the Chinese had been largely absorbed into the East End community – if not socially, then as the main providers of alternative medicine.

In his articles in 1960 on the rebuilding of the East End, Tom Pocock thought that there was probably only one regular Chinese opium smoker left in Limehouse.[34] Others were perhaps not so sure:

There was opium dens well after World War Two. Then in the sixties the Chinese moved up West. Before they moved to Soho they were a very strong force in the East End. They

[31] PRO MEPO 3 1047.
[32] See *East End News*, 14 February 1930. She may well have been correct about Charlie Brown's public house. Although he was a popular figure in the East End there were stories about gentlemen visiting the back rooms. One of his possessions was the opium pipe Billie Carleton used before her death, and it was questioned from where he had obtained the item.
[33] 'Traffic in Human Cargoes' in *Empire News*, 12 February 1928.
[34] Tom Pocock, 'The New East End' in *Evening Standard*, 17 November 1960.

didn't sort of integrate, kept their own counsel. They'd go off to Gerrard Street to gamble. There was a lot of Chinese gambling down there.

Then there was the Chinese herb shops. If you were ill you went to them to cure boils.[35]

[35] Michael Bailey: conversation with the author, April 1999.

8

Oswald Mosley meets Jack Spot – or does he?

The rise of Jack Spot to be one of the two Kings of the Underworld – the other was Billy Hill – in the immediate post-War era can be traced to the mid-1930s and the rise of Sir Oswald Mosley's British Union of Fascists. More particularly it can be traced to the so-called battle of Cable Street when it seems that the whole of Stepney rose as one to prevent a march by the Fascists. Spot claimed he played a great part in stemming this tide of evil which threatened to engulf the East End, and there is no doubt whatsoever that he traded off the story of how he felled Roughneck, a professional wrestler bodyguard of Mosley – so becoming the Champion of the Jews, which he undoubtedly was. As the years have passed, however, it has become clear that he did no such thing and his story, as indeed much of the battle, is simply folk legend. Perhaps more importantly it is becoming increasingly accepted that the so-called battle between the East Enders and the Fascists which resulted in the expulsion of the latter never took place. There was certainly a confrontation, but it involved the police on one side and left-wing sympathisers on the other.

Mosley was born in 1896 and educated at Winchester before going to Sandhurst. In the First World War he was commissioned in the 16th Lancers and was sent to Ireland from where, on his application, he was transferred to the Royal Flying Corps. In 1918 he was elected to Parliament as Conservative member for Harrow and for a time was regarded as a young high-flyer. By 1922 he had quarrelled with the hierarchy and stood as an Independent, defeating the official candidate. In 1920 he had married Lady Cynthia Curzon, daughter of the statesman Lord Curzon, a lady of Jewish extraction who was an ardent Socialist. Under her aegis he converted to Socialism and won the Smethwick seat for the party in 1926. In 1928 he succeeded to the baronetcy and from then on moved right and was duly expelled from the party. In 1932 he founded the British Union of Fascists, known as the Blackshirts – the uniform was said to have been copied from that worn by fencers at which sport Mosley, despite a limp following a flying accident, was of almost international standard. At its height, the movement had some 20,000 members, mostly young and from white and light-blue-collar workers, in 400 branches throughout the country.

A meeting at Olympia in June 1934 provoked considerable opposition from Communists, and with police presence at a minimum there were angry complaints at the way demonstrators and hecklers were handled by the Blackshirt security forces. In September of that year Mosley endeavoured to hold a meeting in Hyde Park, but with an estimated 150,000 anti-Fascist demonstrators present this meeting broke up before he spoke.

Then, after a series of well-supported marches through the East End which had attracted little opposition, Mosley decided to hold a major rally on 4 October 1936 to mark the fourth anniversary of the founding of the party. The intention was that the Blackshirts should assemble at Royal Mint Street at 2.30 p.m. for an inspection by Mosley. This would be followed by a march through the East End and he would speak at Salmon Lane, Limehouse, at 5 p.m.; Stafford Road, Bow, half an hour later; Victoria Park Square at 6 p.m. and Aske Street, Shoreditch, at 6.30 p.m. Even his greatest detractors regarded him as a charismatic speaker and the meetings were bound to be well attended. Now opposition was mounted against him and his march.

The popular view is that it was the local community which rose spontaneously against this right-wing leader, but that is not so. It required a great deal of organisation by the Communists to achieve their undoubted success. Speaking a decade later H.W. Carver, chairman of the Stepney Borough Communists, took the credit on behalf of his party:

> It was the Communist Party which organised that struggle and it was in the face of the opposition of their own leaders that many Labour people joined the fight.[1]

Appeals by the mayors of the East London boroughs for the march to be banned were ignored by Sir John Simon, the Home Secretary, who relied on the police to keep the potential combatants apart. The Commissioner, Sir Philip Gale, set up field headquarters off Tower Hill and 6,000 constables and the whole of the mounted division were drafted in to the area.

The Blackshirts began to assemble at 1.25 p.m. but they had been pre-empted by a group of some 500 anti-Fascists who were already there, with the *Daily Worker* being sold in Leman and Cable Streets. By 2.15 it was estimated that there were around 15,000 anti-Fascists in the Aldgate area, about half of whom had blocked the Commercial Road at Gardiner's

[1] *ELA*, 26 December 1947.

Corner, making clenched-fist salutes and shouting in echo of the French at Verdun, 'They Shall Not Pass.' At 3 p.m. it was thought that the Blackshirts, still in Royal Mint Street, now totalled around 1,900 including women and cadets and four bands. About 300 of them were in ordinary dress.

Mosley arrived to review the troops at 3.30 p.m. and shouting by his supporters was countered by the singing of the 'Internationale'. Now Sir Philip decided things had gone far enough and forbade the march. Instead Mosley would be allowed to march West through the deserted City and the Blackshirts moved off at 4 p.m. ending at Somerset House in the Strand at 4.30 p.m. Later Mosley spoke from the BUF Headquarters in Great Smith Street:

> Brother Blackshirts. Today the Government of Britain has surrendered to Red Terror. Today the Government of Britain has surrendered to Jewish corruption. The British Union will never surrender . . .

And more in the same vein.

The actual battle did not concern them. A barrier had been erected in Cable Street and a lorry was overturned; timber was expropriated from a builder's yard, along with bricks with which to pelt the police. Broken glass was strewn across the road to hamper and injure the police horses.

> [So] we went along to Aldgate and saw for ourselves the Communists with their clenched fists rolling marbles under the police horses' hooves and stuffing broken glass up their noses to bring the mounted police down and we were really disgusted. I made up my mind from then on to be an active member.[2]

The so-called Battle of Cable Street never took place.

2 Gladys Walsh, *Comrade*, August 1999.

The only people involved were Tommy Moran and a few who had arrived with him to set up the assembly point. Hundreds fell on them.

I had just arrived in London from Lancashire and went to the place of assembly. None of the thousands of supporters there were involved. The battle was between the police and the Communists who had been organising all over the country for a fortnight.

Mosley's attitude was to obey the law until we could change it so when Sir Philip Gale ordered him not to march he obeyed that order.[3]

For Mosely it was a case of *reculer pour mieux sauter*. Ten days later he did march effectively through the East End. According to John Warburton:

He held a meeting in Victoria Park Square; an unannounced meeting but people knew Mosley was coming that night. The message flashed through. At the end he was going to speak in Limehouse. He was told he couldn't march there. 'Very well,' he said, 'I'll walk.' And the crowds followed him. As he walked the couple of miles there were crowds behind him and singing. Shouts of 'Good old Mosley', people leaning out of their downstairs windows to try to shake his hand. There was this great mass movement of support. I don't suppose there was more than 50 people wearing black shirts that night.

A Special Branch report of November 1936 concluded:

The general cry was that the entire population of East London had risen against Mosley and had declared that he and his followers should not pass and that they did not pass owing to the solid front presented by the workers of East London. This statement is, however, far

---

[3] John Warburton, interview with author, July 1999.

from reflecting accurately the state of affairs . . . There is abundant evidence that the Fascist movement has been steadily gaining ground in many parts of East London and has strong support in such districts as Stepney, Shoreditch, Bethnal Green, Hackney and Bow.

There can be no doubt that the unruly element in the crowd . . . was very largely Communist-inspired. A number of well-known active communists were seen at, or near, points where actual disorder occurred.

While attempts by the Communist Party to raise enthusiasm over the 'Fascist defeat' were comparative failures the BUF, during the week following the banning of their march, conducted the most successful series of meetings since the beginning of the movement. In Stepney, Shoreditch, Bethnal Green, Stoke Newington and Limehouse, crowds estimated at several thousands of people (the highest being 12,000) assembled and accorded the speakers an enthusiastic reception; opposition was either non-existent or negligible and no disorder took place.[4]

There is no doubt, however, that conditions in the East End following the Depression were appalling:

My father was out of work for ten years. I couldn't say what he actually did for a living. He didn't have any specific trade. You chanced your arm and you got a shilling where you could. He laboured to keep our heads above water.

He would earn a shilling as a bookie's runner or a look-out for a game of dice or a tossing-ring. It was his job to be able to recognise the police in plain clothes. Then he'd shout, 'Split,' which was the word then for a policeman.

[4] PRO MEPO 2 3043. The report went on to say that membership of the BUF had increased by 2,000 since the march. Other meetings during the month held by anti-Fascist bodies such as the Young Communists League had been closed by the police to prevent breaches of the peace or because of lack of support.

We were means tested. I used to sell papers as a kid
and I got a penny a night and tuppence on a Saturday
because it was the football edition. My family was brought
to the means test because of that and they had to go before
the Board.

You had to sell everything before there was any money.
If there was two of you and four chairs you had to sell
two of the chairs because you didn't need them.[5]

It was as a result of these conditions that Mosley undoubtedly
gained a foothold in the East End.

For a fledgeling party the turnout in the East End in its
favour was high, and old members of the Movement believe
that had there been no war Mosley would have received
greater support. Part of his appeal was undoubtedly the anti-
Semitic feeling in the East End. Mosley had by now shed his
Jewish wife and, moving ever further right, had married Lady
Diana Guinness, the third of the Mitford sisters, at a ceremony
in Joseph Goebbels' private home in Berlin. In his 1938 leaflet
Tomorrow We Live, he suggested that the Jews were forming a
state within a state and that those who regarded themselves
as Jews first or who 'engaged in practices alien to the British
character' must leave the country. The 'Final Solution' was a
home in some waste but potentially fertile area.[6]

There was terrific support in the East End for the British
Union from 1936 to 1939. How else can you explain
the high percentage of votes we received in the LCC
elections? These voters weren't wild young men because

[5] Fred Bailey, interview with author, July 1999. In the March 1937
elections the BUF polled 23 per cent of the vote in Bethnal Green;
16.3 per cent in Limehouse and 14.8 per cent in Shoreditch. '. . . the
size of their vote was a surprise even to those in touch with the East
End', *The Observer*, 7 March 1937.
[6] *Tomorrow We Live*, p. 109. See also *Action*, 21 January 1939, 'Let the
Jews beware, for the whispers may very well become a great shout for
the removal of his race from our shores.'

only householders could vote and so they were steady married men. I think it was because rightly or wrongly they didn't like the people who a generation earlier had come from Russia and Poland and who now lived in Aldgate and Whitechapel. They saw anti-Union fighting as an attempt to smash people speaking British working-class sense.

What did they hope to get from Mosley? Forget his policies of what should be done. He brought them hope. In those days the ordinary working-class father was out of work. There was not enough to eat. They'd been forgotten. There was no hope. The one thing they had was patriotism and to them Mosley brought that hope.[7]

As it was, there was little reporting of his meetings even by his champion Lord Rothermere of the *Daily Mail*. The Public Order Act 1936 banned the wearing of political uniforms and Mosley was also suffering, as has many a gang leader, from defections by his lieutenants. William Joyce, who would become Lord Haw-Haw, and John Beckett were sacked by him and formed a splinter group, the National Socialist League. After one final major rally at the Earl's Court Exhibition Hall on 16 July 1939 he toured the country offering the choice: 'War, or peace by negotiation.'

Mosley was interned along with a considerable number of other senior officers of the movement on 23 May 1940 under regulation 18B. He was released in 1943 on the grounds of ill-health. Others who were sent to a camp at Ascot racecourse encountered the Sabinis along with their henchman Papa Pasquale who assisted in keeping order.[8]

After the War the BUF tried without the same success to re-establish itself in the East End. In fact the British Union

[7] John Warburton, *supra*.
[8] For an account of internment under Regulation 18B see A.W.B. Simpson, *In the Highest Degree Odious*. Mosley retired to Paris where he died on 3 December 1980 at the age of 84. William Joyce was executed as a traitor.

Movement, son of BUF, grew out of the British League of Ex-Servicemen who held a number of meetings throughout the East End and indeed, South and North-west London. They were opposed by the 43 Group which had also started up after the War.

> It was supposed to have been 43 Jewish ex-Servicemen but some had never seen the war. Most of the violent battles in Ridley Road were not with Mosley but with the League which eventually was taken under Mosley's wing.[9]

BUM marches were held, notably a May Day march in Dalston in 1948, and there were a number of public houses such as the Rising Sun, the Bladebone and the Green Gate, all in Bethnal Green, which for a time welcomed the Movement. The town halls, however, did not. Bethnal Green followed the Limehouse stance.

Union organiser Fred Bailey asked:

> Is it because the Union Movement dared to challenge and expose the Stepney Council and the Councillors in the housing scandal of Cayley Street?

But no one replied.[10]

> The British Union faded away simply because Mosley's ideas of union in Europe were too far advanced for people to understand. He was interested in tomorrow. People aren't visionaries. They're captured on bread-and-butter politics. He was always twenty years advanced in his thinking. It was very hard for members of the movement to grasp what he was advocating. But now more and more people are grasping the idea of Europeanisation.

---

[9] Fred Bailey, 25 August 1999.
[10] *ELA*, 28 August 1958.

He wasn't the ogre with horns sticking out of his head as they made him out to be.

He was never anti-Jewish. He attacked certain Jews and Jewish things they did but he didn't attack, say, Jewish fish-shop owners. It was people who were working against the interests of this country. He would attack anyone like that. It's the same today. If you are attacking a black drug dealer it's interpreted as you're being against all coloured people. That's rubbish.

I suppose there was a certain amount of anti-Semitism. People resented what was going on and the way the East End was being used as a sweatshop. It was particularly because people couldn't get jobs. It wasn't violent. It was verbal more than anything else. It's the same today with the Kosovans. The resentment was an economic thing.[11]

Many may think that this shows a capacity for self-deception or that time does indeed dim the memory.

When it came to it, Jack Spot may not have had the national appeal Mosley attracted for a time but he reigned far longer. An East End figure recalls:

Spotty's father's name was Comacho and he could not speak English. He was given the name Colmore which was changed to Comer. He lived in Myrdle Street parallel with Romford Street.

Jacob (sometimes John) Colmore, also known as Jacob Comacho, also known as Jack Comer and best known as Jack Spot was around a long time. Not as long as the Sabinis, but getting on for 20 years as one of the 'Bosses of the Underworld'. In fact that title was a contributing factor which led to the violence which ended his reign.

One of four children, Spot, so called because he liked to say he was on it if help was needed – either that or more

11 Fred Bailey, 25 August 1999.

prosaically it was a childhood nickname because he had a mole on his cheek – was born on 12 April 1912 in Myrdle Street, Whitechapel, the son of Polish immigrants. His brother was a tailor, his sister a court dressmaker. At 15 he became a bookie's runner and the next year joined forces with a leading figure of East End protection rackets. Strictly small-time, together they protected the Sunday-morning stallholders in Petticoat Lane. He fell out with the man and they fought, leaving Spot the winner. Now he called himself the King of Aldgate.

After a short spell as a partner with Dutch Barney, an East End bookmaker, he joined forces with a housebreaker, acting as his look-out and minder. This ended with an appearance at Middlesex Quarter Sessions when amazingly, since he admitted to around forty offences, he was bound over. He returned to bookmaking and the racecourses.

For a time he ran a typical fairground scam called 'Take a Pick' at the major race meetings. The mug punters paid 6d. to pull a straw with a winning number from a cup. If they were extremely fortunate they won a cheap prize, whilst Spot cleared between £30 and £40 a day. Later the enterprise was extended to Petticoat Lane where 'Take a Pick' earned him another £50 a morning. He was also an active bookmaker on the free course. On a bad day he welshed, leaving before paying out on the last race. The old-time jockey Jack Leach may well have had Spot in mind when he wrote in advice to racegoers, 'Never bet with a bookmaker if you see him knocking spikes in his shoes.'[12]

Certainly he protected the Jewish shopkeepers against Mosley's Blackshirts when over the next few months there were marches through the East End, but they were obliged to pay up to £10 to ensure their premises were not damaged

---

[12] Welshing was common. When Alfred Solomons was accused of the murder of Barney Blitz, the prosecution proved three cases of welshing at Windsor races to show his bad character.

in the demonstrations. In 1937 he was sentenced to six months' imprisonment for causing grievous bodily harm to a Blackshirt during one such march. It was to be the only prison sentence he received in his career. When he was released he became an enforcer, collecting subscriptions for an East End Stall Traders Fund run by Larry Sooper. This was a private association formed by stall owners who kept the Depression at bay by refusing to let any other new trader break in and set up a stall.[13]

His reign in the East End was not without skirmishes. The father of Bernie Perkoff, who established the fashionable London firm of solicitors Peters & Peters which represented Spot throughout most of his career, ran a pub in Whitechapel patronised by Spot in his earlier days and which was once wrecked by the Sabinis looking for him. A contemporary recalls:

> Spotty wasn't a coward. I met him many times and by then he'd had some fucking terrible seeing to's. Jews weren't liked in the East End and Spot was known by the Jewish mob as a protector. There wasn't a Jew straight or crooked in the East End who didn't know Spot and if a Jew was in trouble he sent for him. On a Sunday I used to see the Jewish stall holders at a café across from Ziggy shouting out in their Jewish accents, 'Is Jacky Spot in here?' They would be queueing up to give him various sums of money which was for what he called Market Traders Associations but which was then just protection money.

One of the many things held against him by supporters of the alternative king, Billy Hill, was his readiness to take his disputes to the courts. He may well have taken a beating from time to time as well as handing them out, but he would also enlist the aid of the police to prosecute his assailants.

---

[13] Hank Jansen, *Jack Spot, Man of a Thousand Cuts*.

During the War he served for a short time in the Royal Artillery stationed in Cornwall, but was given a medical discharge in 1943.

Now it is impossible to trace the accuracy of some of Spot's stories but, according to him, after his discharge he returned to London. Certainly he had an interest in East End gambling because his name appears in the lists of those charged in raids on gaming houses.[14]

But these were relatively small-time operations and Spot gravitated to the West End where the big money was and where he became involved in a fight in a club in the Edgware Road. The man, Edgware Sam – in all Spot's stories the men are Manchester Mike, Newcastle Ned and so forth – ran out of the club, some said to get a gun. Whether Spot believed this or thought that Sam had gone to the police, he feared a prison sentence and fled north to a land where the black market and organised crime were rampant.

Goods were being stolen from the ships at Hull docks and the cash had to be spent somewhere. Where illegal gaming and drinking clubs are established, protection is sure to follow. Spot helped a club owner, Milky, of the Regal Gaming Club in Chapeltown, Leeds, clear out a Polish protection racketeer from his club, then became the owner's bodyguard and, as a reward, was given a pitch at the local greyhound track. He worked as what he described as a 'troubleshooter' for various Northern clubs until he heard that Edgware Sam, with whom he had fought, had been jailed for fraud.[15]

---

[14] See p. 183.

[15] Perhaps fraud is too grand a word. The conviction seems to have been for working the tweedle, the standard short-time con trick of taking a ring into a jeweller's for valuation and then declining to sell it. At the last moment the grifter changes his or her mind and offers the ring once more. This time, however, the ring appraised by the jeweller has been switched and he is now offered a fake in the hope that he will not bother to examine it a second time. In any event Spot returned to London, pleaded self-defence and was acquitted.

Now he was in great demand. He was regularly called back to the North to help club owners in the major cities – so, possibly, earning his nickname. He was 'on the spot'. According to his account of his life he assisted in establishing the proper allocation of pitches at Northern bookmaking tracks, having to deal with such as 'Fred, leader of a big mob in Newcastle' along the way.

> Newcastle Fred was not only a gangster but a racecourse operator as well. He thought he had the say-so on flogging out bookmakers' pitches, but he made a mistake when he tried to get nasty with me and a few of my pals at Pontefract races. There was a battle . . . a proper free for all, and we had settled it before the police and racecourse officials got wise to it. We'd settled Newcastle Fred's business too.[16]

There were other accounts of the story including one from an eyewitness. One bookmaker recorded:

> What Spot doesn't tell is that old Fred celebrated his 65th birthday a few days before Spot bravely kicked him with his pointed shoes into the racecourse dirt covered in blood. That's how courageous Spot was.[17]

Again it is difficult to assess the accuracy of the story. It could be said that the bookmaker who had 'scars tearing across the top of his scalp – relics of the days when he had to fight the slashing gangs who terrorised Britain's racetracks between the wars', was not wholly disinterested. He was Harry White, the son of Alf White who had challenged the Sabinis during the 1930s.

Shortly after the end of the Second World War Spot ran the Botolph Club, a spieler in Aldgate, reputedly taking £3,000

[16] *Daily Sketch*, 29 September 1958.
[17] *Daily Herald*, 8 October 1955.

a week tax-free from illegal gambling. The figure may be accurate; large sums of money changed hands there.

A solicitor's elderly managing clerk remembers:

There was a burglar known as Taters, best screwsman in London.[18] He once went out and did a job, pulled in £7,000 and then went and did it all in a night playing chemmy with a Jewish bookmaker in Spot's club in Aldgate. It was a straight game but mugs always want to beat the finest and they never succeed. Tragedy really.

'We didn't serve drinks,' said Spot, 'drinks interfere with business and they can lead to people taking liberties or starting a battle.'

Spot, who saw himself as a Jewish Godfather in the East End, left an account of how his version of protection worked:

I didn't have to buy nothing. Every Jewish businessman in London made me clothes, give me money, food, drink, everything. Because I was a legend. I was what they call a legend to the Jews. Anywhere they had trouble – anti-Semitic trouble – I was sent for: Manchester, Glasgow, anywhere. Some crook go into a Jewish shop, says gimme clothes and a few quid, the local rabbi says, Go down London and find Jack Spot. Get Jack, he'll know what to do. So they did and I'd go up and chin a few bastards. The Robin Hood of the East End, a couple of taxi drivers told me once. 'You helped everyone,' they said.[19]

But he was still interested in racecourse bookmaking:

In 1948 Teddy Machin took a chopper to Jimmy Wooder at Ascot Races for Spotty. It was all part of a long feud. Before the war him and another beat Spot up and he nicked them,

18 This was George 'Taters' Chatham.
19 Michael Ewing: *Evening Standard*, 6 January 1986.

and both got some bird. That wasn't enough for Spot. In
1943 he cut Jimmy Wooder in a club in the East End,
a very bad cut. Of course Jimmy didn't nick him but
from then on Jimmy could never stop talking about how
Spot had give evidence. That day at the races Jimmy was
working on the bookmaker's box and Teddy Machin just
started cutting him off at the ankles. Jimmy never nicked
him and he didn't retaliate neither. Spot was really above
Billy at the time and Jimmy Wooder just didn't have the
power himself or anyone to go to for help.[20]

The White family had had control of the pitches on the free
course at Ascot, Epsom, Brighton and at the point-to-point
races not yet under the aegis of the Jockey Club and the
National Hunt Committee. It was an arrangement which had
been going for more than 30 years.

Over the years Alf White, Harry's father, had been collecting £2 a pitch from each bookmaker working at the
point-to-points, something which went as a voluntary contribution to the hunt committees which organised the meetings.
Later Harry White expanded the job to include keeping
out welshers and pickpockets as well as a more structured
organisation of the pitches. It was apparently a semi-formal
arrangement which appealed to police, hunt committees and,
no doubt, to Mr White.

Now Spot took over, though exactly how it happened
depends upon the version preferred. This is Harry White's
account as related by Sidney Williams in the *Daily Herald*:

> His fear of Spot began in January 1947 in a club in
> Sackville Street, off Piccadilly. He was drinking with
> racehorse trainer Tim O'Sullivan and a third man.
>
> Spot walked in with ten thugs, went straight up to Harry
> and said, 'You're Yiddified' – meaning he was anti-Jewish.

[20] F. Fraser, *Mad Frank and Friends*, p. 27.

White denied it. He said: 'I have Jewish people among my best friends.' Spot wouldn't listen, and hit him with a bottle. As White collapsed in a pool of blood, the rest of Spot's men attacked O'Sullivan and the third man who was employed by White. O'Sullivan was beaten unconscious and pushed into a fire in the corner of the club. The other man was slashed with razors and stabbed in the stomach.

It is not totally surprising that Spot's version of events is a different one. His account in the *Daily Sketch* reads:

> But the biggest, toughest and most ruthless mob was the King's Cross gang, led by a bookmaker named Harry who had taken over the racecourse protection racket from the Sabini Boys. Their word was law, not only on the racecourses but in the clubs and pubs – even in the fashionable night-clubs of the West End.

He goes on to record that in an unnamed Mayfair club a challenge was thrown down and the King's Cross Mob 'partly wrecked' the place. A few nights later the 'same crowd' returned and were told that Jack Spot was a friend of the Guv'nor. 'F— Jack Spot,' came the answer. 'He doesn't work for us – when we want him we'll call him.'

There were other encounters until:

> We finally ran them down at a place in Sackville Street off Piccadilly. Harry had seven of the toughest of his boys with him when I led my pals into the room. There wasn't any politeness this time. They knew what I'd come for. And I sailed right in.
>
> At the first smack I took at them Harry scarpered. You couldn't see the seat of his trousers for dust . . .[21]

---

[21] *Daily Herald*, 3 October 1955.

Clearly they are both talking about the same incident.

If one accepts White's version there was another fight, this time at the point-to-point races at Bletchley in February 1947. With little difficulty Spot cleared the decks: the £2 pitch fee became £7. For the next eight years he exercised such strict control over point-to-point bookmaking that, for example, at the Puckeridge Hunt meeting in 1955 he refused to let betting take place on the Grand National which was broadcast to the meeting over loudspeakers. Meanwhile Harry White paid him 25 per cent of his winnings.

According to both Hill and Spot, the Whites were finally routed in the week of 9 July 1947 when Hill and Spot united to clear them out of their interests. There had been a previously scheduled meeting as a preliminary to the main event at the Baski–Woodcock fight at Harringay Arena on 8 April that year, but the police had wind of this and had warned both sides to stay out of trouble. Now, according to both Spot and Hill, huge armies were summoned and searched for the Whites. In Spot's tale Harry simply vanished and the gang faded away. Hill has a rather more colourful version which included roasting one of the Whites over the fire.[22]

Each tells the story in almost identical terms, with the emphasis placed on the teller's organisational qualities. This is not actually surprising. After all, each was writing for a different publication. It was this vanity which was finally to tell against Spot.

According to Spot he received a pull from Chief Superintendent Peter Beveridge who had explained that the police were not going to have gang warfare in London.

> When I got back to Aldgate I called the heavy mob together
> at once. 'We've got to pack it up,' I said. 'Get rid of the

---

[22] For the rival versions of the cleansing of the Whites, see *Daily Sketch*, 3 October 1955 and Billy Hill, *Boss of Britain's Underworld*. It seems the Whites were eventually left in control of the greyhound tracks.

ironmongery.' So we collected all the Stens, the grenades, revolvers, pistols and ammunition, loaded them into a lorry and dumped the whole lot into the Thames.[23]

The West End had new owners who ran it for nearly a decade. Both Hill and Spot were essentially businessmen. Accommodations could be reached with anyone and since neither had any serious interest in vice it was easy to continue the *laissez-faire* arrangement with the prostitute-running Messina brothers.

They were peaceful and highly profitable years in 1950 and 1951. Visitors and strangers must have found the West End a rather dull place with no running gang-fights and feuds . . . The truth was that we cleared all the cheap racketeers out. There was no longer any blacking of club owners and restaurant keepers. In fact so peaceful did it all become that there was no gravy left for the small timers.[24]

[23] *Daily Sketch*, 3 October 1955.
[24] Billy Hill, *Boss of Britain's Underworld*, p. 155.

9

Wartime

Amongst East Enders, along with other docklands and to a lesser extent other communities, the Second World War not only produced incredible heroism in the face of repeated bombing which resulted in the destruction of their homes, but also ushered in a new attitude amongst those who would not normally have consorted with criminals.

In terms of wartime criminality the East End was really no different from other cities in Britain. It shared the problems of pilfering from the docks with Glasgow, Liverpool and Belfast. Edward Smithies in his *Crime in Wartime* lists the types of crime committed, adding only the black market to the usual suspects – theft, betting and gaming, prostitution and violence. In theory, under the Defence of the Realm Act the looting of buildings carried the death penalty, but in practice deterrent sentences of up to five years were being passed in 1942.

The *Police Review* thundered against the looters as being 'Human Ghouls ready to profit from the suffering of their fellow men and women'.[1] Its columnist, 'Watchman', went on to remark on the increase in the number of women criminals during the first years of the War, something which had been in decline for some years. The women were charged with looting and fraud. 'Watchman' wished to see a flogging for a first offence and shooting for the second or third.[2] Smithies, however, gives the crime only two brief mentions, pointing out that of 228 cases in the Romford area some 43 per cent were carried out by men in official positions or positions of trust such as ARP (Air Raid Precautions) wardens, police and auxiliary firemen. One of the reasons for the relatively small numbers was that the authorities had anticipated the looting of bombed buildings and consequently had committed their resources to guarding them, leaving unbombed factories and warehouses at the mercy of thieves.[3] So breaking and entering increased during the last years of the War.

What was clear was that there was an inordinate amount of pilfering from the workplace, to a great deal of which employers turned a blind eye. It was only when the level became unacceptable and, later in the War, companies were required to account more closely for the raw materials they obtained, that the losers began prosecuting. In the early years of the War in the Hackney area alone those firms and organisations which suffered included the ARP and borough councils, Ever Ready, tobacco companies, milk depots, London Transport, Bovril, the Post Office, Berger Paints, the Co-op, cinemas and the Metropolitan Police canteens. At the Ever Ready plant in Stoke Newington 13,000 batteries were stolen during a five-week period in 1941. Paint from Bergers, which cost

[1] 'Watchman', 'More notes on the Blitz' in *Police Review*, 7 February 1941.
[2] ibid.
[3] Edward Smithies, *Crime in Wartime*, pp. 49 and 53. The statistics are from the *Romford Recorder*, 31 January 1941. One such case in the area was a 28-year-old removal contractor who, found guilty of looting a house, received a year's hard labour. *Romford Record*, 3 January 1941.

30 shillings a gallon retail, sold for 15 shillings with four shillings going to the insiders. A group known as the Silver Ring was clearing £40 a week. At Shoreditch Sanitary Towels a whole shift of girls was stopped at the exit and their bags searched.[4]

It was not, of course, a phenomenon unique to the area, but with rationing and food shortages it created whole new markets in which the criminal and quasi-criminal could flourish.

> If anyone could get a bit of extra bacon then they were involved in the black market. My wife she would go all the way to the Elephant [from the East End] to buy silk stockings if she heard there were some on offer.[5]

Alcohol and tobacco were prime requirements, as were clothing and material which otherwise required coupons, themselves a target. In 1942 a tobacco company based in Hackney was losing some two million cigarettes a year at a cost of about £8,000, at that time the price of a small row of houses. Some of these thefts were of course for personal use and some for small-time barter, but a very large percentage of the goods found their way onto the black market.

It was now that the target of the professional criminal changed. As Smithies points out, no longer was the private home of the rich man the prime target; now the factory, the warehouse and the distributive network were the objectives and the proceeds went to supply the black market. And

---

[4] ibid, p. 31. Melanie McGrath recalls her grandfather was an ARP warden who spent his nights fishing and poaching game in Essex. 'By the late forties he was the only café owner in the East End to drive a Cadillac,' 'In Grandfather's Footsteps' in the *Guardian Weekend*, 20 September 1997.

[5] Fred Bailey in conversation with the author. Bailey also recalls a remark made by a tenant whose flat he visited, commenting on a supply of meat: 'The butcher – he's shagged everybody in this block including me.'

those who worked the black market were often deserters; either British or, in the later years of the War, Canadian and American servicemen.

Once a man had deserted he became almost *ipso facto* a criminal, for he would no longer have access to ration books and he would be forced to the black market if he wished to survive. By 1947 it was estimated that there were some 20,000 British, let alone American and colonial, deserters. It would be impossible to say how many took to crime, but it must have been a high percentage.[6]

Of course, the call-up was there to be avoided and a salesman in Brick Lane with advanced heart disease not surprisingly obtained an exemption certificate. He turned his illness into a cottage industry and successfully impersonated nine people, relatives and friends before he was unmasked and sent to Borstal. He had obtained up to £200 a time but had lost his money gambling. Those he impersonated received 2 years' imprisonment.[7]

It was only a repetition of the pattern of behaviour during the First World War, according to Horace Cancellor:

> In the East End where young Russian Jews and Poles born of alien parents on British soil had acquired a British nationality they refused to obey the calls to colours and raised the plea of being conscientious objectors . . . by hook or by crook they mean to let the British soldiers fight for them and stick to their soft jobs in the markets of East London.

The hooks and crooks included the assistance of solicitors since their parents were wealthy; forgery of special certificates, lies about their ages and faking diseases. Cancellor recalls

---

[6] John C. Spencer, *Crime and the Services*, p. 52.
[7] *Brighton & Hove Gazette*, 29 June 1940.

that towards the end of the War one young man was given albumen so that his organs might appear unsound. He was kept in custody for two days, by which time all traces had disappeared. He gave evidence against his doctors and one was acquitted at Quarter Sessions on appeal; he had been defended by an eminent King's Counsel. If all else failed, Cancellor believed they fled to Ireland where as a bonus there was still horse-racing.

One home-grown crime involving visiting servicemen took place at Ilford in 1944. When American servicemen came on leave from bases in East Anglia, a gang posing as taxi drivers would take them to a secluded area and rob them. They claimed that they had done so because 'it was so easy'. The ringleader was sentenced to 21 months' imprisonment.[8]

Perhaps because he did not wish to admit the extent of its existence Lord Woolton, the wartime Minister of Food, was somewhat dismissive of the black market which went hand in hand with rationing:

> The penalties for infringements of the food regulations were literally ruinous . . . and the consequence was that [black marketeering] became so perilous an occupation that few indeed dared to embark on it.[9]

In fact his Lordship was probably in a minority of one. The essence of successful crime is that it is not detected. As for the deterrent element, when pickpocketing was a capital offence it was still going on at the foot of the gallows of those convicted of the crime. Whilst black marketeering may never have reached the heights it did in America, it was still a very worthwhile and lucrative trade. It began to emerge in 1941 in Petticoat Lane and flourished also in markets such

[8] *Ilford Recorder*, 5 October 1944.
[9] Lord Woolton, *Memoirs*, pp. 230–31.

as Romford and Chelmsford, both of which had reasonably easy access to the East End.

Smithies gives Romford as an example of the attitude of the authorities to the black market. Apart from a thriving market in coupon-free clothing, it was a centre for black market food. In theory the poultry on offer was for breeding, but a reporter found that many of the birds were less than prime physical specimens and, blind and unable to stand, were good only for the pot. The controlled price in the shops was 1/10d. whilst in the market it was 3/6d. Farmers from East Anglia and the purchasers from the East End had known each other from pre-war days and it was not long before word was passed around and West End restaurateurs turned – swiftly followed by pickpockets, thieves and three-card tricksters – to the market. For some time prosecutions were scarce and fines imposed by magistrates in no way a deterrent.

In sharp contrast with this was the case of a 15-year-old whose mother had died some weeks previously. While her fire-fighter father was out at work she inadvertently left the light on in their home. Despite her father's plea that it was almost a week of his wages, the local bench fined her £2. Following comment in the local paper, readers paid her fine.[10]

By the end of the War, black market goods available in the East End included the then exotic oranges and bananas, and people were prepared to pay a shilling an egg with no questions asked.[11]

The authorities were also desperately keen on saving. Those found betting could expect a severe ticking-off, with substantial fines for the promoters. The North London magistrate,

---

[10] *Romford Recorder*, 3 and 10 January 1941. *Police Review* was appalled by the general lack of enthusiasm for fining thoughtless people who left lights on in the blackout, suggesting that 2/6d. was derisory compared with the risk to life such behaviour engendered. *Police Review*, 17 January 1941.
[11] *Hackney Gazette*, 22 March 1946; 9 August 1946.

Blake Odgers, commented in the case of a prosecution of a number of men betting on a boxing match at a Stoke Newington cinema:

> I think the wickedness of this sort of thing is that here we are in a war, and we have had to stick it for nearly six years. You, all of you, ought to know that every spare pound ought to go either to war savings or be put into the bank and here you are going off with hundreds of pounds between you to a boxing match . . . and not only betting yourselves, but encouraging other people to bet. I cannot help noticing that nearly all the defendants took the oath in the Jewish fashion and cannot help remembering what people of that race and creed have gone through during these years. I think it is disgusting that people of the same race and creed who have not had the bad time they have had should behave themselves in this way, instead of doing what they can to finish the war.[12]

And a month later, fining Hyam Hyams £25 for allowing betting on snooker at the Vogue Social Club, opposite Stoke Newington Police Station, the same magistrate said:

> Do you mean to say that in these days of national savings these men could find nothing better to do with their money than take it to this club?[13]

Throughout the pages of local newspapers faces old and new appeared. On 5 January 1944 Jack Comer, described as a doorman at the Apex Social Club, Beaumont Grove, was fined 40 shillings along with his cousin Solly Kankus and another dozen or so punters who, when asked, chorused, 'We all plead guilty.' Two weeks later Mrs Ettie da Costa, the proprietress, was fined £250. On 3 May that year, William G. Kray along

---

12 *Hackney Gazette*, 28 March 1944.
13 *Hackney Gazette*, 12 April 1944.

with seven others was fined 5 shillings for playing Two-Up in Worgate Street.

Thomas Holland had 'Roll 'em Down' tables at a bombed-out site in Stockmar Road. His great offence was encouraging juveniles to play this old fairground game which paid odds of 4–1. The fear was, as with fruit machines at a later date, that they would become addicted and go on criminal sprees to obtain the necessary funds. Holland was fined £5 with an alternative of two months' imprisonment. His appeal that the wooden boards should not be destroyed in view of the wartime shortage was granted by the stipendiary magistrate, Daniel Hopkin, on his undertaking not to use them for gaming.[14]

Generally there had been worries about fairgrounds being breeding places for crime and in 1941–42 the London Diocesan CETS undertook a survey of fairs in London, many of which were in Hackney and Stepney. They found that 71 per cent of patrons were youths under 16. One of the principal games was a crane which could pick up packs of cigarettes, which in turn could be sold back to the management. Unfortunately the survey found that it might cost eleven shillings to win four packs of cigarettes which could be sold for three shillings. The estimated profit on a crane game was 75 per cent.

In his foreword to the survey, the magistrate Basil L.Q. Henriques, who later had a street named after him, told how the previous week he had dealt with a boy who had stolen £20 from his employers, all of which had been spent gambling at a fair in Aldgate over two nights.[15]

Food hoarding and wasting were great sins. In the summer of 1942 Rose Denyer was given a two-month sentence by Rowland Thomas KC for wasting food.

[14] *Hackney Gazette*, 23 February 1944.
[15] London Diocesan CETS and Churches, *Commission on Gambling, Funfairs and Delinquency: A Survey in London 1941–42*.

I regard this as a most revolting, disgusting and outrageous case. You look well fed, you are 35 years of age and I am assured there is nothing wrong with you mentally and yet, in these days, when men are giving their lives on the high seas in order to bring us food, you are wasting enough food to feed many families. It's no good fining you. I should not get the money. The only thing I can do – and I do it without hesitation – is to send you to prison, where you will be fed at the expense of the State, free to yourself and I am sure with no waste.

The Bethnal Green Food Officer had found 25 large and 32 small loaves in varying stages of mould on her table along with spoiled prunes, jam and margarine. In a cupboard there were a further 17 loaves.

An essentially East End crime was associated with the docks; the bribery by the police of foreign sailors. On 24 June 1940 officers went to the Hotel Central in Aldgate High Street to see two Dutch seamen, Hermanus Sneek and Pieter van Teijligen from the SS *Kelbergen*. Neither had permits to be absent from their ship and they were arrested. At Bishopsgate Police Station while Sneek's fingerprints were being taken, he said that it was cheaper to stay at 'an Hotel' than to stay on the ship overnight. Asked what he meant, he said that on 20 June when he returned to the Victoria Docks with van Teijligen they had been stopped by a policeman inside the gate who had taken away their passes and then demanded 14 shillings and 12 shillings respectively to get them back.

The next day they returned at 11.30 but the policeman said it was an hour late and that while he would let them in on this occasion in future he would charge £2. This appears to have been a steady little racket, with Dutch seamen handing over whatever change they had left at the end of an evening to gain entry to their ships. On one occasion a bottle of gin was extorted.

Both the seamen were discharged at Mansion House Justice

Room and the victims now became valuable witnesses. The
offences were denied by the officers who were not picked
out on an identification parade, but once the case of Sneek
had come to court the game stopped. One constable was
dismissed from the service and two had their pay reduced
by 5 shillings a week for six months. Two others had their
good conduct allowance of 2/6d. withdrawn, and these and
three other officers were transferred.[16]

One of the benefits to the wartime criminal, both amateur
and professional, was that absences could be more readily
explained by the bombing and bodies could be buried in
the rubble. The one-time Mosley supporter Frederick Lawton,
who went on to become a Lord Justice of Appeal, believed he
owed his successful career to being in Lambeth Magistrates'
Court at the moment when Harry Dobkin appeared, charged
with the murder of his wife Rachael. Theirs had been an
arranged marriage in 1920 and although a son was born it
was not a marriage which was in any way a success.

They had separated three years after the marriage and
Rachel Dobkin had obtained a maintenance order. Over the
years Dobkin, a poor payer at best, served a number of short
prison sentences designed to remind him of the necessity of
keeping up the payments. When he was out and about he
seems to have been violent towards her. She took out assault
summonses on four occasions, but the magistrates dismissed
them all.

The Dobkins met in a Dalston café for tea on Good Friday,
11 April 1941, and after they left about 6.30 p.m. Rachel
was never seen again. The next day her sister reported her
as missing, blaming Dobkin, but the police did not interview
him until 16 April, the day after a small fire broke out in the
cellar of the Baptist Church in Vauxhall Road, South London,
where Dobkin was a firewatcher. On 16 April 23 people were

killed when a land-mine was dropped 250 yards from the church, which had already been blitzed in August 1940. The police circulated a description of the missing Rachel Dobkin and there the matter rested.

Then on 17 July 1942 a workman demolishing the remains of the church found her body. Professor Keith Simpson, performing the post-mortem, discovered the hyroid bone had been fractured, signifying strangulation. Dobkin was arrested. At his trial much play was made on Rachel Dobson's height. The corpse was 5′ 1″, but there was some evidence that Rachel had been 5′ 3″. If this had been the case Dobkin would have been acquitted. Eventually her sister, who maintained she was the same height, was measured. In shoes she was 5′ 1″. The jury took only twenty minutes to return a verdict of guilty.

Lawton defended in another East End wartime murder. Lilian Hartney was found dead at about 5 a.m. on 6 August 1945 in Rich Street with her feet pointing to Grenada Street. Her dress had been neatly folded back to her stomach as if to deliberately expose her pubic hair because she had on neither pants nor stockings. She had bite marks around her nipples which appeared to show that the biter had two teeth missing in the lower jaw. She had been strangled.

The prosecution case was that she had been killed by her consumptive husband, Patrick, who had tired of her being out in Chinatown night after night. From a patch of urine in the matrimonial bed it was argued that she had been killed at home. When the police called they found her husband fully dressed. The major, probably the only, point to be made for the defence was that this consumptive husband could not have carried his wife's body 200 yards down the East India Dock Road. The jury agreed with Lawton that he could not. In any event, although he did not know it, Hartney had only a few months to live.

10

Vice

Serious vice problems began again in the East End at the end of the Second World War, and in 1944 local churchmen produced a report into conditions amongst the coloured people. Naturally, sex featured prominently.

It was thought that in the Stepney area there were a minimum of 400 resident people described as coloured, of whom 136 were children and 12 were women. All except 20 of the children had white mothers; 78 of them were under five years old and 58 were between the ages of five and sixteen.[1] The floating population rather appropriately depended on the number of ships in the docks at any one time. The section on the health of the men found that a high number signing off from the Merchant Navy pool had both venereal disease and a general distrust of hospitals and treatment clinics.

The report continued:

[1] Phyllis Young, *Report on Investigation into Conditions of the Coloured Population in a Stepney area.* The report gives a breakdown of the nationalities in the area. Of the group described as colonials which comprised just under half the survey, 69.4 per cent were West Indians, with the British West Indians providing another 17 per cent.

Attitude to white women

When the coloured man first arrives in Stepney he is attracted by the white woman who wishes to trade on him; only after he has lived with her for a short period does he realise this. Thus, in the vast majority of cases, he very soon begins to adopt this attitude towards the white woman who associates with him.

When he has money he is generous and as long as the woman pleases him, affectionate: but this does not prevent him from beating her if she displeases him or even turning her away and taking another woman if he feels so inclined. Even superstition may influence him towards her: a Negro in a café one day explained that he had lived with three different women and although a dark woman had been the most beautiful, he had had to beat her and throw her out because her black hair had brought him bad luck in betting: he had been luckier when living with fair women.

. . . In most instances the coloured man has taken the woman to administer to his physical needs only, for either a short or a long period.[2]

The next section was devoted to the white woman:

Among the women married to coloured men in the area there can be found a few of the nicer type who have been genuinely attracted to the man and have married him for affection, but the vast majority have come into the district with the deliberate intention of trading on the coloured men.

The report found that some of the women were themselves daughters of prostitutes who, having had an illegitimate child, had lost their self-respect:

[2] ibid, p. 21.

Almost all of these women are below normal intelligence and, according to officials who have dealt with them, over-sexed.

With the exception of those few who have married, these women have very little moral sense. They will leave one man to go to another if the second will give them more. While accepting a monthly allowance from one man while he is at sea, they will live with others until he returns, and will encourage men in any activity, such as black-marketing, that will help to provide more clothes or food.[3]

This section of the report concluded that a large number of the women also suffered from venereal disease and that syphilis was on the increase.

It then turned its attention to café society, something which would trouble the clergy and authority for the next 30 years. There were 34 cafés, 32 of which were within the area, used by coloured men and white women. They were often run by 'men from Malta' who usually provided a wireless set. Although the cafés operated as local clubs, their main function was as a rendezvous between coloured men and white women. There were often rooms over the cafés which were let at 5 shillings a week – and more if a woman was brought to stay. If there were no rooms, then the man would be directed to a nearby house. If a woman joined him, part of the additional rent would be paid to the café proprietor. The cafés catered separately for Muslims or for 'Negroes', but all were frequented by white women. In 1943 there had been 12 prosecutions for brothel keeping; in 9 cases women were the keepers. There was also some evidence of trade between similar cafés in the Tottenham Court Road area and as far afield as Coventry.[4]

[3] ibid, p. 22.
[4] It should be remembered that two women working from the same premises constituted a brothel.

Although the figures seem ludicrous by today's standards, the cafés were highly profitable and when they were sold the goodwill could reach as much as £1,000. A manager might receive £9 a week and a share of the profits. Street soliciting, however, did not become a serious problem until the 1950s. There were 2 cases in the Stepney area in 1946; 9 in 1949; but by 1965 the figure had grown to 500.[5]

It had been a growing problem for some time. In October 1947 a 3,000-strong petition was presented out of the blue to Stepney Borough Council, protesting about the conditions in Cable Street between Christian Street and Leman Street:

> . . . Grave moral and physical danger exists for both young and old people in this area, and we demand that the Borough Council take active steps in consultation with the Home Office and the Food Ministry to rid us of this pestilence. We express the opinion that the contributory causes are the excessive number of cafés in the street open at a late hour and the disgusting conditions in some public houses.[6]

This brought protests and counter-protests in the Council chamber. The police representative said that there was no evidence to support the contentions raised and as for suggestions that women were afraid to – and perhaps more importantly their husbands were afraid to let them – walk in Cable Street, not a single complaint of molestation or assault had been lodged.

The reply to this was an invitation for councillors to take off their rose-tinted glasses and to go to Cable Street or the top of Pell Street to see for themselves. The demarcation line between 'good' and 'bad' Cable Street was the traffic lights at, appropriately enough, Christian Street.

[5] See Gilbert Kelland, *Crime in London*; James Morton, *Bent Coppers*.
[6] *ELA*, 31 October 1947.

Taking up the scent of a good story, Harry Procter in the *Daily Mail* wrote:

> The girls who haunt the cafés and pubs are not London girls, they come from South Shields, Newcastle, Cardiff, Liverpool: many of them are on the run and some have escaped from remand homes. They are safe in Cable Street. Most of them are teenagers, they get drunk, and the coloured seamen they are with get jealous.[7]

He went on to say that the cost of living in Cable Street for a week at that time was between £100 and £150, the sum the coloured seamen had when they came off the boats. In the flats around Cable Street he estimated there was a gang of about 150 men and some 200 women who preyed on the seamen, saying that sometimes the gangs would arrange fights during which the unfortunate sailors would be robbed.

The ever crusading *John Bull* weighed in that December with some comments which fifty years later might cause problems with the Commission for Race Relations.

> Seamen from all over the world know of Cable Street, and if their tastes lie that way, make for it as soon as their ships dock. Some of them are coloured boys just off their first ship. A few months ago they were still half naked in the bush. You can pick them by their speech and the awkwardness with which they wear their unfamiliar clothes.[8]

It took the local clergy a little while to muster a reply, but when they did it was to emphasise that the difficulties were not of a wholly racial nature. They suggested that the problems

---

[7] Harry Procter, 'Street Scene' in *Daily Mail*, 31 October 1947.
[8] Vivien Batchelor, 'The Citizen versus Vice' in *John Bull*, 6 December 1947.

had been grossly exaggerated and

> . . . first, and most important, to make known, with the widest possible publicity the fact that the blame for the immorality and the undesirable conditions in the Cable Street area should not, in the first place, be laid upon the coloured population of the district.[9]

They went on to say that coloured people had not been asked to sign the petition. Not so, said one of the organisers. Many coloured people had been asked. Some had signed, some had declined.

The black journalist Roi Otley, writing in 1952, was appalled by what he saw in Cable Street:

> Today, down by London dock in about a square mile of back streets there exists a dismal Negro slum. The neighbourhood, situated in the borough of Stepney, abounds with brothels and dope pads in tumbledown old buildings. Few slums in the U.S. compare with this area's desperate character, unique racial composition, and atmosphere of crime, filth and decay.[10]

Three years later, M.P. Banton was similarly perturbed if less hostile:

> To the passer-by the area is a strange and definitely a frightening one; if he enters a café or a public house the other customers will scrutinize him thoroughly and there is an atmosphere so hostile that anyone but a coloured man, a seaman, or one of the poorest of the local population will come to feel that he does not 'belong' there and that he is not wanted.[11]

[9] *ELA*, 12 December 1947; 26 December 1947.
[10] Roi Otley, *No Green Pastures*, p. 29.
[11] M.P. Banton, *The Coloured Quarter*, p. 92.

However by 1957, in another church publication, the clergy was displaying its fears over the moral welfare of men from overseas:

> THE ADVENT OF MANY COLOURED MEN IS NOT RESPONSIBLE FOR THE SITUATION TO BE DESCRIBED LATER IN THIS REPORT but it does aggravate the gravity of that situation. It will certainly colour the picture of Christian England that they will send home to their countries.[12]

It is clear that by 1957 the fears of the *Daily Mail* ten years earlier had been realised and that the Commercial Road prostitutes who operated over a long stretch of the street came from all parts of England, although there were disturbing signs that local girls were taking up the game. That year there were 795 convictions for prostitution at Thames Magistrates' Court. Many were younger and less stable than prostitutes in other parts of London and, in a survey of girls in a reception area, over 50 per cent were mentally unstable *per se* or drink made them so.[13]

However, there was evidence that prostitution in Stepney was more organised than simply pathetic and feeble-minded amateurs. In his study of East End crime D. M. Downes suggested that: 'since the early and mid-1950s, the girls have been more organised and a pattern established.'[14]

It was now the Maltese who were the suggested organisers. There was a grain of truth to lend a little substance to the stereotype of the Maltese as profiteer, exploiter and pimp, but not everyone condemned them. The East End priest Father Fitzgerald asked, 'Who taught them to sell their sisters and

---

[12] 'Vice in Stepney,' 1957. Pamphlet in the local history section of Tower Hamlets Library.
[13] Wellclose Square Fund, Progress Report 1962.
[14] D.M. Downes, *The Delinquent Solution*, p. 161.

other girls, but the visiting Imperial British?'

The problem of the Maltese in the East End was that over the years the community had been tarnished severely by the activities of the Messina brothers who had run organised prostitution in London overall.[15] Nevertheless in 1956, out

[15] The Messina brothers – Carmelo, Alfredo, Salvatore, Attilio and Eugenio – began their career as souteneurs and pimps in the 1930s. Their father Guiseppe came from Linguaglossa in Sicily and in the late 1890s went to Malta where he became an assistant in a brothel in Valetta. There he married a Maltese girl, Virginia de Bono. His first two sons, Salvatore and Alfredo, were born there. The family then moved to Alexandria in 1905 where he built a chain of brothels in Suez, Cairo and Port Said. The remaining sons were all born in Alexandria, and their father ensured they were all well educated. In 1932 Guiseppe Messina was expelled from Egypt. Two years later Eugenio, the third son born in 1908, came to England. He was able to claim British nationality because his father had sensibly claimed Maltese citizenship. With Eugenio was his wife Colette, a French prostitute. It was on her back that Messina founded his London empire. More girls were recruited from the continent and as the empire grew he was joined on the management side by his brothers. Property was bought throughout the West End and the brothers turned their attention to English girls. By 1946 with the family's weekly earnings at £1,000, the girls were earning £100 a night and were being paid £50 a week. It was not until 1950 that the Messinas were exposed for what they were, and it was the work of Duncan Webb, a curious man who a little later caused so much trouble for Jack Spot; a devout Roman Catholic, he believed his mission was to clean the streets of London. After one triumph over the Messinas he put an advertisement in *The Times* offering thanks to St Jude. After the murderer Donald Hume, killer of Stanley Setty, had been convicted, Webb married his wife Cynthia. On 3 September 1950 *The People* published the exposure, backing it with photographs of the Messina girls and the flats from where they operated. Eugenio and Carmelo fled, as did Salvatore. Attilio and Alfredo remained. On 19 March 1951 Alfredo was arrested at his Wembley home charged with living off immoral earnings and trying to bribe a police officer. He had offered Superintendent Mahon, one of the arresting officers, £200. He received 2 years' imprisonment concurrent on each of the charges and a £500 fine. Attilio and Eugenio were eventually accepted by the Italian government. Salvatore lived in Switzerland whilst Alfredo, who could claim British citizenship, died in Brentford in 1963.

For a fuller account of the operations of the brothers, see James Morton, *Gangland*, Chapter 6 and for an in-house view Marthe Watts, *The Men in My Life*.

MURDER.
£50 REWARD.

WHEREAS Mrs. Matilda Moore, who lived at No. 96, Green Street
Bethnal Green, was assaulted by a Man on the Evening of 26th
March 1863, and has since died from the effects of the Assault.

£50 REWARD

ill be paid by Her Majesty's Government to any Person giving such
nformation as shall lead to the Apprehension and Conviction of the
Murderer; and the Secretary of State for the Home Department will
dvise the Grant of Her Majesty's Gracious Pardon to any Accomplice
ot being the Person who actually struck the blow, who shall give such
nformation as shall lead to the same result.

About 8.30 p.m., 26th March 1863, a Man, of the following description
ntered the Shop, No. 96, Green Street, Bethnal Green, and, after picking
Mrs. Moore's pocket, assaulted her and ran away, leaving behind him a
Black Cloth Over-coat and a Magenta Woollen Scarf. Age about 20
Height 5 feet 6 inches. Complexion fair. No Whiskers. Dressed in dark
lothes, and Black Hat. Of respectable appearance.

Information to be given to Superintendent Howie, Police Station
rbour Square, Stepney, or at any of the Metropolitan Police Stations.

RICHARD MAYNE,

Metropolitan Police Office. *The Commissioner of the Police of the Metropolis.*

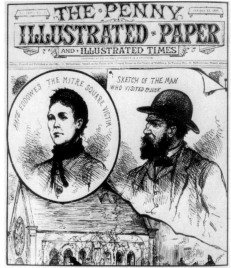

The Hunt for Jack

Fred Wensley, scourge of
Arthur Harding

Wensley's protégé Charles Leeson

Leeson in disguise

Detectives at the siege of Sidney Street